Watt Footprint

Copyright

ISBN: 978-1-910179-80-2

Printed and Bound in Ireland by
eprint limited www.eprint.ie

Cover design: **Eduardo Gonçalves**
Texts and images design: **Eduardo Gonçalves**

Please note that any page cross references refer to the print edition.

eBook Also available.

Visit our website at:
www.wattfootprint.com

"To Teresa, Jenny, Lisa-Jean, and Greg, for your absolute support, patience, and reviving cups of coffee, during the many weeks, months, and years it has taken to write this book."

Publisher's Acknowledgements

I am grateful to the following for permission to use source information and copy materials:

- Image on page 21 reproduced by kind permission of the International Code Council Inc., Western regional office, 3030 Saturn Street, Brea, CA 92821.
- Image on page 43 reproduced by kind permission of ResourceKraft, Innovation House, Glasnevin, Dublin.
- Images on page 59, 61 & 71 courtesy of 2 save Energy Ltd., 9 Grafton Way, Basingstoke, RG22 6HY, United Kingdom.
- Image on page 63 courtesy of Flir Systems Ltd., 2 Kingshill Avenue, West Malling, Kent, ME19 4AQ, United Kingdom.
- Building Energy Rating (BER) image on page 77 and 79, courtesy of the Sustainable Energy Authority of Ireland (SEAI), Wilton Park House, Wilton Place, Dublin 2, D02 T228.
- Screen shot image of HEED software sourced from University of California, Los Angeles, California 90095-1467 on page 81.
- Screen shot image on page 131 and 152 courtesy of Dartwin.
- Image on page 189 courtesy of Climote Ltd., Finnabair Industrial Park, Dundalk, Ireland.
- Image on page 189 courtesy of Nest, 3400 Hillview Ave., Palo Alto, CA 94304.
- Photograph on page 239 sourced, with thanks, from EARTH5R, Raheja Vihar, Powai. Mumbai, India.
- Image of faucet on page 257 sourced from Ideal Standard, Jafza View 18 Building, P.O. Box 261559, Jebel Ali Free Zone, Dubai.

In some instance, despite extensive investigation, I have been unable to trace the owners of certain images and would gladly acknowledge credit in the event that I have the correct information to do so.

Acknowledgements

I would like to thank Eduardo Gonçalves for his work on the graphics and images used through out the book, as well as the cover design and page layout. I would also like to thank Rosemary Horan and Kevin Kirwan for their invaluable assistance editing and proofing my script.

A special thanks to Finbarr Stuart, John Brennan, Damien Collins, Liam Bourke, Colin Bolger, Peter Wallace, Barry Coffey, and Richard Morton, for taking time out of their busy schedules and providing insightful feedback and comments on the more technical aspects of the book. I am also indebted to Denis Heenan for his expertise and feedback, which helped me to fine-tune chapter flow and content.

Finally, particular thanks is due to Gerry Duffy, who made tangible my jumbled goals, helping this book come to fruition. The entire project would not have happened without his unique style of inspirational motivation.

Watt Footprint

The Smart Citizen's Guide
to Save Energy
in the Built Environment

Introduction

"Everybody talks about the weather, but nobody does anything about it."

Attributed to Mark Twain (1835-1910)

A whole new language has emerged to describe how our buildings need to be assessed and upgraded to help meet globally agreed carbon-reduction targets. The baseline statistics and target efficiencies may vary from country to country, but the overriding need for carbon-emissions reductions and fossil fuel energy savings is the same. Today you cannot buy a car, a washing machine, or new window for your home without knowing the carbon-emissions effect of its production, use, and demise. Climate change policy has silently embedded itself in legislation worldwide, and everyone needs to quickly come up to speed with these developments because the price for not doing so will be detrimental to our very existence. We have one world and one problem, where energy waste and carbon emissions in one region can result in consequential detrimental effects elsewhere.

Globally, we have strictly limited reserves of fossil fuels, and we simply must appreciate the consequences of climate change and other devastation that would result if fuel consumption continues. at current rates. We must change course and face our greatest challenge. A transformed thinking and approach is now required of us all.

There are some fantastic emerging technological innovations in the field of energy efficiency and renewable energy production that, together, can measure and control heat loss, prepare computer-generated graphics and plans, and generally optimize new building design and retrofit upgrades. Nonetheless, one simple fact remains: People can save energy more quickly than technology can. Today's smart citizens could take some lessons from the way in which our ancestors integrated their homes and buildings into the environment in a more holistic fashion. We need to become more intuitive about how best to use the natural environment to both heat and cool our buildings without always resorting first to fossil fuels. We also need at least a basic understanding of the relationship between energy use, energy efficiencies, energy costs, and the key role played by time in every energy bill. However, because technology is increasingly controlling energy use, the smart citizen also needs to become familiar with the many forms of smart technology.

The book outlines a simple seven-step approach to saving energy in buildings by combining energy efficiency and renewable energy systems and explaining simple payback periods.

- The first step relates to **mind change** because a failure to accept that this small planet has limited resources and to recognize the extreme consequences of ignoring climate change will result in a failure to fully embrace the transformation needed.
- The second step examines **measurement** because "you manage what you measure." An inability to measure means you cannot monitor, and monitoring is the only effective way to address our climate change challenge and develop systems of measurable accountability.
- The third step explores the importance of making buildings **airtight** and draught-free.
- The fourth step describes the readily understood concept of **insulation**.
- The fifth looks at **temperature control** and renewable heating methods.
- The sixth investigates **electricity demand**, including the role of renewable energy.
- The seventh and final step is the crucial issue of **water efficiency**: too much water, too little water, water in all the wrong places and at the wrong times, and, of course, no water where and when it is needed most.

Climate change is a game changer in the building industry. New players and new opportunities are appearing throughout this most traditional of business sectors. Citizens will need ready access to information on all matters relating to new-build energy-efficiency, renewable energy, and building refurbishment. Sometimes, when governments become involved in an area of business, they can adopt an overly-bureaucratic approach and overly complicate matters. Re-simplifying matters is, therefore, essential and is the matter at the core of this book.

This book aims to help you to navigate the rules, to understand the genesis of regulations governing energy efficiency in buildings, and to make sensible decisions about some very basic issues that significantly affect the quality of our modern lives. I have avoided as much technical jargon as possible and only introduced it where it is essential to explain a subject or a detail. At the back of the book, you will find a glossary of some frequently used abbreviations and terms, as well as a list of some of the more useful web sites, where additional relevant and more technical details are available and easily referenced.

Step 1: Mind Change

"We cannot solve our problems with the same thinking we used when we created them."

Albert Einstein

The climate change challenge is a direct result of the enormous amounts of fossil fuels we choose to burn on a daily basis, leading to a rise in global temperatures. The problem is essentially an energy change one, and a change of mind-set on the issue has become the substantive challenge of the age. This means abandoning our ingrained dependence on fossil fuels, which has evolved over 200 years, equivalent to many human generations. The developed world is designed, built, and engineered to run on a cheap, readily available supply of the primary fossil fuels: coal, gas, and oil. So it's not just our attitude that needs changing, it is also every piece of engineering that relies on fossil fuels, from power stations to manufacturing plant and machinery to transport and home heating. The reality is that we won't solve 21st-century climate change problems with the same 20th-century thinking that got us here in the first place. We need to think differently.

Before we look forward and prepare for the coming energy revolution, we need to grasp the concept of global warming and greenhouse gases (GHG) and understand why buildings currently account for up to 40% of the energy used in most countries. In sum, we need to understand how and why the buildings in which we live and work are effectively in the eye of the climate change storm.

Scientists tell us that mother earth has been around for upward of 4.5 billion years. During this time, the world has undergone many climatic changes, from the Ice Age to warmer interglacial periods. In fact, there were numerous ice age cycles followed by warm periods every 100,000 years. Using data from ice cores, scientists have also established that the warm periods were associated with much higher levels of CO2. There are no definitive answers as to exactly why this occurred, but the temperature cycles are believed to be associated with variations in the earth's orbit and axial tilt, known as Milankowick cycles after the Serbian astronomer who discovered them. It appears that rising temperatures and greenhouse gas fluctuations are part of the earth's natural cycle. So, you might ask, what's all the fuss? And who among us is going to change the earth's orbit? Climate change sceptics will certainly win all arguments on this point.

There is, however, more to the story. Keeping the earth's temperature finely regulated and adjusted is the role of the atmosphere. In effect, the sun acts like the earth's heat source and the earth's atmosphere is its thermostat. The atmosphere plays a key role in regulating the earth's temperature and maintaining its life-sustaining properties. It is a thin layer, and greenhouse gases are its main component. On Mars, for example, where there is essentially no greenhouse gas atmosphere, the temperature is continuously below freezing, too cold to sustain life. By contrast, a thick atmosphere surrounds Venus, where the temperature is too high to sustain life.

The Goldilocks Principle

By burning fossil fuels, we are releasing greenhouse gases that augment and thicken earth's atmosphere, causing temperatures to rise. In simple terms, just like a comfort blanket, the, thicker, the warmer. Now here's the problem. The earth's thin atmospheric layer is being increased daily because of human actions. The more correct, scientific description of this process is anthropogenic climate change, that is, caused by human actions. Although scientists may not be able to accurately predict precise future earth temperatures, there is universal agreement that a temperature rise above 2oC will have a devastating effect on life on earth, as we currently know it.

Sustainability

With over 15,000 new citizens joining the world every hour and only 5,000 departing, the net global population is expected to rise to 8 billion by 2025 and possibly 10 billion by 2050. The sustainability of humanity's existence very much came into focus toward the end of the 20th century, and it raises a variety of issues that demand attention, including:

- The need for greater food supply
- Ever-diminishing natural resources
- Continuously increasing demand for energy
- Decreasing water availability
- Weakening biodiversity footprint
- Rising pollution levels
- Increasing global carbon emissions

There is a remarkable similarity between the "hockey" stick shape of the population graph and the carbon emissions graph, as the time frame moves from 18th century to the present. The direct correlation between population growth and energy consumption is a major challenge to the sustainability of our very existence.

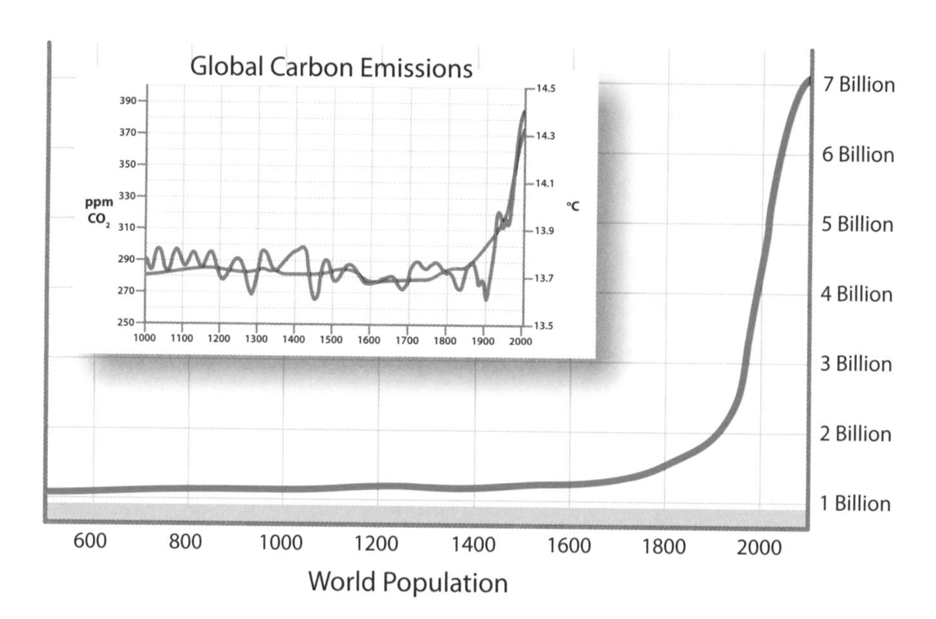

Many graphs and tables also indicate, from an overall sustainability level, how many planets are needed to sustain the current level of global consumerism. Today, it is estimated that humanity requires the equivalent of 1.5 planets to supply necessary resources and space to absorb our waste. If current population and consumption trends continue, by 2025, we will need the equivalent of two earths to support us. In other words, it would take us 18 months to regenerate what we use today and two years to regenerate what we will use in the year 2025. But even these startling predictions don't tell the real story because they are based on the principle that the earth has sustainable, renewable growth. This is a completely misleading correlation and gives us consent to exterminate one earth on the supposed notion that we can live off any number of additional virtual earths. We are in effect eating tomorrow's dinner and living on borrowed water (see also Step 7). If you accept that fossil fuels are nonrenewable because it takes millions of years to replace the oil or gas we burn today, we need to seriously rethink our energy policy based on the exhaustion of fossil fuels.

The Story of Gaia

A radical adjustment is necessary if we are to depart from a business-as-usual frame of mind and take real steps to reduce dependence on the earth's energy reserves. We have renewable technologies and the knowledge to build in an energy-efficient manner. All that is now required is the mind-set to implement the necessary changes. If scientists cannot convince us using rational arguments, perhaps we should search deeply within to revive the intuition exercised by our ancestors, stop being parasites, and become the earth's protectors.

Science tells us that life on earth, as we understand it, exists in the biosphere at the surface of the earth and manifests itself by way of plants, creatures, and all other living organisms. The earth itself is lifeless, composed of air, water, rock, and numerous minerals and gases, all of which support, nourish, and sustain life. An alternative view or theory was proposed in the 1960s by James Lovelock, an independent British scientist. He posited that the earth is more than just a mere life-supporting environment but is part of life itself. This living earth Lovelock names "Gaia," resurrecting the ancient Greek term. I have extracted a quote from Lovelock's discerning book, The Vanishing Face of Gaia, which offers an alternate view of today's climate change problem.

"If we are to understand the climate and adapt to its changes, or even counter them, we have to see the Earth as something able to resist adverse change until the going becomes too tough and then, like a living thing, escape rapidly to a safe haven. Fight or flight is a characteristic of life, and the Earth itself, Gaia, has long been resisting our interventions through negative feedback; opposing the way we change the air with green house gases and take away its natural forest cover for farmland. We have been doing this ever since we were hunter-gatherers equipped with fire, but until the last hundred years there was little or no perceptible change in the Earth's state. Now our intentions are too great to resist and the earth system seems to be giving up its struggle and is preparing to flee to a safer place, a hot state with a stable climate, one that it has visited many time before. A look at the Earth's climate history tells us that in such hot states Gaia can still self regulate and survive with a diminished biosphere."

Our ancestors, who were arguably more in tune with nature than we can ever be, would have had no difficulty in understanding earth as a living entity. Whereas most people today might sense that the earth is more than a lump of rock to be exploited to support 21st-century lifestyles, we are happy to follow mainstream scientific teachings and conclude that the earth is, in fact, just a mass of rock and other materials that has to be maintained. Whatever one's personal opinion, the concept that the earth is a living planet might help us in the quest to reduce the extraction of its precious fossil fuels.

Understanding Greenhouse Gases

Understanding the concept of greenhouse gases is fundamental if we are to take responsibility for our own carbon emissions and reduce our personal carbon footprint. To help with this concept, picture what happens in a garden greenhouse or conservatory when the sun shines. The sun's rays come straight in through the glass and are immediately turned from light into heat when they hit a mass object, which might be the floor, walls, and furniture or it might be you. The glass allows the sun's rays to strike through and bounce off the mass objects, but then the glass prevents a portion of the bounced light/energy, the infrared part, from escaping. This means that the greenhouse becomes warmer than the surrounding area because it has trapped a portion of normally reflected heat from escaping.

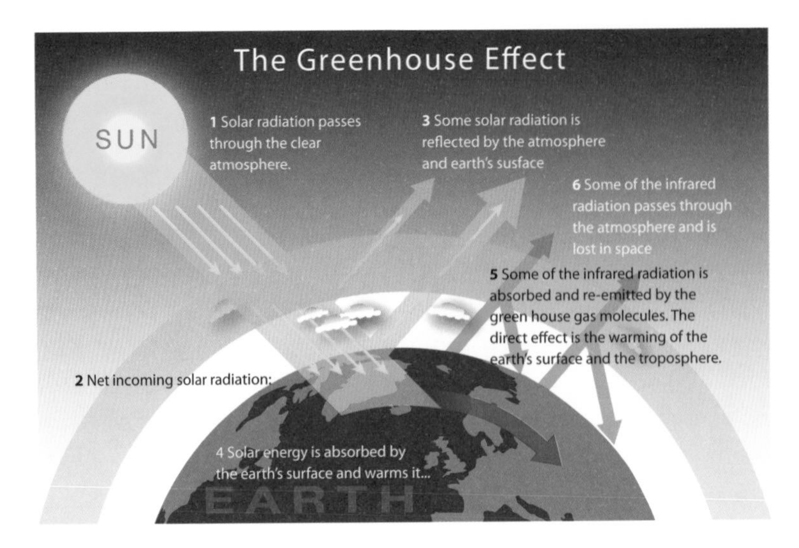

Greenhouse gases got their name because they have exactly the same effect on the atmosphere. They allow the sun's rays to heat the earth. But as the rays bounce back, a portion is prevented from passing through the atmosphere from earth to space. As discussed earlier, having the right balance of greenhouse gases to regulate the earth's temperature is the key. Over time, the amount of energy sent from the sun to the earth should be about the same as the amount radiated back into space, and this would make earth's temperature just right for life as we know it today.

Not every greenhouse gas is carbon dioxide; others are even more potent in terms of global warming potential, including methane, CFCs, ozone, nitrogen, helium, and sulphur, some of which occur in nature from the

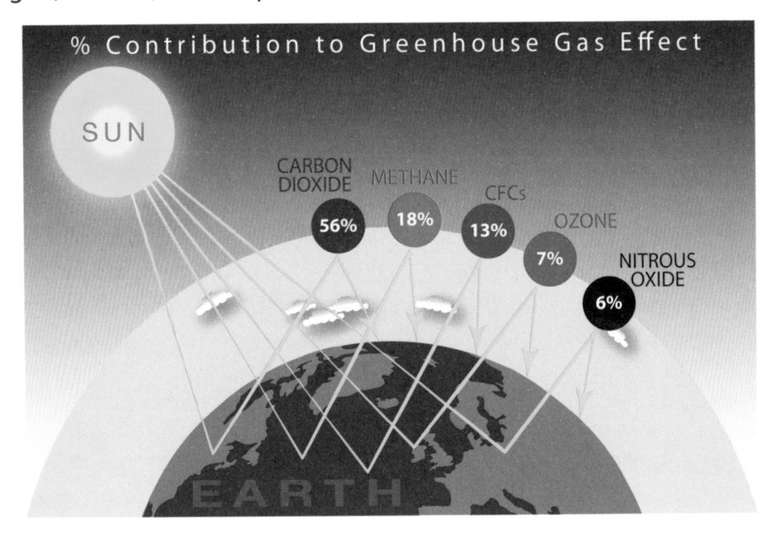

oceans, soils, plants, and animals while others are exclusively human made. These gases have a greater impact on global warming, but their overall abundance is not as significant as that of carbon dioxide.

Because carbon dioxide CO2 is the most prevalent gas, all reference to climate change is in terms of carbon. The term "carbon equivalent" is used to account for gases other than carbon and is denoted by the small "e" after the chemical formula CO2e. The graphic above displays some of these gases and their effect in the atmosphere. Carbon has now become the primary benchmark for climate change measurements; hence we have carbon footprint, carbon trading, carbon emissions, carbon budgets, low-carbon economy, zero carbon, etc.

The Carbon Cycle

There is so much talk today about carbon, prompting us to consider where has this stuff come from and why was it not part of our vocabulary before this, apart perhaps from school chemistry class. Popular awareness of CO2 and its effects on global warming is a relatively recent development. Chemistry classes taught us that carbon forms the basis of all life forms on earth and is the second-most abundant element in the human body, by mass. Carbon, or a form of carbon, is a basic element of all living and breathing animals and plants on earth. Like most other elements in the universe, the amount of carbon is constant. Carbon is not created or destroyed; it is simply cycled and recycled from one form to another in a very similar manner to the water cycle.

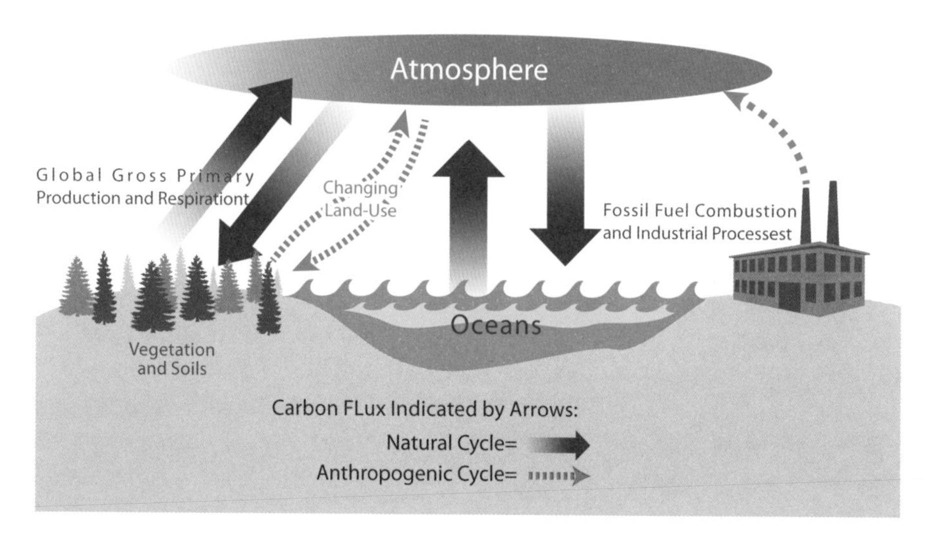

Plants draw carbon dioxide from the atmosphere and absorb it into their own structure to create biomass. During its lifetime, a tree absorbs carbon dioxide through the process of photosynthesis and creates leaves, bark, roots, and wood (all biomass) and oxygen. It is estimated that one large broad-leaf tree over its lifetime can absorb 1 ton of carbon dioxide and produce enough oxygen to support two people for one year.

Fuel is termed a fossil fuel when it is made from the decomposition of organic matter in plants and animals, laid down over millions of years. Mother earth incubated and created these fuels over such a long time frame, but mankind burns them without a second thought, releasing the carbon in seconds to heat our homes and power our buildings. So when we burn these fuels, we release the carbon captured in the original materials. Coal, particularly anthracite coal, is composed of 98% carbon. In fact, the name carbon comes from the Latin word carbo, meaning coal or charcoal. Before the Industrial Revolution, when our need to burn fossil fuels was minimal, the earth's ecosystem was able to balance itself. In simple terms, the carbon absorbers balanced the carbon emitters and the earth's ecosystem was in balance.

Earth Summit

In fairness, the scientific community has provided fact-based evidence for more than a century that draws a direct relationship between burning fossil fuels and raising the earth's temperature. Nonetheless, the threat to the environment of climate change was not well known outside of research communities. Climate change was not truly recognized until 1988, when the **Intergovernmental Panel on Climate Change (IPCC)** was set up to provide governments with a clear view of the current state of knowledge about the science of climate change. The IPCC remit was also to provide advice on potential impacts and options for adaptation and mitigation through regular assessments of the most recent scientific and technical information. In 1992, when the first Earth Summit, held in Rio de Janeiro, took place, the problem of climate change had emerged as the most important single issue affecting global sustainability. While the Earth Summit was founded to address the full remit of sustainable issues affecting the earth, from population growth to water shortages, the main priority that emerged centered on climate change. A key policy agreed at the Earth Summit was the setting up of the **United Nations Framework Convention on Climate Change (UNFCCC)**. The ultimate objective of this convention is the...

...Stabilization of greenhouse gas concentrations in the atmosphere at a level that would prevent dangerous anthropogenic (human-induced) interference with the climate system...

In order to achieve this, the UNFCCC put the onus on developed countries to lead the way. These are referred to as the Annex 1 countries. It also directed new funds to climate change activities in developing nations. The UNFCCC keeps tabs on the problem and tracks remediation efforts using a number of steps, including the preparation of greenhouse gas inventories. It requires all governments that have ratified the treaty to formulate national programs to mitigate climate change. The treaty itself is not legally binding, but it does provide a framework by way of yearly Conventions of Parties (COP), which has been meeting annually since 1994. The first protocol to set mandatory emission limits on national greenhouse gases was agreed at COP3 in Kyoto, Japan.

Kyoto Protocol (COP3)

The Kyoto Protocol, which was adopted in December 1997 and came into force in 2005, is perhaps not something that you might expect to see referenced in a book about the energy efficiency of our buildings. But it has set the ground rules for how nations account for their carbon emissions. Since our homes and buildings are responsible for as much as 40% of all greenhouse gas emissions, these are among the protocol's prime targets. Not all nations have signed up to this agreement, however. Chief among these are the United States and China, leading some to conclude that, because the world's two largest economies have not signed up, the protocol is meaningless. But that is to ignore its true significance, which lies in the obligations that it has effectively established for carbon emissions accounting.

The Japan Times
Conference adopts Kyoto Protocol
Greenhouse gas emissions to be cut by average of 5.2%
Kyoto convention's success open to debate
KYOTO COP3

It has facilitated a sort of UN global police force, setting the rules for measuring, monitoring, targeting, and cutting greenhouse gases. It commits member countries to making specific carbon emission reductions within specific time periods. The European Union has embraced the Kyoto Protocol to such an extent that all of its carbon accounting rules have become ingrained in member state legislation. As a direct result of Kyoto, we now have a common global vocabulary and a new set of measurements to determine how energy efficient our buildings are. In Step 2, I explain what these measurements are and how they have embedded themselves in the legislation of some of the world's most developed nations, becoming integral to our everyday lives. You cannot buy a washing machine, refrigerator, automobile, or house or insulate a home or buy windows without knowing the carbon emissions associated with each item or process. We are already trading in carbon, perhaps unknown to ourselves, and we need to learn the rules of engagement of this new parallel accounting system. We will also need to understand the difference between high carbon emission energy sources and low to zero sources. Carbon accounting is now mandatory in some countries for large industry and is slowly making its way down to all businesses. The term carbon footprint, explained in Step 2, will soon become familiar to all.

If governments have to account for every tonne of greenhouse gas emissions, they are likely to target the construction sector, given that approximately 40% of our energy use and carbon emissions are from heating, cooling, and powering buildings. Before long, everyone will be accounting for our carbon emissions, and the cost of any penalties for noncompliance with Kyoto Protocol-type targets will be levied in taxes. Kyoto is now measuring and monitoring us from afar, and we have less and less control over its embrace.

Most countries are introducing a carrot-and-stick approach. Steps that save on greenhouse gas emissions, such as saving energy in our buildings, improving insulation, and upgrading heating systems, will benefit from grants, tax rebates, and other incentives. But inefficient, fossil fuel-burning properties, dependent on fuels such as oil, gas, and coal, will be penalized through higher taxes. Additionally, the energy performance certificate now mandatorily displayed on properties on sale or for rent in many parts of the world will clearly distinguish between energy-wasting and energy-efficient properties, similar to energy ratings for household appliances and vehicles.

Paris 2015 (COP 21)

As was the case with the previous 20 International Conferences of the Parties (COP 1 to 20), the successful ones are those where the advance preparations were critical to the final outcomes. In other words, all the hard work was done prior to the summit, international positions were adopted, and bargaining was complete. All that's left are the fanfare and optics at the summit, where agreements are finalized and ceremonially signed. Because the host city lends its name to the gathering, the outcome can enhance or tarnish the city's international reputation. The political focus of the host government is critical in the run-up to the summit to ensure that all international leaders are on course for agreement.

Held in Copenhagen, Denmark, in December 2009, COP 15 failed to deliver on any key issues and is regarded by most commentators as a failure. There may have been many reasons for this, from bad timing to a global recession to falling global temperatures, which undermined the case for global warming. There was, however, another factor that most commentators agree was key: The host government played a weak role before and during the summit. Consequently, progress on all matters regarding collective international agreement on carbon emission reductions and climate change responsibility was frustrated. The summit concluded with a series of mixed messages and without a unified deal or accord from all parties. There was one noteworthy outcome, an agreed objective to hold the increase in global temperature below two degrees Celsius. The implementation of this remains the corner stone upon which COP 21 in Paris will be judged.

The Paris gathering positioned itself differently to overcome many of the perceived failures identified from the Copenhagen summit. France, the host country, was acutely aware of the potential impact that failure could have on its image and has been very proactive on the international stage, making sure that everything possible was done to ensure success in December 2015. Much preparation work was done. French president Francois Hollande went on a mission to build global diplomatic momentum and visited many countries in advance, including the Philippines, one of the front-line countries in the battle against climate change. Because of its vulnerable geographic position in terms of storms, typhoons, and rising sea levels, the Philippines' stance on any agreement at COP 21 is considered crucial to the overall success of the summit. In addition, there have been many unique developments that may strengthen the prospects for success.

- Earth's warmest year on record was 2014, according to the World Meteorological Organisation.
- California enters its fourth year of drought, as melting snow in the Sierra Nevada Mountains disappears due to climate change. This snowmelt normally accounts for 60% of California's water supply.
- UNESCO issued a report stating that the planet could face a 40% water shortage by 2030.
- The United States and China made a historic joint announcement in November 2014 to reduce carbon pollution.
- Many countries have demonstrated commitment to Paris 2015 by submitting their contributions to the UN climate change secretariat.
- Key milestones were agreed in Geneva on 13th February 2015, when all 194 participating countries agreed a negotiating text.

According to Christiana Figueres, executive secretary of UNFCCC, "if the trend is your friend, then Governments in Paris will be working against a background of the most climate-friendly conditions the world has yet seen." However, the true success of Paris 2015 will not be determined by grand policies set down by national governments at the conference but by the actions taken by everyone immediately afterward to implement those same policies.

Energy Security

Climate change and energy security are two sides of the same coin. The driving force to find zero-carbon, renewable sources of energy is either a need to find local fuel sources that do not add further to the greenhouse gas effect or an energy supply not dependent on diminishing oil and gas reserves.

Take the United Kingdom, for instance, which has had a comfortable energy supply since the vast coalfields of northern England were discovered in the late 18th century. Coal ignited the Industrial Revolution, and not only did it drive new industries that exported goods worldwide, it was also a leading export, generating high levels of income for the country. By the 1970s, the coal industry was faltering and its future looked ominous. The U.K. government enacted legislation to clean up smog in cities, which spelled the end for dirty fuels, limiting where coal could be burned. More efficient than coal, oil and gas were better suited to powering newer heating systems and electricity generating stations. Just as the coal industry went into decline, the U.K. discovered oil and gas in the North Sea. This find protected the balance of payments on an import-export basis, and the U.K. continued to be a net exporter of energy until 2005, when gas and oil reserves began to decline.

Today, the United Kingdom imports over 75% of its coal needs, 30% of its gas needs, and 20% of its oil needs, at a cost that is thought to be in excess of £5 billion. This is problematic for two reasons: Hard-earned cash leaves the country to pay for what is essentially a day-to-day consumable product and, more critically, Britain is fast becoming wholly dependent on the political goodwill of neighboring countries for its energy supply, referred to as energy in-security. No country can afford to leave itself vulnerable to the whims of neighboring disputes on such a critical issue.

The fragility of such dependency was highlighted in 2006, when Russia turned off a pipeline passing through Ukraine that supplied gas to Central and Western Europe. This occurred because of a dispute over gas payments between Russia and Ukraine, and the net result was that no European country downstream of Ukraine received any gas until the dispute was resolved. Tension subsequently escalated in 2014–15, and Russia now regularly turns off the gas supply running through Ukraine, leaving all dependent European countries at the mercy of the Russia-Ukraine relationship.

Future-Proofing

The rise and fall of consumer oil and gas prices relates directly to the cost of crude oil, which is, to some extent, governed by global demand. There are other dynamics at play in what is the world's largest industry. For example, there are many theories as to why oil prices fell so dramatically in 2014–15, but it is clear that the large oil cartels can, at a whim, control the cost of crude. From 2012 to 2014, prices were high, at $100–$120 per barrel, and many analysts maintained that the price was artificially high, given that the major world economies were in recession. Moreover, at this time, many large solar farms and wind farms started to generate electricity at a cost that was starting to look very competitive relative to the price of oil. The shale gas and oil industry, particularly in the United States, also came of age during this period. The net result was that demand for crude oil was down.

Decreased demand and increased supply meant something had to give. The Organisation of Oil Exporting Countries (OPEC) countries had to choose between reducing supply and maintaining prices or reducing prices and increasing demand. Saudi Arabia could afford to reduce supply to keep the price high, but other OPEC countries such as a recession-hit Russia could not afford the luxury of reduced income in order to keep prices artificially high. Simple supply-demand math won out in the end, and the price per barrel of oil dropped significantly, to under $60. Clearly, any country that is entirely dependent on foreign energy imports places its entire economy at the mercy of a great big Monopoly game played by major oil-producing countries.

The Saudi OPEC governor Mohammad Al Madi perhaps summed the situation up best when, in 2015, as the price per barrel was at $55, he stated *...We understand that all countries want higher incomes... we want higher incomes, but we want higher incomes for us and future generations...* While prices are low, alternative sources of energy struggle to compete. Just when the shale oil and gas industry was starting to provide a real alternative energy supply, its cost-effectiveness was completely undermined by the current low price of crude oil. This is a key consideration for many governments worldwide that were placing their bets on finding oil and gas reserves by incentivizing higher-cost shale explorers. For instance, the U.K. government offered planning authorities increased income from local rates on a type of profit-share basis in the hope that planning permissions would be more easily granted for this process. But, apart from the very controversial and environmentally unfriendly fracking process, shale is not, as a rule, economically viable to pursue. Another quote from Saudi Arabia's OPEC governor should explain the dilemma. *Our vision is simply the following: the producers which have low costs have to have the priority to produce, but those who have high costs have to wait to produce.* In other words, the major players can control not just cost but where and when oil is produced.

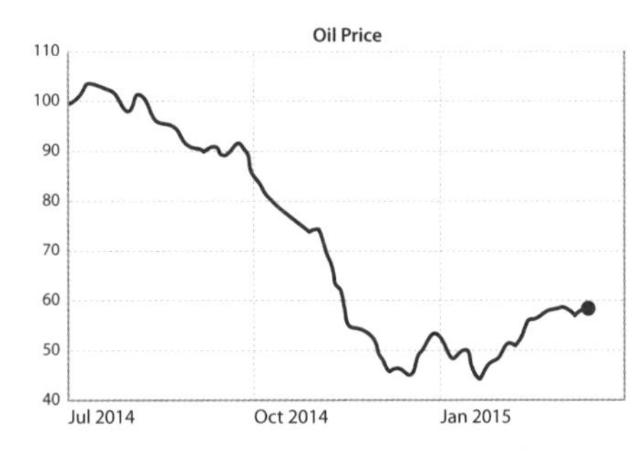

Governments concerned about energy security have two clear choices: reduce national demand or find new, alternative supplies in order to become independent of the fossil fuel cartels. Encouraging reduced demand usually entails strict regulation in conjunction with penalties in the form of taxation/carbon levies or an outright ban on inefficient energy products. Reducing demand on energy imports is not a short-term goal; it needs some very long-term strategic thinking.

The problem here is a clash of interests, as politicians and governments, who are always the cheerleaders for growth, try to grow the economy while reducing energy demand. As economies struggle to overcome this dilemma, it is always the poorest in society who suffer and, in this instance, struggle to meet their ever-increasing energy bills.

Fuel Poverty

Fuel poverty is a relatively new concept, one that is fast making news headlines around the world. It has slightly different connotations in different places, but it basically refers to households that cannot afford to keep their homes adequately warm or cool at a reasonable cost, relative to their income, a figure that is generally assumed to be 10% of income. It's an important concept because, as fuel prices rise, many more households will fall into fuel poverty. There are a number of converging factors that lead to fuel poverty:

- Low income households, including those on state pension or assistance
- Rising fuel and energy prices
- Poor building energy efficiency
- Inadequate and expensive to run heating/cooling systems
- Overly large or underused properties

These criteria for fuel poverty also clearly identify the categories of occupants and buildings in need of energy-efficient upgrades. Because these households, by definition, don't have any surplus income, they need government support and intervention. The elderly are one such category. They are more likely to suffer fuel poverty because they tend to live in older, sometimes larger, properties, which are harder and more expensive to heat and maintain. Additionally, they are more susceptible to the effects of both heat and cold and need more regulated temperatures.

In the United Kingdom, for instance, where fuel poverty is better defined than anywhere else, there is a framework of measures specifically designed to tackle this issue. A fund to support upgrade works comes from levies on the large energy suppliers, which in turn claim the carbon credits generated from the energy-efficient upgrades of targeted buildings, including homes, while fulfilling an obligation of their license. In other words, the energy companies have to actively promote energy efficiency in order to retain their license to operate.

In the United States, low-income families can avail of financial support to combat fuel poverty by way of the **Weatherization Assistance Programme (WAP)**. This fund helps families reduce their energy bills by making their homes more energy-efficient. Fuel poverty is becoming more widespread, with as many as 7 million U.S. families availing of the fund annually. While each state has its own criteria for eligibility, the **U.S. Department of Energy (DOE)** provides all funds centrally. The WAP web site offers a full map of opportunities, projects, and activities, including energy-saving lighting, boiler replacement, and insulation upgrades. (See appendix for WAP references).

Countries that monitor fuel poverty have seen a rise in both numbers and the severity of need. Short-term solutions such as direct aid and supplementary income to meet increasing energy bills will not create any measurable economic benefit. However, longer-term solutions such as improving the energy performance of buildings will protect the occupants, increase the asset value of the buildings, and help governments meet their own strategic efficiency targets in terms of energy security and measurable carbon emissions.

Property Values

In the global property boom of 2000–07, the capital value of property was primarily related to the widespread availability of bank finance. Obviously, location, size, and quality were important fixed factors, but in the places where cash was flowing most freely, property prices boomed. Then came the crash. In many European countries and in the United States, the crash was so severe that metrics used to determine property value were shattered.

That property-market jigsaw is still being put back together, particularly across Europe, as the commercial world re-evaluates the measurements that underpin good property value. A key ingredient in determining value that did not previously exist is energy-efficiency rating and the part it has to play in running costs and loan-payback periods for investors.

In previous years, energy-efficient buildings with low-carbon-fuel heating systems did not command higher sale prices than inefficient buildings. Elements such as good layouts, nice fitted kitchens, and good-looking doors, windows, floors, and ceilings were viewed as more important. This is changing, as building energy ratings and sustainability metrics gain a strong hold on people's perception of good value when purchasing or renting a building. An energy label, like the rating stamps on refrigerators and automobiles, rates the building from A (best) to G (worst) and is becoming mandatory in many countries. When energy cost mindfulness is imposed upon us from every quarter, why would someone buy a building that will be expensive to heat or cool when a similar one with a good energy rating might be locally available?

There is ample research suggesting that a good energy rating on a property increases its capital resale value and helps to secure a premium rent for leased property. With the growth of green building design, investors are recognizing that leading international sustainability certification schemes, which will be discussed below, are becoming essential testimonials for premium-priced buildings.

Breaking Old Habits

While most people like to stick with old familiar habits, change is being driven incrementally, as people strive to survive in this highly legislatively regulated, interconnected world. Change can be government-controlled or may simply come about as people follow the example of others or market trends: If my neighbors have a solar panel on their roof, why haven't I?

Many changes have already taken place. Houses were smaller 50 years ago and many were heated by coal fires and had one or more chimneys. Problems with smog, especially in built-up areas, prompted many governments to place restrictions on open fires. In fact, the first piece of energy legislation enacted in many places sought to improve air quality in cities and towns by placing emission controls on fixed and mobile sources, meaning buildings and automobiles. Tremendous advances have been made with regard to auto efficiency, and emissions have dropped dramatically over the last 25 years. The same cannot be said of the building trade, where changes have been less dramatic to date.

Now, however, construction is set to change in response to legislative changes, but house production, unlike auto production, involves numerous decision-makers and stakeholders, all of them directly involved in the project: various professionals, specialists, and tradespeople. This makes the process more cumbersome and more heavily dependent on the stick than the carrot.

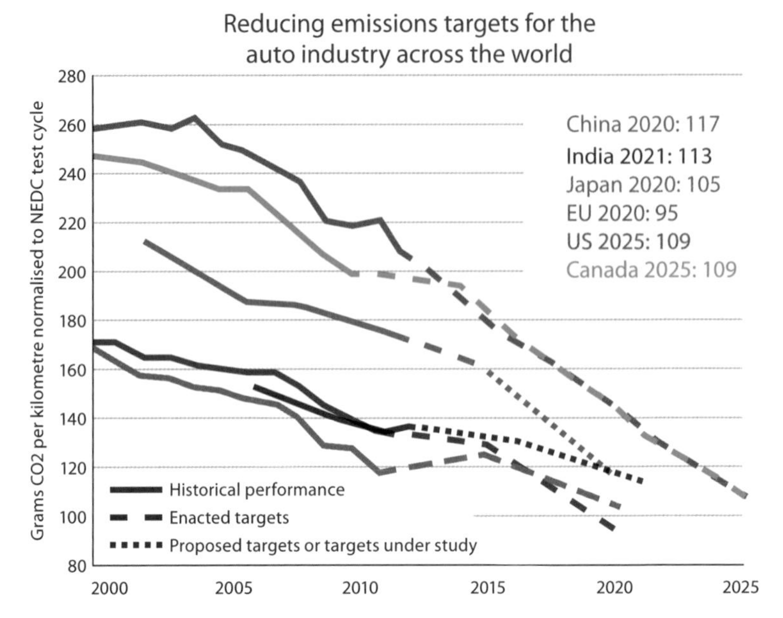

Chimneys are disappearing from our houses as a result of environmental and energy-efficiency regulations. They will be replaced by solar panels, which will trend, even as higher rates of market share lead to a fall in prices. The catalyst for this is not, however, a worthy ambition to save the planet but fear of noncompliance with government legislation. Under a law approved in 2014, rooftops on new buildings in commercial zones across France must either be partially covered in green plants or solar panels. Green roofs help reduce the amount of energy needed to heat a building in winter and cool it in summer. They also encourage biodiversity and reduced runoff to mains sewers by retaining rainwater. Solar panel installations on new commercial buildings are now mandatory in France, and other EU nations are following suit.

Climate Change Legislation

Worldwide, nations are drafting legislation aimed at introducing new economic models to meet the international drive for low-carbon economies, which sounds great and visionary but is, in fact, necessary to ward off from future energy crises. The concerns addressed by low-carbon legislation are energy security, fuel price hikes, and carbon emission penalties laid down by past and future UNFCCC protocols. In effect, the driving force behind climate change legislation is the commercial viability of individual national economies. The stealthy approach of incremental change that governments have imposed on energy-efficient issues has set a challenge for every man, woman, and child in the world.

Knowing how the move toward a low-carbon economy evolved and how it has influenced everyday choices, from buying light bulbs and energy-rated dishwashers to renovating our houses, will help us with the choices we face. Whether or not you believe that humans are responsible for climate change and the rise in global temperatures is probably of little consequence, given that legislators around the world do and are steadily making carbon-reduction principles a fact of life.

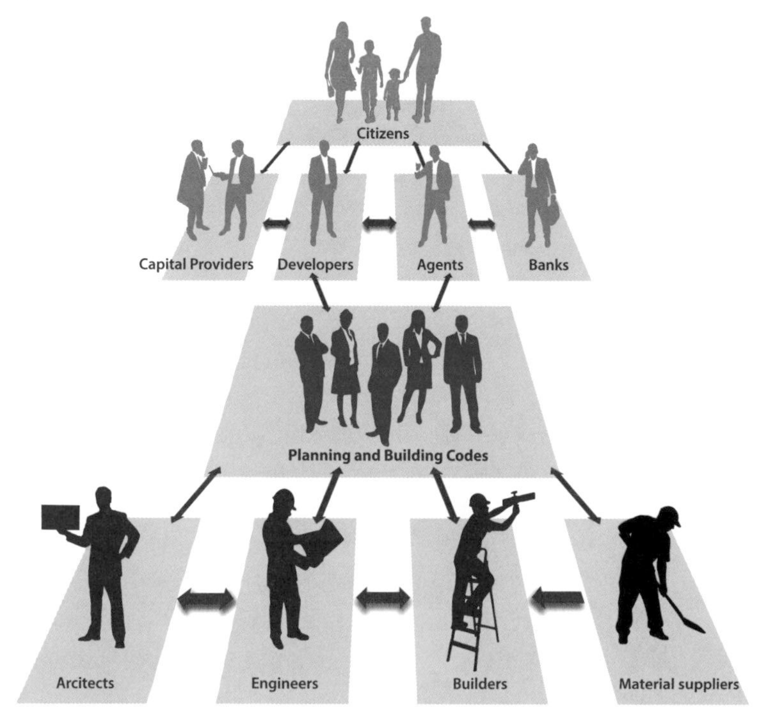

The building industry is undergoing one of its greatest challenges as it tries to keep pace with evolving climate change legislation. Nearly every traditional building technique and skill has become outdated, and the rules and regulations governing energy efficiency, renewable energy, and carbon emissions will decide how the construction sector develops in the future.

During time of great change, it is normally difficult to copper-fasten rules that will apply to a new and emerging set of circumstances. Nonetheless, in most countries, the first place to start is the planning process. Planning permission is traditionally the first permit necessary before any building work commences, whether for a new build or refurbishment work.

Planning Policy

Planning regulations, like most other government regulations, are reactive. Planners respond to emerging trends and formulate policies to curtail developments with restrictive guidelines. In most places, planning policy is mainly concerned with the quality of the built environment. Consequently, grants of planning permission are moving to encourage and favor more sustainable developments. As climate change takes hold, sustainable developments that are measurably adhering to a variety of new international standards (such as BREEAM and LEED, discussed below) are more favorably received. For instance, under Britain's Merton Rule, new commercial buildings over 1000 square meters must generate at least 10% of their energy needs using onsite renewable energy equipment before planning permission will be granted. To better understand where tomorrow's planning laws will take us in an age of climate change, it's worth taking a look at historic drivers of planning policy.

The first planning acts, which were introduced at late as the 20th century to control development, were very much focused on the condition of housing and the effect of poor housing on the spread of disease. Sanitation was a priority, as was curtailing the spread of cholera and typhoid with properly designed sewers and drains. With populations more than doubling in many major cities over the second half of the 19th century, some density and building-height restriction rules were needed. Practical considerations like zoning were introduced, dictating where housing should be built, and new developments were needed to accommodate growing populations without hampering a region's economic development. Another major concern of late 20th-century planners was how to accommodate fossil fuel-based transport, the automobile and its associated infrastructure.

Surprisingly, perhaps, planning policy or planning permissions were not usually prescriptive or proactive in terms of building design, fashion, or trends. So much so that when you look back over the development of an area, planning permission would have left its mark, not for what was built, but for what was not. On the plus side, planning zones protected green spaces, centralized housing, and separated it from industrial areas. High-rise developments and high-density housing was confined to urban areas. The rigidity of planning restrictions meant that compliance with policy was the building trend of the 20th century. What resulted were identical houses, all in straight lines; identical tower blocks; identical windows and doors; the brick finishes on one street in keeping with the brick finishes of the next. Moreover, new builds conformed to the style and finish of existing and previously granted developments, all in accordance with statutory obligations.

We are now in a new era of planning, which has changed considerably in recent years, perhaps most notably in the tightening of regulations to insist on greater use of renewable energy sources such as wind turbines and solar panels. Planning policy in most countries with a low-carbon agenda now favor developments that score high in terms of their green credentials. Planning remains the main overriding factor in refurbishment, but its status is becoming less and less pronounced as climate control policy takes center stage and involves itself in the micro details of building construction.

Building Codes

Complying with building codes is a separate process to planning. Building codes are principally concerned with the standard to which buildings are designed and constructed. They cover everything from structure to electrics, including water supply, drainage, fabric and materials, access issues, fire safety, and, increasingly, fuel and energy conservation as well as reduced carbon dioxide emissions.

Building codes and regulations have evolved slowly since their introduction centuries ago, and little attention was paid to new thinking or to encouraging the latest technology as they evolved. They tend to reluctantly embrace change by retrospective attrition rather than vision. Historically, too, codes were only introduced to deal with some error or faulty building practices discovered in the existing building stock. Globally, building codes have undergone more changes in the last 10 years than they did in the previous 200.

Like planning regulations, building codes came about because of public health and safety issues. For instance, the Great Fire of London in 1666 had tragic consequences that led to the introduction of one of the first-ever pieces of building-control legislation. Because many structures were razed when fires spread from one wooden building to the next, the earliest codes introduced firebreaks to prevent the spread of fire between buildings. At about the same time, New York City was growing and laws governing construction were required to control development. Poor building standards, particularly in relation to sanitation and water supply, were responsible for health issues, notably the cholera epidemic of 1832. Given those circumstances, it is unsurprising that building permits first emerged to ensure best practice in sewer design and construction. Similarly, today's new codes focusing on energy conservation and carbon emission controls are a response to another set of circumstances.

Energy Codes

The same sorts of challenges face all countries that seek to address inefficiencies with regard to new construction and existing building stock. For example, the United Kingdom, generally recognized as a leader in setting new standards, only started to take energy efficiency in building practice into account as late as the 1980s. At first, energy standards developed on a piecemeal basis and were slow to become fully established in mainstream construction. Basic insulation levels were first mandated for roofs and attic spaces, and insulation standards for walls and floors soon followed. Then, single glazed windows were replaced by double and now treble glazing. Minimum boilers efficiencies followed, and a 95% minimum is now standard in most developed countries. Not only were standards incrementally changed over time, they were also incrementally raised. Take attic insulation: When originally introduced, its mandated thickness was 50mm, a figure that subsequently increased to 100mm and 200mm and will continue to rise to 500mm and more, as near-zero-energy buildings and Passive House standards become part and parcel of building codes. Today, there are problems not just with older building stock that predates energy regulation but also with buildings that were constructed to meet early energy codes and can now be deemed inadequate and in need of further upgrading.

	1976	1985	1990	1994		2000	2005	2010
			U - Values W m^{-2} °C^{-1}					
External Wall	1.0	0.6	0.45	0.45	0.35	0.45	0.35	0.35
Roof	0.6	0.35	0.25	0..2	0.16	0.25	0.16	0.16
Floor	1.0	0.6	0.45	0.35	0.25	0.45	0.25	0.25
Windows	NS*			3.0	2.0	3.3	2.0	2.0
Windows as % of external walls	17%	12%	–					
Windows as % of total floor areas	–	–	15%	15%	22.5%	22.5%	25%	25%

*Not Specified

Like other developed nations, the United States struggles to implement a uniform approach to building codes, with individual states at different phases of implementing energy-efficiency measures. What is more, U.S. codes have to cater to a wide range of climatic conditions, from California to Alaska. When designing and specifying building details and products, therefore, the construction sector has to think local and comply with state, as opposed to federal, codes. As the climate changes so much across the United States, insulation requirements, air-conditioning efficiencies, and emissive coatings on glass in windows, etc. have different values according to where the building is sited.

Although traditionally not known for energy-efficient building standards, China, over the past five years, has increased its energy efficiency compliance in new buildings to a staggering 99.5%. In other words, nearly all new buildings comply with the country's new codes. China has managed to achieve this at a time when it is undergoing one of its greatest-ever building booms, with more than 20 billion square feet of new construction added each year. How has this been possible? For one thing, the country doesn't have the level of bureaucratic constraints that can cause paralysis in other countries, including EU nations. But that's not the whole story. China has implemented clear, finite standards as well as measurable and accountable controls. Although China is the target of plenty of criticism with regard to its carbon emissions, Western nations might do well to take some guidance from its success with energy-efficient construction.

The enforcement of building codes and regulations is also vitally important today. Because we are not intuitive about energy efficiency, we are totally dependent on some form of measurement to determine whether or not our building has reached required standards. Contractual relationships with builders are fraught with challenges, and often the only way to successfully complete a construction project is to be guided by design and building standards and then contract builders to do the same. This is difficult to do without metrics to track contract performance. In Step 2, details will be provided of individual performance tests such as airtightness, insulation values, heating system efficiencies, and water efficiencies. In the end, however, an independently certified, overall energy rating for a building is often the best measurable benchmark to establish regulation compliance.

Energy Certificates and Labels

Energy labels, which are becoming increasingly common, are designed to help consumers to quickly determine the energy efficiency of an appliance before they buy. Many appliances such as washing machines, dishwashers, refrigerators, and TVs must display them, as must all cars and motor vehicles that are sold from new. Additionally, energy-efficiency identifiers are mandatory on properties for sale or rent in many countries. There will be a proliferation of such labels as laws extend their reach to all appliances. There are also water labels in the same shape and format as energy labels, designed for products that contain and dispense water such as faucets, WCs, showers, and bathtubs.

Most people are familiar with energy display certificates, and prospective buyers understand what the labels mean in terms of energy use. Indeed, the energy display system has been very successful in influencing people's choice of appliances, and the A-grade category has been refined over time, to A1, A2, or A+, A++, etc. Manufacturers have fully embraced certification as part of their sales and marketing strategies, so much so that there is now tremendous competition between them to be the best in category.

Another success story is the energy display label attached to new automobiles indicating the level of CO2 emissions. In many EU countries, the cost of road tax is directly related to a vehicle's CO2 emissions. Smaller models require less fuel and normally have lower CO2 emissions, which translate into lower road tax. Other energy-saving models include hybrids, which run on both electric power and a fossil fuel and offer considerable savings in fuel usage. In addition, all-electric vehicles command the top certification and qualify for the lowest road tax. The graph on page x shows the considerable progress made by the auto industry in reducing CO2 emissions over the past 40 years.

Building energy certification has a long way to go to catch up with product and vehicle emissions ratings in terms of simplicity and the public's level of comfort with the ratings system.

Comparison of Fuel economy factors for cars and buildings	
Engine size	Type of building
Number of seats	Floor area
Number of passagers carried	Occupants
Luggage / Trailer	Servers and other special loads
Distance driven	Hours of occupancy
Economy driving	Energy management
Tyres maintenance	Maintenance
Engine tuning	Recommissioning systems
Fuel gauge	Energy meters

Perhaps the best place to start when trying to get to grips with building energy ratings is to compare them to the fuel efficiency of a vehicle. It is generally understood that the more miles/kilometres a vehicle can travel per gallon/litre, the more economical it is to drive. So a car that travels just 20 miles per gallon (U.S. mpg), or 11.7 litres per 100km, would be considered a fuel guzzler compared to a more efficient model rated at 75 mpg, or 3.2 litres per 100km.

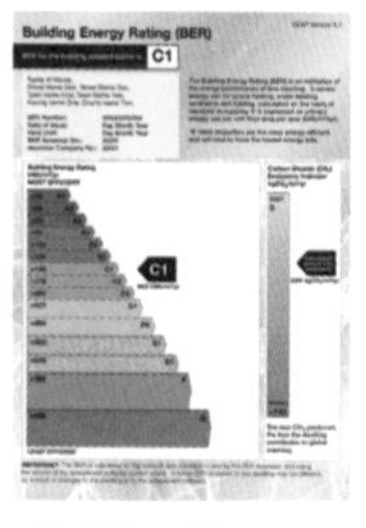

Building Energy Rating

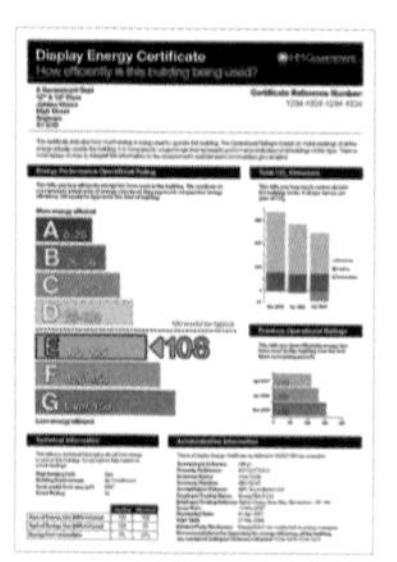

Display Energy Certificate

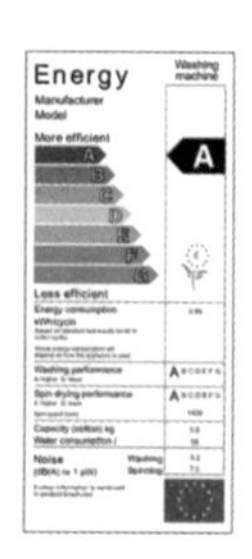

Dishwasher Label

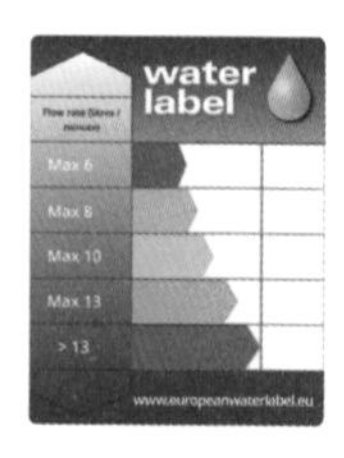

Water label

In a building, the accepted basis for energy rating is the amount of energy used per meter square of floor space per year (kwh/m2/yr). In most countries where the building energy rating system is adopted, the label is a simple design, with a color-coded system that goes from green for good to red for poor. Of course, this simplicity masks the very complex set of criteria and standardized assessment methodology that inevitably underpins the accuracy and relevance of the label. While there is much critical review around the methodologies used to calculate label values and the levels of training needed by energy assessors, the label is nonetheless fast gaining universal recognition. Each country has adopted a unique version of the building labeling system, but they all follow the same basic format. Some of the more popular energy rating labels are displayed above.

Sustainable Leadership

Real progress in energy efficiency and sustainability can only be made when commercial interests have a stake. Government regulations, by their nature, are reactive so do not provider leadership. Building regulations and codes can really only pass or fail, where buildings are set minimum standards below which noncompliance is the considered outcome. Above a pass, however, there is no incentive or measure of what higher-than-building-code compliance might even look like. This represents an inherent weakness in any government-led legislative regime.

Today, many of the key players in the building and property industry realize that having a verifiable sustainability rating is good for business. If you carry out a web search for green buildings, you will return an overwhelming amount of information, making it difficult to distinguish the superficially green from the legitimate, fully designed and built green sustainable developments. The growth of this new and emerging green industry is rapidly becoming a business opportunity worldwide. Indeed, there are numerous new green business opportunities in promoting greater efficiencies across the full spectrum of sustainability concerns such as water, natural resources, biodiversity, pollution, and reduced greenhouse gas emissions.

Building Environmental Assessment Methods (BEAMS)

Building environmental assessment methods originally developed as a voluntary market-driven benchmarking system. They offered a structured means of measuring the environmental credentials for building projects that sought to surpass the minimum building code regulations but still gain credit for achieving higher standards. Over the years, the emphasis has changed to meet the challenges of today, with water and energy now very much key weighted factors. The colder northern European countries place greater emphasis on energy, whereas water-stressed countries such as Australia and the Middle East place greater weighting on water efficiency. However, there are generally seven main categories for each assessment tool: site conditions, energy efficiency, water efficiency, materials, indoor environmental quality, waste, and cost economics. There are now numerous environmental assessment tools in use worldwide, to reflect local climatic and environmental issues. It is also clear that building assessment methods will quickly migrate from "nice to do" to "must do" standards as governments everywhere follow the example set by the original voluntary standards and make them part of national standards.

International Certification Rating Tools

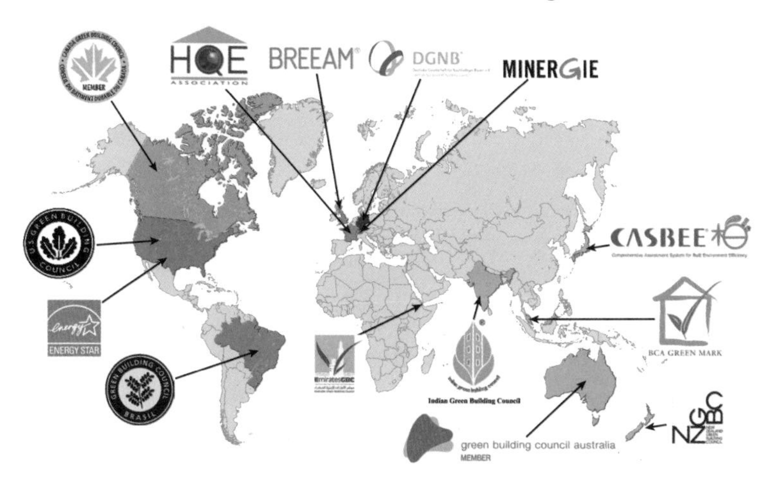

As discussed under planning policy above, new developments that are moving toward measurable building environmental assessment methods are becoming more favorably considered in terms of planning, as climate change takes hold. Consequently, a minimum grading under a locally preferable BEAMS system is required by certain planning authorities before they will consider granting planning permission for developments. Financial institutions and fund managers now increasingly recognize them as benchmarks for risk mitigation in sales and investment transactions.
There are several green assessment systems in use worldwide, but two in particular stand out in terms of popularity and merit further discussion here. They are BREEAM and LEED.

BREEAM

One of the first environmental rating tools was the **Building Research Establishment's Environmental Assessment Method**, or **BREEAM**, which was developed in the United Kingdom in 1990. As the world's longest established building environmental assessment tool, its name is now synonymous with good building practice. Many countries worldwide, including Canada, Australia, and Hong Kong, have adopted BREEAM and versions of it as their national environmental assessment tool. What is more, over one million buildings have been registered with BREEAM since it was introduced.

As an environmental standard, BREEAM covers a wide range of developments, from new-build residential to commercial and from rural community to urban schemes. Over the past ten years in particular, energy, carbon emissions, and water use and the potential for flooding have been added as key criteria within the assessment. There is also a dedicated BREEAM category for domestic dwelling refurbishment, which provides a benchmark for owners, designers, and builders to aspire to when undertaking upgrades. In Britain, home to BREEAM, it is expected that over 80% of the existing building stock will still be around in 2050, which means that the refurbishment sector cannot be ignored if climate change is to be addressed.

All BREEAM-graded buildings are measured against a checklist of compliance standards, and depending on the score, they are awarded ratings on a scale from "Outstanding" to "Pass." Points are awarded for each element the standard considers important, with energy in refurbishment taking the lion's share of the points: A total of 42% of the category weighting rests with energy. Most of the traditional building stock in Britain has solid brick and block walls, solid floors, roof spaces without insulation, and ornate windows and doors. Given that all of these are difficult to treat, energy upgrades are heavily weighed in favor of reducing energy loss. This may not be the case in every country, so the adoption of BREEAM standards must be adjusted to suit local climate and building methods.

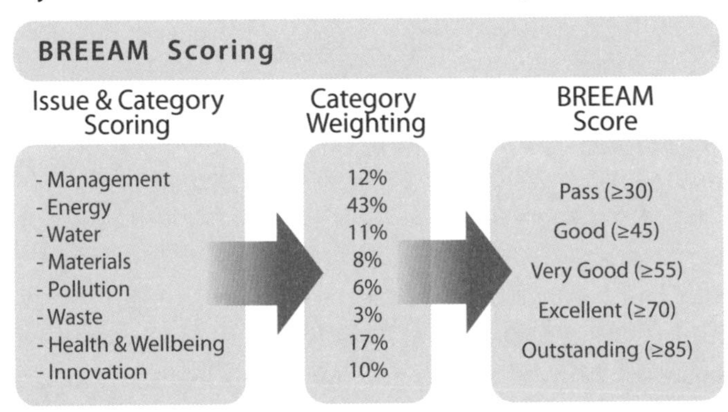

There is no direct link between energy rating certification and the BREEAM rating, but the latter is much more detailed and represents a more comprehensive evaluation for a whole building. Because of BREEAM's high weighting for energy in refurbishment properties, an outstanding rating usually correlates to an A-rated standard on a building energy certificate.

LEED

Leadership in Energy and Environmental Design, or LEED, is the U.S. version of BREEAM. It was developed by the U.S. Green Building Council in 2000 and is now considered a first-generation assessment system, one that is widely used internationally for green building certification. LEED and BREEAM both hold the prestigious position as the world's leading design and assessment methods for sustainable buildings, and justifiably so because they are far ahead of the competition. LEED is a flexible system that can be applied to most building types: commercial, industrial, residential multi-story units, single homes, and refurbishments.

The LEED Green Building Rating System issues points across nine basic categories, including sustainable site issues, energy efficiency, water efficiency, materials, resources, and indoor environmental quality. The more points scored, the higher the level of certification achieved and the more sustainable the building is deemed to be. There are four levels of certification awarded by an independent certifier: Platinum, Gold, Silver, or simply LEED certified.

Zero Net Energy (ZNE) and Nearly Zero Energy Buildings (NZEB)

The common thread in developed countries is that traditional buildings consume 40% of the total fossil fuel energy and are significant contributors of greenhouse gases. While there might be different terminology used worldwide to describe the conditions needed for buildings to be defined as zero-energy users, the underlying driving force is the same: the need to reduce energy consumed in buildings. All new building energy codes are leading towards net zero-energy use. The definition of net zero-energy consumption usually involves a combination of high energy efficiency with the balance of required energy coming from renewable sources created on or local to the site. California was the first U.S state to implement a plan for all residential buildings to have Zero Net Energy (ZNE) by 2020, with all commercial buildings required to be ZNE by 2030. The ZNE building in California is defined as a structure that produces as much energy onsite as it consumes on an annual basis.

The EU has mandated all member states to implement a nearly zero-energy buildings policy for all buildings by 2020. It defines nearly zero-energy building as a building that has a very high energy performance.

The nearly zero or very low amount of energy required should be covered to a very significant extent by energy from renewable sources, including energy from renewable sources produced on-site or nearby. Because zero-energy definitions vary in each country, the International Energy Agency (IEA) has developed an evaluation tool that helps bring together some of the criteria that define net zero-energy buildings. Details of the evaluation tool are available from the agency's web site (see Appendix 2).
Whether focused on new or existing buildings, achieving net zero-energy involves three fundamental steps:

- Optimize passive building design
- Maximize energy efficiency
- Use onsite (local) renewable energy to cover balance of energy needs

Details for optimizing the passive design of buildings together with the criteria for selecting appropriate renewable energy supply sources are discussed in Steps 5 and 6. However, the best place to start to understand the ultimate in passive building design is to study the German Passive House standard.

Passive House

Passive House building, or "passivhaus," was developed in Germany in the 1990s and is now an internationally acknowledged standard for energy-efficient buildings. The word "haus" in German means building (as well as house), and passive refers to the fundamental heating for the house. Passive House certification is widely viewed as the ultimate standard in energy-efficient construction, and it doesn't just apply to houses; it can apply to any building. However, Passive House certification only applies to the energy-efficient aspect of the building and not to the wider environmental issues covered by standards such as
BREEAM and LEED.

Passive houses are essentially highly insulated and airtight buildings, in which the form and shape has been optimized to suit the appropriate climate zone and local weather conditions, and attention to construction detail becomes a priority. The structure and fabric of the building envelope are finely designed and built to a standard more akin to a premanufactured process than is normally possible outside of factory conditions.

Passive House Principal Details

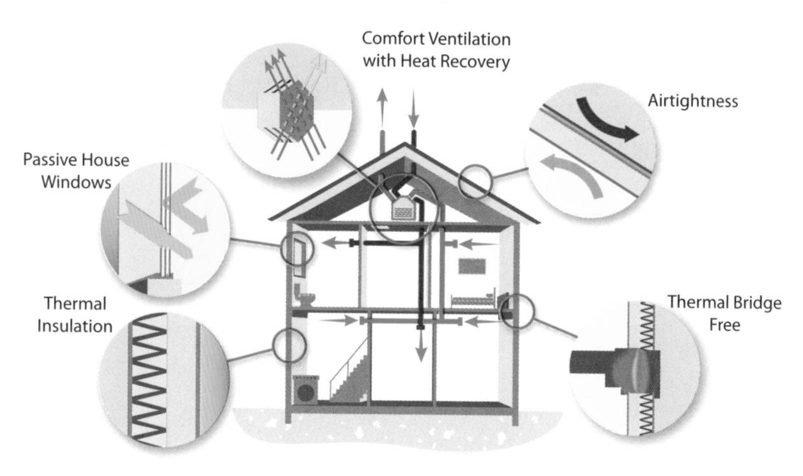

There are five basic principles to which every passive house must comply. After the building form and shape have been optimized to suit the particular climate zone and local weather conditions, attention to construction detail becomes a priority. The standard of detail involved really did not exist until the advent of Passive House. The element that most people find difficult to come to terms with is the level of airtightness needed. The more airtight the building, the better the insulation can perform. Passive House criteria are heavily weighted toward complete blanket-like insulation of the building envelope. Here again, this entails a level of detail and analysis that was new to the building industry, in that there is a nearly forensic elimination of cold bridging also know as thermal bridging (see Step 4) throughout the building.

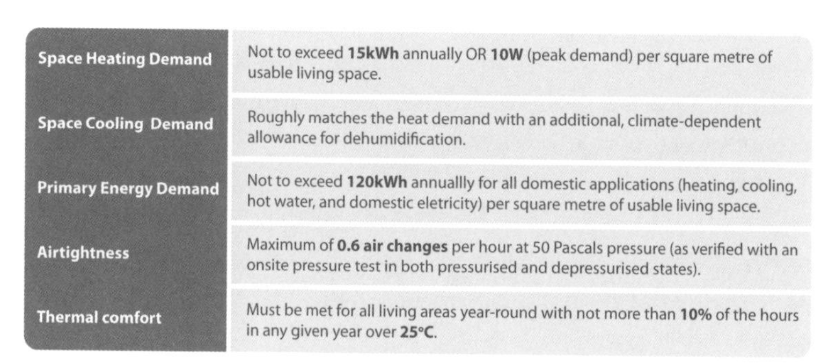

Space Heating Demand	Not to exceed **15kWh** annually OR **10W** (peak demand) per square metre of usable living space.
Space Cooling Demand	Roughly matches the heat demand with an additional, climate-dependent allowance for dehumidification.
Primary Energy Demand	Not to exceed **120kWh** annualIly for all domestic applications (heating, cooling, hot water, and domestic eletricity) per square metre of usable living space.
Airtightness	Maximum of **0.6 air changes** per hour at 50 Pascals pressure (as verified with an onsite pressure test in both pressurised and depressurised states).
Thermal comfort	Must be met for all living areas year-round with not more than **10%** of the hours in any given year over **25°C**.

Triple glazing is mandatory in all Passive House buildings. Ironically, the traditional weak points in buildings are the windows, but in Passive House design they become heating assets. The final detail essential to all Passive House buildings is ventilation, or more specifically heat recovery ventilation

(HRV). There is a perception that HRV adds a continuous electrical load to the building's energy costs, but this load is actually small and should only amount to between 2 to 3 kW/m2.

Passive House and Retrofit Upgrades

As the global retrofit market became increasingly important, a Passive House retrofitting standard emerged. It is slightly less onerous than full new-build Passive House certification because it takes into account the difficult and costly nature of deep refurbishment. Passive House principles can be applied during the upgrade of existing buildings but only with a full understanding that a deep retrofit is required, whereby the building is completely gutted and rebuilt to meet the same high standards as a new-build passive house. With retrofitting, there are some relaxations of standards and a different certificate, called EnerPHit, which was introduced in 2011 in cold climates and in 2014 for hot climates. Only existing buildings that are deemed by structure or form to be incapable of complying with full Passive House standards are eligible for EnerPHit certification. Although slightly more relaxed than full Passive House standards, it is probably the world's toughest upgrade standard. The key issue in any deep retrofit project is moisture movement, which is specifically addressed in EnerPHit analysis. The relaxations of EnerPHit compared to Passive House are as follows:

- Annual heat demand allowance increased 10 to 25kW/m2
- Airtightness criteria increased from 0.6 to 1.0 ach. (See also Step 3)
- Moisture movement calculated and addressed.
- U-values for walls, roofs, floors, windows, doors, and individual components have to meet slightly more flexible standards. (See also Step 4)

Retrofitting existing buildings to Passive House principles can have significant savings in terms of future energy running costs.

From 2014, Passive House allows for the use of solar panels to augment a building's energy supply and demand. If there was criticism of Passive House in the past, it centered on the inflexibility of integrating renewable energy into the certification process, but this new development will make the system more acceptable to a greater number of developers. The allowance for solar panels also serves as a basis for complying with the "Nearly Zero Energy Building" mandated for all new builds throughout the EU as of 2021.

There are currently over 50,000 buildings worldwide certified to Passive House standards, and there are a wide variety of designs to suit both hot and cold climates. While most Passive House structures built to date are residential new builds, a growing number of other building types such as schools, offices, supermarkets, hotels, and leisure centers are also becoming certified to Passive House standards.

Early Passive House designs were the target of some criticism because of their boxy shape. This calls to mind the film Crazy People, in which Dudley Moore starred as an advertising executive on a mission to tell the truth and creates an ad for Volvo, promoting a slogan to the effect that Volvo cars are boxy but good. The same could be said for early passive houses, which were very simple, with flush facades and no balconies, verandas, or elements that protrude and recess, thereby avoiding difficult cold bridging details. The elimination of places where cold bridging occurs is part of the preliminary design process for a passive house. The easiest way to achieve this is by designing walls and roofs that make the outside envelope flush and streamlined. Although Passive House designs have become increasingly imaginative over time, they still retain that boxy shape.

Passive houses, like Volvos, are arguably boxy but good!

A whole industry has grown up around the design and certification of buildings to Passive House standards. Software packages, technical guides, building training courses, certification training, and numerous research documents and literature are available from the Passivhaus Institute in Germany and its branches in various countries.

Green Funding Opportunities

There are numerous sources of funding available in most developed countries for green projects that involve energy efficiency and renewable energy. The primary objective is to support the development of new and emerging technologies that reduce greenhouses gases. While the major part of incentive-based funds target large energy-generation opportunities, including carbon capture and storage, a percentage of many funds is also set aside for the smaller domestic and residential markets. No single guide covers the multitude of grants, subsidies, funding opportunities, feed-in tariffs, tax rebates, loan guarantees, etc. for climate change mitigation factors. To properly navigate any funding opportunity, it will always be necessary to consult local government offices and web sites relevant to a particular area.

In the United States, for instance, numerous sources of funding for green building projects are available at national, state, and local levels for industry, government, nonprofit organizations, and homeowners. So anyone considering even a small job such as installing a new boiler or water heater should investigate whether the technology is eligible for financial incentives. The criteria for inclusion in any scheme will be specific to the local area.

Feed in Tariffs (FITs)

Renewable energy is not sufficiently competitive to encourge its uptake and so still needs some form of government policy or incentivized financial support to allow to compete with traditional fossil fuels. One of the most popular incentive programs, particularly for wind and solar energy generation, is feed-in tariffs (FITs). The United States was the first country to bring in FITs in the 1978 National Energy Act, which allowed renewable generators to connect directly to the national grid. This crucial piece of legislation paved the way for small systems to play a role in national power generation, and the success of the policy led to its emulation elsewhere, notaby in Germany, which now has what is considered best practice in FITs policy.

Feed-in tariffs work by providing price certainty to renewable-energy generators by way of a guaranteed price for each unit or kilowatt hour of electricity produced. FITs represent government management of the energy pricing market to encourage the uptake of low-carbon technology and reduce dependency on fossil fuels. Each country that introduces

FITs sets its own rates and incorporates varying levels of flexibility, cost, certainty, and contract durations to best suit its national energy markets. The payment received by suppliers depends on the size and type of technology used, and the feed-in tariff rate generally fluctuates with inflation for the guaranteed period, which can be up to 25 years. Most successful feed-in tariff schemes have a degression clause whereby the earlier you join the scheme, the better the rate achieved. This is designed to encourage early uptake while allowing for reduced payments to reflect reduced costs as the technologies gain wider mass-market appeal.

The renewable energy sector referred to here is not the large scale stuff such as wind farms, major hydroelectric dams, and ocean wave technology, but their micro counterparts. They are known as micro generation solar, hydro, wind, anaerobic digestion (AD), and combined heat and power (CHP). Micro suggests small, which they can be, although some systems can also generate up to 5 MW of electricity, or enough to power a large town. In fact, one of the optimum ways of generating electricity from a micro source is when a village or community can pool resources and needs and install a large wind turbine, AD plant, or CHP plant. The larger the plant, the greater the efficiencies and payback under the FITs scheme. However, the simplest and easiest technology to install and the most popular in most countries is solar Photovoltaic (PV). Under the FITs scheme, the payback can be under ten years and the PV panels required can be small enough to fit on the roof of a two-bed terraced house.

All of these micro methods are fabulous zero-carbon ways of generating electricity. The choice of renewable system often follows the rural-urban divide. Wind, hydro, AD, and, to some extent, CHP need space and comfortable distances from neighboring properties, which makes them most suited to rural settings. So those living in a city or town with small gardens are left with just one likely option, solar PV. All that is required is a good area of south-facing roof. Geographically, the more southern the location in the Northern Hemisphere or the more northern in the Southern Hemisphere, the more efficient the the output from the PV will be.

The German Experience

Germany was the first European country to adopt laws on feed-in tariffs and grid connections, in 1990. The guarantee that renewable electricity producers could supply electricity to the grid was fundamental to the success of the origional scheme. In its early years, the system was not sufficiently incentivized to encourage the uptake of renewable technologies, so a revised scheme with higher rates was implemented in 2000. This proved to be very effective and accelerated the uptake of micro generated electricity right up until 2015.

The new system set in place a framework of prices and tariffs that has now been copied the world over and forms the basis of all feed-in tariff regimes. The key elements of the new feed-in tariff policies are:

- The feed-in tariff reflects the generation costs. Hence, there are different prices for wind power, solar power, hydro electric, and AD and for projects of different sizes.
- The term of agreement was extended to 20 years, making projects attractive to banking instutitions.
- The tariffs had a degression schedule, which effectively means that the sooner a project is ready for connection to the grid, the better the rate.

The beauty of this system is that there are no advantages given to existing market-leading branded technologies over new technology. The feed-in tariff method pays for the energy delivered, not for the technology. In a sense, it is an energy procurement contract (EPC) and if no energy is delivered, measured in kilowatts, there is no payment. The system has been highly successful, and it has driven the emergence of many new technologies, placing Germany in the pivotal position as a global leader in renewable energy technology.

It hasn't, of course, been plain sailing all the way. FITs have many detractors, namely the utility companies and the coal and oil industry, which have consistently lobbied governments to reduce the tariff payments, succeeding in 2015. The tariffs in Germany have been lowered, but that follows over 25 years growth in renewable electricity generation. It is estimated that Germany today produces more than 25% of its electricity from renewable sources, which places it ahead of all the countries that share the 80% target set for renewables by 2050.

Renewable Heat Incentive (RHI)

Unlike the FITs scheme, RHI is payment for usable heat rather than electricity. A renewable heat incentive scheme is a relatively new concept. In 2011, the British government became the first to introduce a long-term financial support program for renewable heat. The practicalities of this scheme are still working themselves out, and to date no other country has followed the U.K. lead and introduced an RHI. Many countries are, however, watching the British progress and will undoubtable follow. The RHI scheme is best suited to more northerly, cooler climates, where heating demand accounts for a bigger percentage of carbon emissions and energy usage.

In order to increase the percentage of heat generated from renewable sources, some form of RHI is going to be needed, particularly for countries that are about to sign up to the new Paris protocol. Because the U.K. system currently represents best practice, newcomers are undoubtably going to track its structure. So it is therefore worth exploring how it works and which technologies are likely to be eligible. In the British system, the RHI has two versions, one for domestic homes and the other for nondomestic dwellings such as industry, businesses, and the public sector.

Domestic RHI. Allowing the RHI to apply to single domestic homes is one of the key aspects of the success of the whole process. In order to change the public's mind-set to address climate change, the individual must become involved. Far too many of the other financial incentive schemes miss this point. Another strategic advantage of the U.K. system is that it is also the first to start linking renewable energy (heat in this instance) to the energy efficiency of the building. In other words, the building must have a minimum building energy certificate before joining the RHI scheme. There is little point in generating renewable heat efficiently if it is allowed to go to waste because of poorly insulated building fabric.

The domestic RHI applies to biomass boilers, solar water heating, and certain heat pumps such as air and ground source types. Payments are made for seven years and based on the amount of renewable heat measured in kilowatt hours generated by the heating system. The payment amount is estimated by an RHI payment calculator, which is available online. Because heat meters can be relatively expensive, particularly in domestic heat installations, the payment amount can estimated based on a number of factors such as the building size, number of occupants, and the energy output of the heat-producing unit in kilowatts. The payment method for larger comercial installations must, however, relate to the measured heat delivered, as confirmed by a certified and verified heat meter.

Nondomestic RHI. The nondomestic RHI scheme is designed to tackle the U.K. government's comitment to produce at least 15% of its energy from renewable sources. The domestic RHI scheme will help to kick-start the process and allow for individual and community buy-in, but the real impact will be felt when industrial and commercial properties, including small businesses, hospitals, and schools, come onboard.

A large range of renewable technologies are available and for a guaranteed minium period of 20 years. Like in FITs, there is a degression period, which means the amount of payment is reduced as greater uptake forces prices down. However, once you join the scheme, prices are gauranteed and index-linked, which acts as an encouragement for early involvement. The renewable heat technologies supported by the scheme include:

- Biomass
- Ground and water source heat pumps
- Geothermal
- Solar thermal
- Biogas
- Biomethane
- Combined heat and power (CHP)

The RHI is a relatively young system and there are still many glitches to be sorted out, particularly with regard to tariff payment amounts. But the overriding principles surrounding the implementation of RHI systems to tackle climate change are here to stay and will undoubtably spread to more countries.

Tax Incentives

Providing tax-based incentives for the purchase of energy-efficient products or services is government policy in many countries. The tax incentive process, also know as a tax credit or tax rebate, is open to any individual who pays tax. The business version is usually referred to as an accelerated capital allowance because the tax rebate is returned to the business in one year rather than over a number of years. The scheme is popular because it allows national governments to promote and control energy efficiency without necessarily having to commit any upfront payments. The actual cost of maintaining the relevant database of approved products and services suitable for inclusion in the scheme is often paid for by the product manufacturers and operated by sub-government agencies and nonprofit organizations. The tax incentive schemes can also extend to renewables such as biomass boilers and solar thermal arrays.

Another advantage of tax-based schemes is that they allow for an element of quality control, which is especially relevant when new products come on the market. Documents and specifications can vary to meet national building code requirements such as minimum efficiency standards for boilers or insulation values for windows. Before embarking on any energy-efficiency-based upgrade works, it is always worth checking local government web sites for the latest information. This will reveal whether tax incentives have an end of year completion date or changing eligibility dates depending on when works commence. Because tax-incentive based schemes rely on databases of approved suppliers and products, it is also important to ensure that any product or service you intend using is approved.

The types of energy efficiency products and services that normally qualify are:

- Highly efficient boilers and furnaces. The minimum standard efficiency will vary from region to region so its important to make sure that your selected equipment meets the appropriate local standards.
- Biomass stoves usually have a minimum requirement of 75% efficiency. The allowable size may also be defined relative to the property, meaning that the unit should not be oversized for the occupancy needs.
- Ground and air source heat pumps are often included on tax-incentive-based schemes, but it is also worth checking whether separate incentives are also available from a renewable heat incentive program.
- Certification for windows will generally specify a minimum insulation value for the complete unit, including glass and frame. It's important to ensure that the window certificate includes the appropriate value relative to your area.
- Insulation added to walls, floors, ceilings, and roofs must meet local code minimum standards.

A list of web site addresses to help navigate through compliance is included at the back of the book.

Step 1 Summary

Twitter Summary
Step 1 is about the Mind Change challenge every citizen faces today. The old analogy of frog in gradually boiled water is the ultimate situation the smart citizen must quickly avoid.

Smart Citizen Summary
Climate change policy has silently embeded itself in legislation worldwide. You cannot buy a car, a washing machine or even a new window for your home without knowing the carbon emissions associated with every stage of the process. To underestimate this fact might be unwise, as the leading car brand VW found out to its cost in late 2015.
The smart citizen must:

- Take immediate action to reduce our dependance on fossil fuels.
- Understand that burning fossil fuels causes greenhouse gases which are a form of pollution that causes the earth to heat up which will have devastating consequences.
- Be aware that there is now piles of international legislation that mandates international governments to account for their carbon emissions
- Understand that building owners and tenants will be targeted by this new legislation because approximately 40% of energy use and carbon emissions worldwide come from heating, cooling and powering our buildings.
- Embrace the education and training necessary to acquire the skills to embrace the new energy efficiency and renewable technologies that may assist in future energy savings.
- Be aware that a "carrot and stick" approach underpins the policies of most governments to encourage/force change in how citizens account for their energy use. The carrot usually takes the form of financial incentives, grants, tax rebates etc. and the stick usually, carbon taxes, minimum energy efficiency standards and outright embargos on some inefficient products.

Step 2: Measure

"Measure three times before you cut once"

Old Proverb

Life was much easier when energy was cheap. Measuring it rarely taxed our brains. Coal was measured by the bag or, at its most complex, bags per week. Oil and gas were measured by the gallon or fill at the pump, to the tune of what you could afford. Electricity and mains gas were reckoned on the basis of the bill. Although every building had its own meter, it wasn't even necessary to know where it was located because the meter reader would magically call once in a while to read it for you. Gas was supplied by the bottle or tank if you weren't on the mains supply, and there were just two measurements: full and empty. The term energy efficiency was not in our vocabulary. With such a lack of awareness, it's little wonder that the humanity will soon need the equivalent of two planets to survive.

Energy in all its forms has been delivered so effectively to our doorsteps and further, right to the actual point where it's required. If you need to boil water, you don't have to go out to the yard and find energy, attach it somehow to a pot, and heat it. You simply flip a switch, and the water starts to boil. We are still many steps away from asking and understanding where that energy has come from, what type of energy it is, how much we need, and, until recent times, how much it costs.

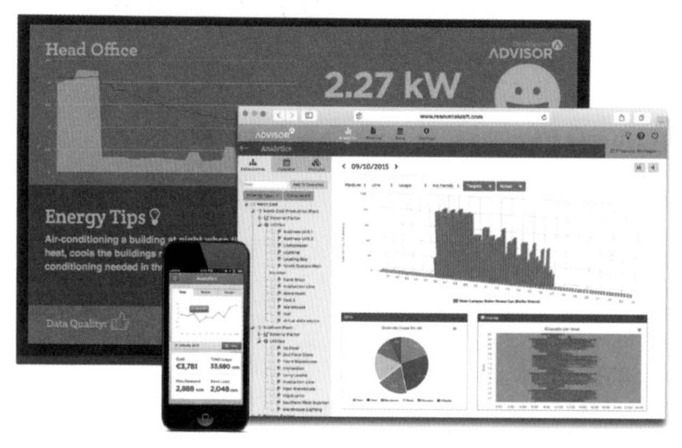

What has emerged over the last few years is a new language of energy measurement to describe how we must cope with a climate-changing world. The sooner we learn the new ways in which energy is measured and accounted for, the better chance we will have of avoiding an inevitable spiral of upward-only costs that are associated with the wasteful fossil fuel era. There's a saying in business that "what you can't measure, you can't monitor." So the first step, which is often the most inspiring, is to set down what needs to be measured. A fairly obvious thing to do, you might say, but it's surprising how many people don't even read their utility bills, never mind try to take a measurement.

Where Do We Get Our Energy?

The origin of all the energy sources that we rely upon is in distant, little-known places. The sun, moon, and earth itself, or rather its core, have a major influence on available energy resources. Some of that energy is freely accessible and continuously renewable. For example, the sun is an abundant supplier of both solar thermal and solar PV energy (see Steps 6 and 7). What is more, the sun sustains our ecosystem, which in turn provides many more sources of energy, including hot and cold air movement to drive wind turbines; moisture and rainfall, which are good for hydroelectric power; and plant growth, which supports biomass energy and more.

The moon also provides potential energy through its magnetic pull on the tides. By harnessing the ebb and flow of the waves and currents, we can generate continuous and renewable energy.

The more energy we harness from sources beyond earth, the more sustainable and less harmful it will be to the balanced ecosystems of this fragile earth. This energy is commonly referred to as renewable energy because it does not diminish earth's scarce and finite resources. Non-renewable energy, on the other hand, generally refers to the earth's limited store of oil, gas, coal, and peat, sources that cannot be re-created in our lifetime, or even multiple lifetimes. These resources are known as fossil fuels because, like fossils, they were laid down and compressed into the earth's crust millions of years ago. The earth, over time, consumes and digests all matter, plant and animal, that once grew and lived off its rich, biodiverse resources, in a sense fattening all of its guests so that it can trap their shared key ingredient, carbon. All living things – trees, grass, flowers, weeds, crops, animals, birds, flies, bugs, bacteria, micro-organisms, and, of course, humans – absorb carbon, directly or indirectly. The direct process is known as photosynthesis, whereby plants, algae, and bacteria extract energy from the sun to convert carbon dioxide into biomass. The indirect process is where animals, including humans, eat carbon-rich plants.

It can be difficult to comprehend that plants grow fed by energy from the sun and the atmosphere. In the 17th century, Jan Van Helmont became one of the first scientists to discover that the bulk of a plant's biomass comes from photosynthesis and not from the soil. We can see this if we consider how quickly a plant outgrows its pot and has to be repotted in a bigger container or in the ground. This growth would not be possible if the container soil were the only source of nutrients for the plant. Imitating this process is now part of the latest thinking in terms of creating sustainable renewable energy.

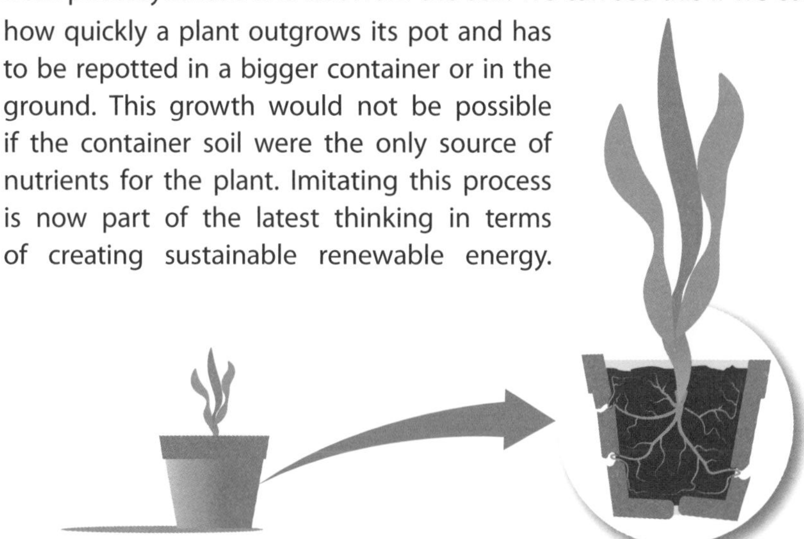

Research is still in its infancy, but if artificial photosynthesis can simulate the natural process, potentially, the energy produced can be deemed renewable.

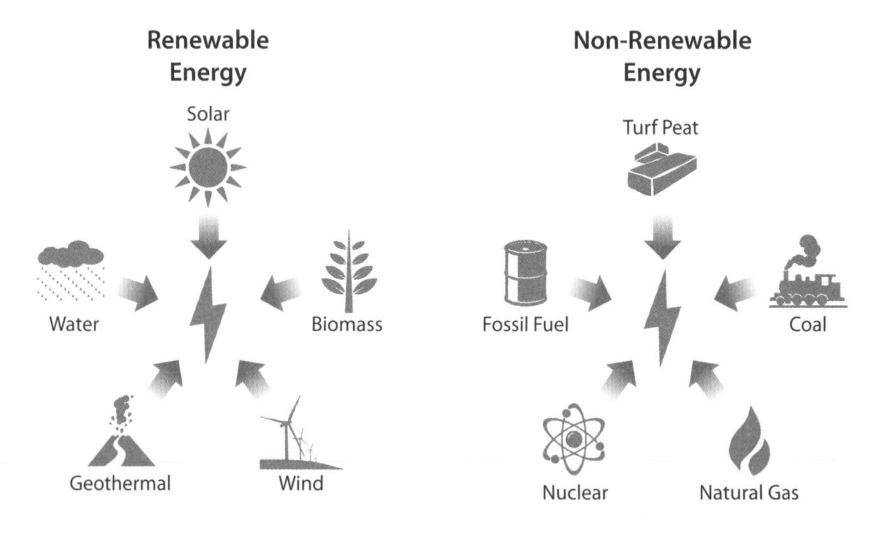

Nonrenewables

Nonrenewable energy sources come from the earth in the form of liquids, solids, gases, minerals, and heat and not all of them are fossil fuels. Think of the uranium ore used for nuclear power or pure heat from geothermal natural sources within the earth, for example. However, once they have been extracted from the ground, these resources cannot be replenished in a human-scale period of time. Crude oil, which accounts for over 36% of all the world's primary energy, according to the Energy Information Administration (EIA), is one of the best examples of this.

With both renewables and nonrenewables, before we try to measure them, its important that we become conscious of how and where they were originally formed. This is particularly important with regard to fossil fuels. Because the smart citizen must realise that these resources are so precious to the very essence of this earth that their further removal irrespective of what quantities may/may exist must be reduced to zero.

Oil

Oil, like gas, coal, and peat, is a fossil fuel, one that has been exploited heavily since the 19th century. Oil and gas are believed to have mostly formed under the oceans over millions of years, as marine organisms died and became entombed in the sediments of the seafloor. The organisms were heated and pressurised over eons, evolving into compounds of carbon and hydrogen. Depth and pressure have a major influence on the quality of these hydrocarbon deposits. Generally, most oils are found at depths of between 1 and 4 miles and the best gas deposits are found at depths greater than 6 miles. Because of the fluid and gaseous nature of the deposits, they naturally migrate toward more porous and permeable rocks.

Petroleum and Natural Gas formation

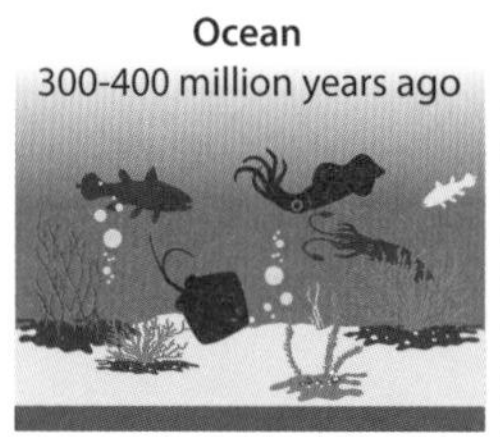

Tiny sea plants and animals died and were buried on the ocean floor. Over time, they were covered by layers of silt and sand.

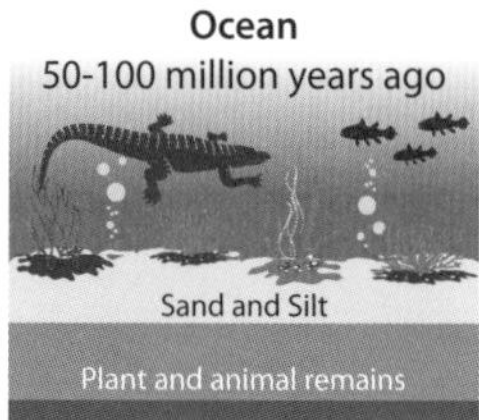

Over millions of years, the remains were buried deeper and deeper. The enormous heat and pressure turned them into oil and gas.

Today, we drill down through layers of sand, silt, and rock to reach the rock formations that contain oil and gas deposits.

Crude oil extracted from the ground is processed and refined into many different fuels, including gasoline, diesel, jet fuel, kerosene, heating oil, and lubricating oil. The average age of the fuel in an automobile's tank is 500 million years, the length of time it has taken for the organic remains of prehistoric plants and animals to compress and metamorphose into crude oil. Most of the easily accessible deposits have been found and exploited by now. These are the oil deposits that explorers can get to by drilling wells, with natural pressure sending the reserves to the surface.

In the search for more deposits, explorers are becoming more daring, drilling to greater depths and in more difficult deep-sea locations. These gambles do not always pay off, as demonstrated in the Gulf of Mexico in 2010, with the explosion of BP's Deepwater Horizon drilling rig. The disaster caused many deaths, both human and wildlife, and a major oil spill that resulted in millions of dollars in environmental clean-up costs.

Natural Gas

Natural gas was formed in a similar manner to oil, as the remains of plants and animals decayed below the seabed, over millions of years. The decayed organic material was, essentially, consumed and digested by the earth, with the sands and silt parts transformed into solids, i.e. rock. The pressure and heat in the now-entombed anaerobic environment changed some of the formerly organic material into oil and some into natural gas. Not surprisingly in such a process, the main component of this natural gas is methane. Geologists and engineers study the structure and processes of the earth to locate the rock types that most likely contain gas and oil deposits. Dynamite is first used to create the necessary vibrations in order to determine underlying rock densities. Seismic surveys are then used to identify the easiest places to drill, and rock sampling determines how best to create shafts that will allow the gas flow to the surface and into the pipelines for processing and cleaning. At this point, some gas byproducts are separated and sold for specific uses, including butane for small heaters and cigarette lighters and propane for some domestic heating systems, patio heaters, and barbeque grills.

Natural gas from the depths of the earth should not be confused with biogas, which is extracted from anaerobic digesters (ADs). The process is very similar, but the time frame is dramatically different. Extracting gas from an AD unit takes just days. This process is discussed in more detail in Step 6.

But if you believe that oil and gas drilling are environmentally unfriendly, welcome to the new era of fracking, a term that was not in popular usage a few short years ago. Fracking is a relatively new way of chasing difficult-to-extract shale gas and oil deposits. This costly process usually involves igniting the shale where the deposits lie, thereby fracturing the ground layers and releasing the oil/gas deposits. There are numerous negative environmental effects associated with the process, including contamination of watercourses, surface vibrations, oil and gas spills, and mixed atmospheric pollution. But as oil and gas reserves diminish and the world price for oil rises, fracking will become more common. Although fracking became economically unviable in 2015, when the price of oil dropped to below $60 a barrel, it will be back in some form or other because the energy balance requirement is simple: reduce energy usage or accept fracking as a necessity.

Coal

Coal was the first fossil fuel to be exploited in vast quantities, and it powered the Industrial Revolution in the 18th century. Today, it accounts for approximately 30% of world energy, but its days are numbered because its environmental credentials are poor, from the mining process to the pollutants associated with its burning. The challenges associated with coal include:

- Coal is the most carbon-intensive of all fossil fuels
- Carbon emissions and their role in climate change
- Sulphuric acid drainage from mines, which pollutes watercourses
- Burning coal, which produces smog and acid rain
- Water, air and land pollution by a range of heavy metals contained in coal deposits
- Coal fires are at best only 10% efficient in traditional open fires and, coupled with poor chimney design, they can vacuum up most of the rest of a building's heat

How coal was formed

Before the dinisaurs, many giant plants died in swamps.

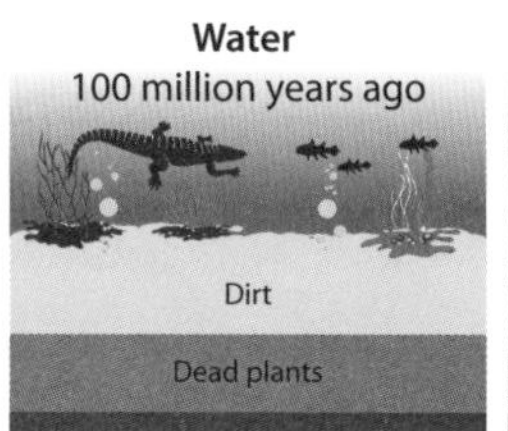

Over millions of years, the plants were buried under water and dirt.

Heat and presure turned the dead plants into coal.

Although there are new technologies to scrub, clean, and filter coal for burning and reduce its polluting effect, these are labour-intensive and costly. In the end, coal contains up to 97% carbon and, with emerging strategies to keep fossil fuels in the ground, will undoubtedly find itself in number one position when it comes to eliminating the major offenders in terms of carbon emission.

Geothermal Energy

Geothermal energy is heat from the earth. It's generally considered clean and sustainable, but is it? Just like the sustainability issues that arise with wood and other natural biomass materials, it can only be considered renewable if used in a sustainable and balanced ecological way. Geothermal is classified as either deep or shallow, depending on the depths involved and the source of heat. If that source is the sun, i.e. the heat of the sun warming the ground, and the depths are shallow, harvesting this energy can potentially be considered renewable. However, the temperature generated is rarely hot enough for heating or cold enough for cooling and usually requires a heat-pump process to increase or decrease the temperature for use in temperature control in buildings. (Geothermal energy should not be confused with ground-source heat pumps, discussed in some detail in Step 5).

Deep geothermal energy refers to the heat energy generated and stored in the layers of rock below the earth's crust and within its core. This heat energy is, in part, a by-product of the earth's formation 4.5 billon years ago and, in part, a result of the continual radioactive decay of materials. To some extent, it is sustainably renewed, but, otherwise, it is continuously leaked to the surface through hot springs, fault lines, and volcanic activity. The amount of heat available varies worldwide, with the greatest heat energy available in regions with active volcanoes or tectonic plate boundaries or places where the earth's crust is thinner and allows heat to escape. In

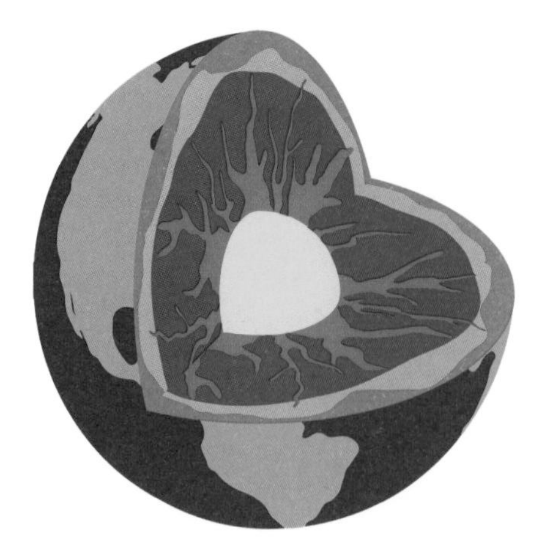

many regions, this energy is being harvested; Iceland, for example, generates more than 25% of its electricity from such geothermal plants.

Harvesting geothermal heat is cost-effective and potentially sustainable, and it produces clean energy, free from carbon emissions. On the downside, although geothermal may help to address climate change, extracting too much heat from the earth's core may lead to a consequential new dilemma for future generations.

Nuclear Energy

Is nuclear energy renewable? Probably not, principally because the basic fuel needed is uranium, a naturally occuring material and a finite resource. Does nuclear energy produce greenhouse gases? Most environmental analysts would concur that it does not, at least to any significent extent. So, really, the acceptablity of nuclear energy is an ethical matter that must balance the environmental benefits from a climate change perspective with the obvious risks, everything from accidents to the ability to safely handle radioactive waste. Ultimately, nuclear power has a role in electricity generation worldwide. It accounts for 11% of the world's electrical energy needs, 30% of Europe's requirements, and 75% of electricity production in France.

Nuclear energy has been controversial since the first commercial nuclear power plant opened in Sellafield in the United Kingdom, in 1956. Some people believe that nuclear energy is the only viable short-term solution to climate change because it releases fewer greenhouse gases than burning fossil fuels. Others believe it to be dangerous if things go wrong, such as in Chernobyl. Because nuclear power plants need to be very large to be economicaly viable, they are vunerable and need to be protected from earthquakes, flooding (Fukushima, Japan), and terrorists attacks. Having a voice in the debate about the merits or otherwise of building more nuclear power stations will become more important as the effects of climate change take hold on the planet.

There are no simple solutions for producing sustainable energy in sufficent magnitudes to satisfy the ever-increasing global energy demand. All of the current renewable solutions such as wind, solar, biomass, and hydro also have environmental risks and local objections. The fossil fuel sector is depleting the world's finite resources without having to account for the damage its carbon emmissions are doing to the environment. Ironically, nuclear energy is currently the only power industry that is mandated to fully account for all of its environmetal effects, including that of its wastes. Indeed, there will never be a level playing field for an informed debate on the merits of all forms of energy until the ecological footprint of all energy-producing processes receives a mandatory cradle-to-grave analysis.

Bioenergy: Is It Renewable?

Bioenergy is essentially energy from organic materials, and its sources are all around us. They include plants, crops, trees, grass, wood clippings, animal waste, food waste, and more. Although biofuels may seem like low-value energy products, they can be very energy-efficient when used in the right circumstances.

What about timber? Is it renewable or non-renewable? It is carbon-rich? Can it be considered part of the clean-tech industry? The oak tree spends its lifetime absorbing carbon dioxide from the atmosphere and creating biomass. Year on year, it also sheds its leaves, and these are integrated, mixed, and sealed into the soil where, if deprived of oxygen, they start the unimaginable million-year journey through shifting soils, entombed in the rolling and heaving layers of earth's crust. These once organic leaves are metamorphosed into peat, for instance, which we might find with a little digging. Deeper down and more encrusted, we may find the leaves have become coal. In the right location, where this once organic matter has been allowed to mature longer under some additional stresses, strains, and compressive forces of earthly digestion, we may strike oil and gas. So when we cut down trees and use the timber for construction and furniture, we are depriving the earth of future reserves of carbon.

There's probably not a lot we can do about that; we have more immediate concerns. However, by using timber and recycling it, we are preserving the carbon embedded within. Burning the timber for heat and energy is a different matter because the carbon dioxide is released immediately.

There are livelihood and sustainability concerns associated with the use of biomass for energy purposes. This is especially the case where crops grown for energy compete for land that might otherwise be used to grow food. Like wood fuel, there is also uncertainty about whether biomass is really carbon neutral. For biomass to be considered renewable, there is an inherent assumption that the quantity of biomass consumed can be balanced by regrowth in an ecologically managed way. As everything is now becoming measurable, the carbon footprint of a biomass production facility will dictate the carbon-neutral credentials in the biomass for energy production process. So today, all biomass is effectively considered a renewable energy source. As standardization of sustainable practices becomes more mainstream, only stamped and certified processes for the production of the biomass material will qualify as renewable.

The popularity of biomass is set to rise exponentially with the introduction of renewable heat incentive schemes. This approach, introduced in the United Kingdom in 2012, pays people an incentive per kilowatt-hour for producing heat from specified low-carbon technologies.

Biomass is not solely for burning in stoves. There are many advanced technologies such as anaerobic digestion that can extract gas from biomass material in sealed digestion chambers. Additionally, more basic forms of anaerobic digestion are currently operating on millions of small farms and homesteads in rural China and India. The developed world has not yet perfected the small-scale biogas plant. But when you consider that there are over 15 million individual such units operating in rural China, adjusting the design with some advanced technology cannot be too far away for a more urban society.

Another bioenergy fuel, biodiesel is also considered renewable. It is made from a mix of feedstock, including vegetable oils, corn, soybean, and animal fats. Biodiesel is renewable insofar as it comes from plants and animals that can be replenished through sustainable farming practices and recycling. It can work as an alternative to diesel made from fossil fuels, but it can also be blended with fossil fuel diesels to help make standard engines more compliant in terms of meeting carbon emission reduction targets. Because it can be used in standard diesel engines with very little modification, it makes perfect sense to use it as a pure or blended fuel. Biodiesel blends are denoted as "BXX", where B stands for biodiesel and XX for the percentage of biodiesel contained in the blend. Hence B20 is 20% biodiesel and 80% fossil-based diesel.

Renewable Energy

Renewable energy is generated from natural resources that are continuously replenished. These may include sunlight, wind, water, tides, and, potentially, bioenergy and biofuels. Renewable energy has, in general, been more expensive to produce and use than energy produced from fossil fuels. This is starting to change, particuarly since the advent of solar hot water and solar electricity generation, but renewable energy arguably needs some sort of government incentive to help encourage its uptake and make it more comercially viable, particularly in the short term to cover the capital conversion costs from fossil fuel. When you consider that as little as 10% (this percentage varies dramatically depending on the source) of total energy generation today comes from renewables, there is a long way to go. This means that fossil fuels along with nuclear energy are supplying over 90% of the world's energy needs. Sun, wind, water, and bioenergy are the perfect energy sources and, with the right incentives, can be developed to balance the environmentally negative effects of fossil fuels.

Total World Energy Consumption by Source (2015)

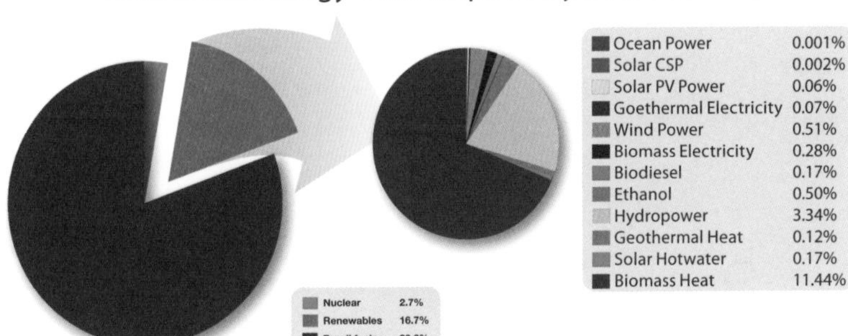

Renewable energy as a source of heat and the generation of combined renewable heat and power (CHP) are discussed in some detail in Step 5. Renewable energy as a source of electricity is examined in Step 6.

Understanding Energy Units

Energy is a complex subject with specialist terminology, which has particular meanings and conversion rates as you move from one country to the next. Countries measure fuel differently, and even when the same measuring unit is used, such as the Btu, it can have different values depending on where the fuel originates. The situation becomes even more complex when you factor in time, which can become the most important unit in determining the cost of any potential energy upgrade. A small amount of power used over a long period of time can cost more than a large amount used over a shorter period.

To help understand the frequently used units, it is probably necessary to first understand the difference between power and energy.

What is Energy?

The simplest generic definition of energy is the ability to do work. Work relative to buildings usually has something to do with such activities as heating/cooling, lighting, cooking, playing music, operating TVs, and doing laundry. The most regularly used energy units are the kilowatt-hour (kWh), the British thermal unit (Btu), calories (Cal), and joules (J). Energy units can be bought and sold, and their measurement directly determines how much we pay for our energy. Some forms of energy are delivered through wires (electricity), measured in kWh. This is energy in its most convenient form, supplying power to run today's technology and appliances. Other forms are supplied as gases, liquids, or solids and are generally burned to generate heat.

What is Power?

Power is the rate at which energy is generated or used, or how quickly something is generating or using energy. To ascertain the consumption rate, all we have to do is divide the energy unit by the unit of time. So using the energy units referred to above, we get the power units Btu/hour, calories/minute, and joules/second. Interestingly, taking kWh and dividing by time in hours (kWh/h = kW), we simply get kW. Whereas kWh represents energy, kW represents the unit of power. You might ask how can that be? It's because the watt already contains a unit of time; it is, in fact, just another name for joule/second. It's a little confusing, so considering the definition of each unit in isolation may help.

$$\text{Energy} = \text{Power} \times \text{Time}$$

$$\text{Power} = \frac{\text{Energy}}{\text{time}}$$

Watts and Kilowatts

One thousand watts, a **kilowatt (kW)**, is fast becoming the accepted standard unit of measurement in all areas of energy efficiency. It is associated with nearly everything related to the new clean-tech, energy-efficient world of property, defining all the key measurables.

By definition, the watt is a derived unit of power that performs work or

generates heat in the international system of units (SI). It is named after the Scottish engineer James Watt who lived from 1739 to 1819. Power in watts is the rate at which energy is consumed (or generated), and, as described above, one watt is equal to one joule per second. In terms of electricity, one watt is the product of voltage multiplied by the current.

The mandatory energy labels found on new electrical appliances record the power requirements in watts per hour (W/hr). Building energy rating labels provide the comparison metrics in kW/m2, and the lower the figure, the more energy efficient the property. In fact, the Passive House standard target figure is defined by kW hours, with the optimum target figure of 15kWhr/m2, or the amount of energy that the house consumes in kW per hour, rated against the square metre area of the building. Insulation for walls, floors, ceilings, windows, and doors is defined in terms of the rate that one watt of energy can pass through the material (the U-value), measured in W/k/m2.

Power x Time = Energy Consumption
Electrical Power: P(watts) = V(volts) x I (amps)
Kilowatt = 1000 watts

Similarly, renewable energy key items are all rated in terms of their kW output. A small wind turbine might be referred to as a 15kW, for instance, which would indicate that the rated output is 15kW per hour at a designated wind speed. Solar PV panels are bought and sold on the basis of their wattage output. Manufacturers' panel sizes are, for example, 600W for, say, a 1m panel. Additionally, international feed-in tariffs are paid for every kW of electricity produced.

A classic example of 1kWh is the electric heater (some readers may not remember them!). When one bar of this appliance is switched on for one hour, it will use 1kW of electricity (or 1kWh). When both bars are turned on together for one hour, 2kW (2kWh) will be used. Because heat is energy, it is also possible to use the kilowatt unit to measure heat, and this can make life much easier when considering and comparing the many energy-efficient materials and devices on the market.

Joule (J)

Named after the physicist James Prescott Joule (1818–89), the joule is the standard international unit of energy. By definition, it is equal to the work done by a force of 1 Newton, acting through a distance of 1 meter. In electrical applications, it is also defined as the energy needed to maintain a flow of 1 ampere for 1 second at a potential of 1 volt.

Now I'd say you are none the wiser as to what the measure of a joule really is. To get a sense of the size of a joule, I'll use the analogy of the apple falling 1 meter, supposedly the precise event that prompted Isaac Newton to develop his theory of gravity. Food-product energy labels are often expressed in both joules and calories.

Calorie (Cal)

As a unit of energy, the calorie, correctly speaking, should have no place in the vocabulary of building energy efficiency. By definition, it is the approximate amount of energy needed to raise the temperature of 1 kilogram of water from 0°C to 1°C at a pressure of 1 atmosphere. The reason for its exclusion is that, since the adoption of the international system (SI) of scientific units in the 1950s, the joule is now the only defined SI unit of energy. The reason for the calorie's inclusion in this book is that most people have an awareness of the size of this unit. Our bodies need energy, and by retaining the Cal, nutritionists have adopted a common-sense approach to the energy balance of food. Food labels in most countries now have mandatory nutritional information, including the number of calories per portion. In the European Union, food labels display both calories and joules.

The calorific value of a fuel is an important measure of the amount of heat produced by combustion of a specified quantity. Lower calorific values of, say, softwood timbers can have their heat-producing capacity measured and compared for cost purposes against, for example, higher calorific value hardwood timbers.

The calories in these items could:

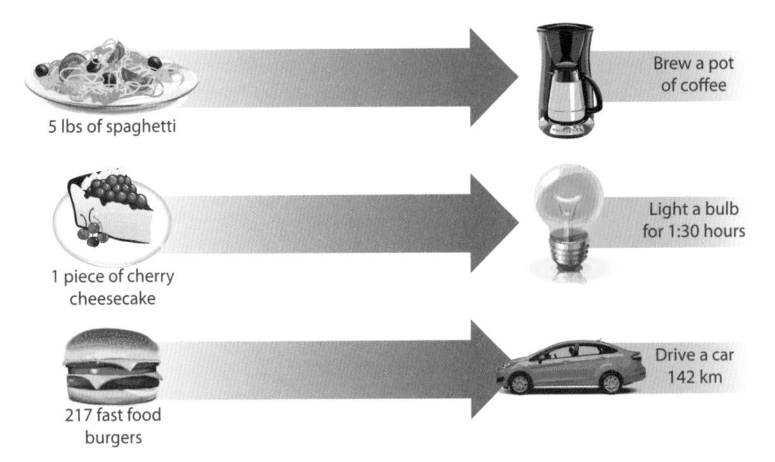

British Thermal Unit (Btu)

The British thermal unit is the standard unit of energy principally used in the United States and Canada. Most other countries use the joule, including the United Kingdom, where the Btu originated. The Btu is grounded in imperial units, insofar as it is defined as the amount of energy needed to raise the temperature of one pound of water by one degree Fahrenheit. In countries that use the metric system, the Btu is been phased out but is still sometimes used to describe the power output of boilers and furnaces. To get a sense of the size of 1 Btu, it is often approximately equated to the heat given off by burning a single match.

Btus are commonly used to compare the heat content of different fuels per unit weight. For instance, coal has a typical heating value of 24 million Btu/ton.

Barrel

As a basic unit, the barrel of oil has more to do with pricing and oil reserves than with the accurate measurement of volume. A barrel can technically be used to specify any volume and can have multiple values depending on its contents, including beer, whiskey, water, and flour. On average, it is said to represent 42 U.S. gallons, or about 159 litres, or 35 imperial gallons when referring to oil. When estimating production rates and oil reserves, financial analysts often use the term barrels per day. However, the real value in the metric of a barrel of oil is for cost-tracking purposes, principally by national economies when future-proofing energy supplies and verifying energy security issues, as discussed in Step 1.

The thermal energy content or heating value of a barrel of crude oil depends on its composition, but it generally averages about 6 million British thermal units (mBtus) or 1,700 kilowatts hours (kWh) or 6.5 x 109 joules (6.5 gigajoules).

Measuring Instrumentation

Metering, monitoring, and measuring energy use in buildings has undergone a revolution in recent years. There are some astonishing technological innovations in this area that allow for assessing and controlling heat loss, preparing computer-generated graphics and plans, and optimizing new building design and retrofits. As technologies have evolved, costs have dropped considerably. Today, for a relatively small sum, we can access technology and software to measure most conceivable energy conditions:

- Electrical current, voltage, and power
- Fuel consumption
- Temperature
- Temperature differences
- Air movement
- Relative humidity
- Heating efficiency
- Water flow

As the electronic wizardry behind metering, monitoring, and reporting has become increasingly sophisticated, its usability has dramatically improved. Meters and monitors can now communicate wirelessly and are cloud-based, with automatic reporting functions built into the software. They are a far cry from traditional meters that required cabling and power, were more costly and time-consuming to install, and were visibly intrusive. In this new era, data loggers seamlessly integrate and collate all sorts of information gathered from different meter sources, including electricity, water, and gas meters. Using standardized international protocols, they can perform all sorts of extra tricks by communicating directly with lights, sockets, heating controls, valves, motors, and most of the other technologies that power our buildings. Data loggers and meters also bring affordable and smart energy-efficiency control to the home.

Take, for instance, simple energy monitors, which cost from as little as $20 but can provide instantaneous information on electricity usage and costs.

Electrical Monitors

Energy monitors are one of the cleverest and most useful inventions for helping us to navigate our way around power usage at home. Every home and, indeed, every building should have a monitor. They are small handheld or countertop devices that measure electricity usage in real time. They are easy to install and can be purchased from most builders' suppliers or online.

They simply help you to monitor your energy usage at home or work by helping you to understand:

- How much electricity is been used
- Where energy is used in the building
- What are the big electric eaters
- How to reduce energy usage
- How to demystify and get to grips with your energy bills

Armed with such information on energy usage, you can quickly act to reduce consumption. Slightly more expensive monitors can be connected to your PC to record energy usage year-on-year, and this is very useful for tracking savings, increasing awareness of energy use, and helping to predict utility charges with reasonable accuracy. However, energy monitors are very different from smart meters, which are discussed separately below, in that they do not send data to the energy supplier, and play no role in verifiable power usage. Energy monitors are not expensive, but when buying one it's important to:

- Get one with a clear display that is simple to use. Often the selection of monitors is a personal choice, and there are now plenty of well-designed models on the market.

- Get readings in kWh because that's what the utility company charges for. Some will also give readout in CO2, which is useful. However, only some power companies supply green, low-carbon energy. So for the reading to be meaningful, there must be an adjustment on the monitor to set the carbon emissions per kWh of electricity actually supplied. The monitor will likely be supplied with an inbuilt generic conversion factor that should provide good indicative CO2 figures.
- Seek a readout in your own currency. It may take a little time to set the exact rate charged by your energy utility for each kWh of electricity. Unfortunately for consumers, the way most companies charge for power can make it difficult to set the monitor to exactly record the multiple and often confusing rates.
- Have the ability to connect to a PC and display historic usage. These features can be worth the extra cost; the more you pay, the more you get.
- Get instantaneous usage data. It is very important to get real-time readings. So what is real time? A few seconds delay is fine, but a few minutes delay is useless. Ideally, when you turn on the toaster or kettle, you want to see an almost instant surge in the monitor's reading.
- Have mobility. Ideally, the monitor should have mains supply with a battery backup, allowing you carry it around the house or building. So, for instance, if you're checking the energy requirements of a shower, you can turn it on and get an almost immediate reading of power usage.
- With solar PV becoming very popular as a supplementary power source in many homes, some electrical monitors can also measure and display the solar power generated, the solar power exported, and the electricity imported from the grid. This feature is particularly useful for maximizing energy and allows the home/building owner to calculate the amount of battery storage that may be needed to potentially leave the property with an overall net-zero electricity import requirement.

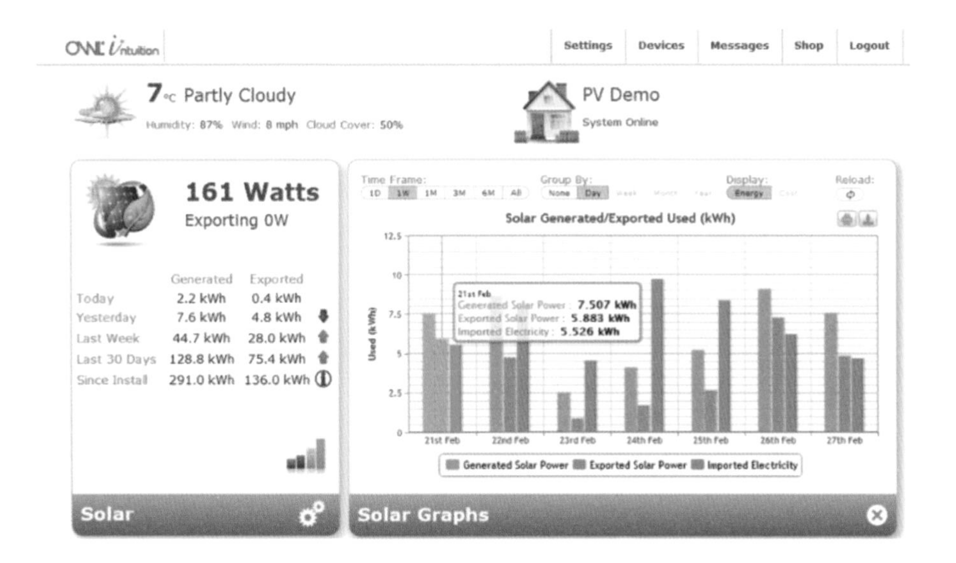

Moreover, a monitor is difficult to ignore, particularly if it is in a living area in the home, niggling away at your conscience. It's also a great item to get everyone involved in conservation. Kids, in particular, will get an early understanding of the relationship between power, energy, and cost. My kids were fascinated by how everyday household items such as a hairdryer could cause a surge in the meter readings. More importantly, they realized that the electric shower had the highest reading of all household appliances, which persuaded them to take shorter showers, something I couldn't have achieved on my own.

Fuel Meters

Fuel consumption is not as easily measured as electricity. Gas or oil meters are expensive. This is particularly the case with gas, which can only be installed by qualified and certified experts. Installation costs can be high, in part because in-flow meters may need the fuel line isolated before connection. At the same time, costs are continually falling and clamp-on meters that are sensitive enough to take pulse readings are also available. Because fuels are normally measured and charged for by volume, most meter data loggers will have inbuilt conversion factors for outputs in Btus, kWh, and, the always necessary, CO2 emissions.

Measuring the quantity of liquid fuel in a metal or plastic tank is the challenge faced by most small-property owners if heating costs are to be monitored. There are many smart devices on the market that will remotely measure fuel levels in outside tanks. They also have such extra features as anti-theft alarms that go off if the fuel level drops suddenly. In addition, they can facilitate the remote measuring of the volume of fuel remaining in a tank and alert both the owner and fuel suppliers when a refill is needed.

Temperature

Temperature measurement and control in buildings is perhaps one of the most important but least appreciated tasks in the energy-efficiency process. Temperature monitoring is taking place all around us, and we depend much more than we may think on correctly set and regulated temperature controls and thermostats. Refrigerators and freezers have built-in temperature controls that we rarely ever adjust from the day we purchase to the day we discard the unit. Typically, most building heating and cooling systems are controlled by a set of internal and external temperature measurements. The accuracy of the measuring device is only one element in the overall efficiency of temperature control. In many cases where energy audits take place, the biggest offenders in terms of wasted energy are inappropriate temperature settings, set either too high or too low. People rarely take the time to understand and adjust temperature control settings. There are many rules of thumb regarding energy efficiency, but a key one states that every 1°C in temperature correction can have a 5% reduction in energy costs.

Heat Meters

In the past, heat meters were really only used in large-scale industrial settings for measuring the heating efficiency of plant and machinery. That has changed of late, particularly since falling prices mean that it's now more economically viable to install them to measure the energy efficiency of a building's heating system.

A heat meter usually consists of two temperature sensors, a flow meter, and a data logger for collecting the information. The sensors, one on the outflow and the other on the return flow, measure the heat delivered to a building from a boiler. The data logger will automatically calculate the amount of heat (Btu or kWh) that has been dissipated in the pipework loop and work out a boiler's efficiency based on its heat capacity.

Being able to check, at reasonable cost, the actual heating efficiency of such equipment as biomass boilers, solar thermal units, under-floor systems with heat pumps, and combined heat and power units (CHP) is a tremendous asset in the armory of those tracking the energy efficiency of products in performance mode.

Thermal Infrared Imaging

If ever there was a piece of technology that can monitor the flow of heat around a building, it is the infrared camera image. It is simple to use, and the images it produces are easy to interpret because it depicts temperature differences using different colors. An inspection of a home is quick and definitive, and the resulting thermal image can pinpoint various previously undetected problems in any building, old or new.

The image highlights places where heat might be leaking from a house, with lighter colors indicating warmer areas and darker blues indicating cooler areas. In regions where it's important to keep the internal environment cool, the brighter red to yellow infrared image will indicate where heat is entering through the building fabric. It's an extremely valuable tool and one that is also very successfully used in diagnostics. It can identify areas in attics and walls where there is no insulation and, more importantly, where there are gaps or minimal cover. It can also detect cold bridging in and around windows, doors, and wall junctions. The thermal infrared image is a fantastic post-installation survey tool because it allows for the inspection of all building elements, including anything built upon or covered up. Indeed, it is perfect for detecting shoddy workmanship and malfunctioning heating systems.

Air Movement

Measurement of air movement may be needed for a number of reasons, including testing for air leakage in ducts, rooms, and entire buildings. The monitoring of air movement in buildings is becoming ever-more important, given the need for greater energy efficiency and to account for either heat gain or loss. For that reason, Step 3, is devoted solely to this topic. The process of measuring is normally left to professionals who may need to make numerous calculations involving pressures, volumes, and flow rates as well as carrying out some onsite measurements using vane anemometers and blower-door tests. There are, however, some simple and inexpensive instruments such as smoke pens that can be used to detect air movement.

Relative Humidity

Moisture content and relative humidity are two interlinked and very important measurements that are necessary as buildings become more insulated and airtight. Individual measurements can be made using the traditional wet-and-dry bulb hygrometer. There are also some handheld electronic instruments that use sensors to determine local humidity levels in rooms, walls, or fixtures and fittings. Air quality and moisture levels are discussed in more detail in Step 3.

Water Meters

Chapter 7 of this book is devoted to water and the central role it plays in the climate change process. Water is a scarce resource, but, instinctively, most people living in temperate climates believe it is renewable. This is not the case, so we need to be fully aware of how much water we use, which means measuring. Water meters are the device of choice for the water utilities because, naturally, they provide the data to support a billing regime. When introducing water meters for charging purposes, most countries have minimum regulatory standards. If, however, a meter or sub-meter is desired purely for measurement and flow rate information, it can be sourced very cheaply. A sub-meter can be positioned at any accessible location on a property to gather evidence of current flow and cumulative flow, which will help to reduce usage and can monitor the utility-grade meter.

How to Measure

If you were asked how much your heating and electricity bills are, would you know? What is your peak time for energy use and do you know how much your annual bills are? How much fuel do you use and are there seasonal variations? Is your building well insulated and, if so, to what depth and effectiveness? How efficient is your boiler and when was it last serviced? These are some of the issues that must be ascertained in order to get an idea of how much energy you use. By performing simple checks in all energy usage areas, you can identify potential ways to save energy and money.

One key factor that must be taken into account when considering the cost of energy is that energy is power multiplied by time. It's a bit of a misnomer to label things energy-efficient; they can only be power-efficient. The biggest factor in all energy-cost equations is time.

Over time, a light bulb can use more energy than a powerful dishwasher if the bulb is continuously left switched on. A unit on standby consuming, say, 1 watt is often considered too small to bother accounting for. But a forgotten watt used 24 hours a day, 7 days a week, 52 weeks a year amounts to nearly 9kW. (1x24x7x52 = 8736) whereas a 1000w (1kW) electric toaster which takes, say, 3 minutes to toast bread would need to be used 175 times to draw the same amount of energy as the item on standby in the corner. The energy-efficient control in this scenario is you because you can control the length of time the power is used.

The Savings Puzzle

Building and refurbishment and energy-efficient installations are no longer exclusively based on traditional skills and experience. Worldwide, a whole new set of skills and training are now needed to design and build the most basic domestic dwelling. The old process was much simpler. The builder pulled together a team of individuals, specialist subcontractors, in a sort of pick 'n' mix fashion from a small pool of locally available trades. This approach was successful because the building work was traditional and each tradesperson knew what the other trades did and there were no gaps or mysteries that couldn't be addressed afterward.

Today, there are specialist trades that never existed before: solar specialists, heat pump specialists, heat exchange specialists, external insulators, voltage optimizers, power correction specialists, smart heating controls specialists, and many more. In each case, the underlying technology is getting more complex and must be individually proven, tested, certified, and installed by trained and certified professionals. They arrive on site with range of high-tech systems that affect the whole house, but there seems to be a gap when it comes to explaining how best to integrate the technologies.

The challenge becomes more acute in refurbishment projects because the various specialists have to adjust their technologies to suit the imperfect conditions met onsite. Because the specialists all work as individuals, they can only, with some degree of accuracy, tell you what savings can be made using their particular process. What they can't tell you is how their process

Description	% Saving	% Total
Measure & Manage	20%	20%
Draft Proofing	20%	40%
Insulate Roof	20%	60%
Insulate Floors	5%	65%
Upgrade Windows	5%	70%
Boiler Controls	30%	100%
Heating Controls	15%	115%
Voltage Optimisation	15%	130%
Power Factor Correction	10%	140%
Heat Recovery	10%	150%
Solar Thermal	20%	170%
Biomass	15%	185%
Heat Pumps	15%	200%

interacts with other processes and what the overall savings may be. This leads to the impossible situation whereby more than 100% of savings can apparently be achieved by adding together all the individual savings claimed by the specialists.

Some energy saving procedures will always work, including attic insulation or installing efficient motors and fans. Other options, such as voltage optimization and power factor correction, will only work in the right circumstances. Still other systems such as heat recovery and heating controls must be sized and commissioned accurately. While they may work perfectly when first commissioned, they may cease to operate efficiently if the homeowner does not have full working knowledge of the controls. In all cases, particularly when installing renewable energy systems where grants or feed-in tariffs are involved, it is essential to have the installation verified under a national certified measurement protocol, which will be discussed later.

Being able to compare like with like when discussing energy-efficiency measures in buildings is key to understanding the cost benefits of the numerous different systems and the savings that can be made. The old adage of only being able to compare apples with apples is very relevant here. Thankfully, the kilowatt-hour is fast becoming the apple of the energy efficiency world.

Energy Balance

One of the oldest laws of physics is that energy can neither be created nor destroyed; it can only be converted from one form to another. When it comes to energy use, traditionally the only part of this equation we paid any particular attention to was the energy input part, i.e. the part relating to the purchase of fuels for heating and the electricity to light and power our buildings. There are other elements in the energy equation or energy balance that should be examined. These are discussed in more detail in Steps 4, 5, 6, and 7, but essentially they relate to the energy balance, and heat input from passive solar gain, waste heat loads from refrigerators, freezers, cookers, motors, fans, lighting, PCs, and even body heat. This energy cannot simply disappear, though many people may think it does. It is absorbed into the structure and fabric of the building before making its way outside.

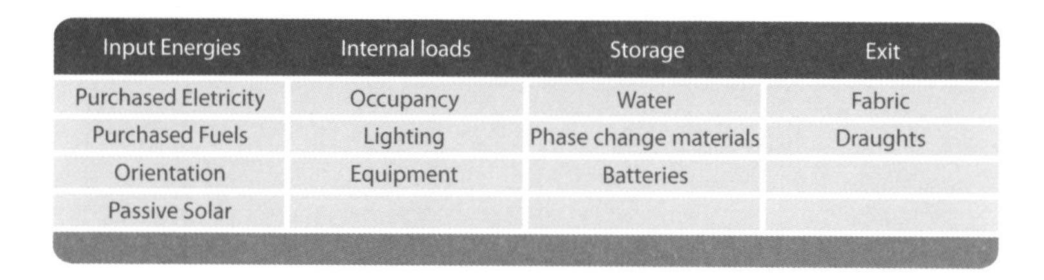

Input Energies	Internal loads	Storage	Exit
Purchased Eletricity	Occupancy	Water	Fabric
Purchased Fuels	Lighting	Phase change materials	Draughts
Orientation	Equipment	Batteries	
Passive Solar			

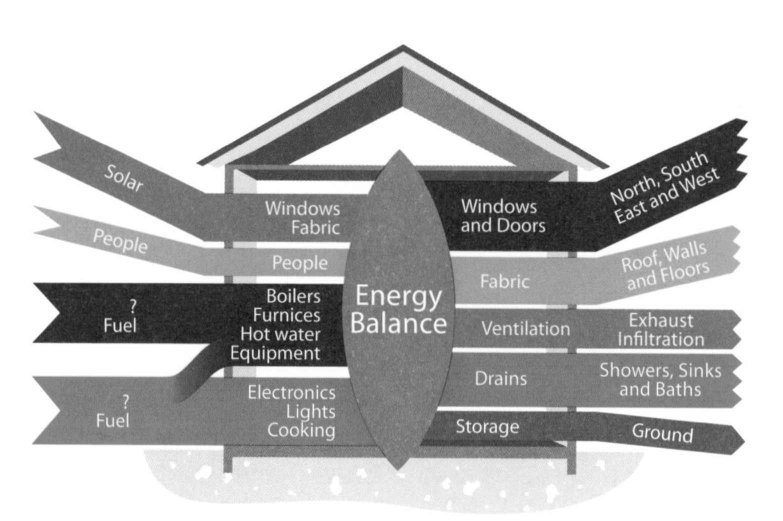

The Sankey diagram shown above is the visual aid most used by the energy-efficiency industry to display energy balances.

Advances in technology have found many ways of reclaiming and reusing this once lost heat. Heat recovery from all sorts of locations is becoming more feasible as primary energy costs continue to escalate. This may involve installing single heat recovery ventilation units in rooms or aggregating the heat from a series of space cooling units in one location and transferring the heat to another location. There are many examples of this, including a project in one popular nightclub, where a heat recovery process was added to the air-handling units to heat all of the building's hot water requirements.

In plain terms, energy in equals energy out, and the key to success in energy efficiency projects is to reduce the level of lost energy, having them as close to zero as possible.

Understanding Where We Use Energy

Energy use in homes pretty much follows the same pattern in all developed countries. The greatest domestic energy use, amounting to over 40%, is on space heating and/or cooling. In colder, northern hemisphere regions such as Canada, northern Europe, and parts of the northern United States, most energy is expended on heating systems. In hot countries, such as in the Middle East and Mediterranean, cooling and air-conditioning are the priority. In more temperate climates, particularly in major world cities such as London and Paris, where there is less fresh air flowing, a combination of heating in winter and cooling in summer accounts for the greatest energy usage.

Residencial Energy Use

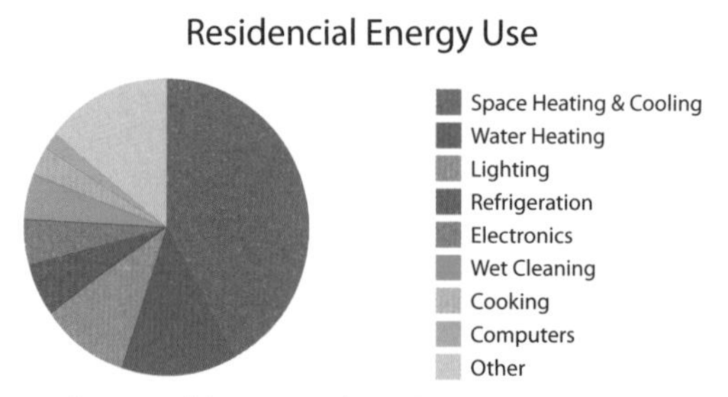

The next largest demand is water-heating, at an average of 20% of overall energy use. So heating, cooling, and hot water account for a whopping 60% of overall building energy usage. Consequently, more efficient heating and cooling systems can have the single most significant impact on the size of home energy bills. In fact, the amount of energy we use cooking at home is remarkably low, at 2%, varying little across developed nations, but our refrigeration needs continue to rise, amounting to an average of 6% of energy use.

In supermarkets, by contrast, refrigeration costs can account for up to 50% of overall energy use during the day and 80% of night usage. Refrigeration has to run 24/7, and inefficient units are known energy eaters, particularly older models with well used compressors, worn insulation, and often degraded seals. As a result, the unit always struggles to keep the food contents cool and has to work flat-out. During energy audits, one of my first suggestions is often to replace an old refrigerators/freezer, but that advice is not always acted upon.

Another fairly uniform pattern is the frequency with which we use the numerous modern appliances and gadgets in the home, which can amount to 6% of energy use. More importantly, TVs, computers, microwaves, security systems, etc. quietly draw power all day every day, even when apparently turned off. Most houses have localized clusters of units on standby, with arrays of small green, red, and orange indicator lights. In many countries, it is obligatory for manufacturers to account for all power use and carbon emissions for recording on energy labels. The new energy labels, discussed in more detail in Step 5, also show standby power consumption. Beware of older equipment, which drains higher amounts of power.

Lighting accounts for about 3% of energy usage, but costs can creep up very quickly if some of the basics of lighting and power are not understood. Even as low-energy bulbs reduce energy usage, more bulbs are being used: spotlights in the home and around domestic buildings and external floodlights, which have serious power requirements. When I carry out energy audits, I have encountered a growing belief that external lights must be left on all night for security reasons. This is more of a comfort than a security measure, and there are many more economical and effective ways of securing buildings other than flooding them with light. A single 500W bulb can cost as much as $250 a year to run and numerous light fixtures can multiply this figure.

Of course, average energy consumption values are influenced by geographical and climatic conditions. They will also vary depending on family size and living patterns. Attitudes to energy efficiency are changing at a different rate in different parts of the world. When governments and their citizens become like-minded about energy efficiency, real progress is possible. For instance, Sweden as a whole is on track to be carbon neutral by 2020.

Acknowledging your energy consumption quantities and patterns is a first step toward realizing how you can adapt to energy-saving behavior. There is also no cause for concern that reducing energy consumption might compel you to buy expensive energy-efficient equipment. In fact, there are many easy, low- or zero-cost steps that you can take to save money.

Energy Audits

An energy audit is essential to ascertain the energy balance of a building. It is an investigation carried out by a homeowner, business owner, or professional into the energy entering and leaving a building. Although some auditing tasks are best left to professionals, particularly in more complex buildings, owners are often best placed to carry out the audit, especially at home. The main aim of the process is to identify areas where potential energy savings can be made and then make sure these savings are achieved.

A good energy audit should offer financial, maintenance, and environmental benefits, which would generally include:

- Reduced electricity bills
- Reduced heating/cooling fuel costs
- Longer life spans for boilers and other plant due to reduced running times
- Improved comfort levels
- Better data on the reallocation of saved funds to other possible renewable energy generation options
- Improved carbon footprint

Whether you hire a professional or undertake the audit yourself, the process must start with a full inventory of everything in the building that uses energy. You can, of course, call upon a professional energy auditor to undertake a survey and present you with the findings, an option with both merits and drawbacks because auditors can only measure current and past usage. The future usage is totally your responsibility and cannot successfully be delegated to someone else. There is a place for a professional survey, but only after you have carried out a self-assessment that will give you at least a basic understanding of your own energy usage. Key to completing a successful energy audit, is having access to your bills from the at least past 12 months.

Thereafter all the fundamentals necessary for analysing the energy usage can be computed.

Base Load

Do you know what your minimum power usage is? This is the most fundamental question of all in terms of reducing energy costs. You must find a point in the day or night when the power load is zero or can be reduced to near zero. This may be unachievable in many cases because such essentials as refrigerators, freezers, security systems, and broadband may demand a continuous base load. But in establishing your minimal power usage, you might be very surprised at just how far from zero it actually is. Most people have some awareness of the big power users in their home or place of work, but what we pay for is energy use and energy is power by time. Like the constantly dripping tap, a small amount over a long period can lead to the greatest wastage. The quickest, easiest, and most telling way to establish energy usage is to install an energy monitor, which can pay for itself in a few weeks. Bottom line, if you don't know what your costs are, it's quite difficult to figure out what your savings may be.

All of the tables and graphs produced above can be prepared without any special measuring tools or instrumentation.

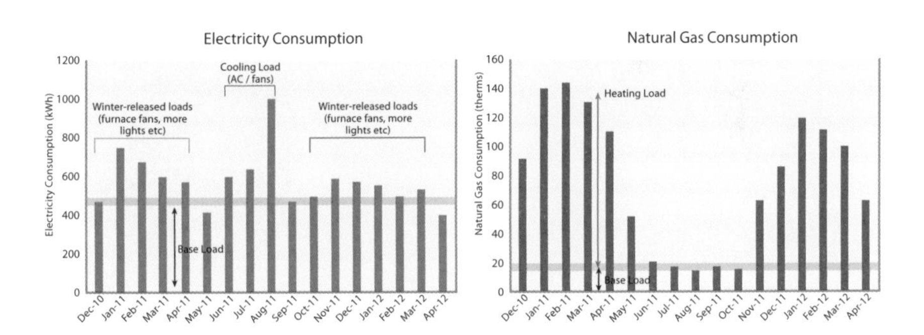

They are generated from bills and receipts that, if kept and filed, can provide the basis for a quite detailed analysis of a building's energy and usage patterns. However, as the rationale behind the incentives to make buildings more energy efficient evolves, whether that's because access to grants or to finance require more detailed energy data, it is often necessary to install additional meters to monitor the building's performance over a given period of time.

Read the Bills

The most valuable step anyone can take to reduce energy costs is to read their bills. This may sound obvious, but it is surprising how many people do not take time to understand bills. This applies to homeowners, tenants, and leaseholders of both commercial and residential properties. Even large corporations neglect this and simply pay the bills as presented. Energy bills can, at first, be difficult to interpret, so a little time should be taken to fully understand them. The small print fulfils the obligations of the energy supplier to clarify contractual aspects of the billing system but does little to empower the bill payer to take control of the amount of energy used.

We have to take stock of what bills we are paying, how the bills are constructed, what the rates are, and whether and what control we have over their amounts. Simplifying the energy bill format is not necessarily in the interest of the energy companies, which will be reluctant to move in this direction unless compelled to by national governments. So it is the consumer's responsibility to become informed. All energy bills have similar structures and share common features:

- Customer cost
- Energy cost
- Transmission costs
- Seasonal or time-of-day charging

When it comes to electricity bills, we have one particular advantage: benefit from the fact that the universal unit of electricity billing is the kWh. If the mechanisms of this unit, as explained above, are understood, making savings is all the more possible. The basic unit of measure of electric power is the watt, and 1,000 watts equal a kilowatt. If you use 1,000 watts of power in one hour, you have used a kilowatt-hour (kWh). Your electric supplier bills you by the kWh.

The first step in verifying any electricity bill is to determine whether the meter reading is actual or estimated. Knowing where to find your meter and how to read it is fundamental. There are two main types of electricity meter: older style dial meters and newer digital meters, which may or may not be smart meters, as described below.

When reading an older style dial meter, read and record the numbers as shown on the dials, from right to left. When the pointer is directly on a number, look at the dial to the right. If it has passed zero, use the next higher number. If the dial has not passed zero, use the lower number. Record the numbers shown by writing down the value of the dial to your extreme right first and the rest as you come to them. Should the hand of a dial fall between two numbers, use the smaller of the two numbers.

Reads 39804 KWh (Units of electricity)

With newer meters featuring digital displays, you simply read the numbers from left to right in the normal fashion. The difference between one month's reading and the next is the amount of energy units that have been used for that billing period.

Reading a gas meter is a similar exercise except that a conversion factor is then used for billing purposes because gas is measured by volume, usually cubic feet or cubic meters depending on where you live and how old the meter is. It is then converted to calorific value to display the energy delivered. In many countries, including in Europe, the conversion is to kilowatt-hours (kWh) for billing purposes. In the United States and Canada, gas is commonly measured in mega joules (MJ) or Therms.

Building Energy Assessments

No two buildings are exactly the same, and even if they are similar, their occupants will differ, not least in terms of energy usage. Even within individual countries, climatic conditions may vary widely, from a snow-capped mountainside in one location to a temperate seaside holiday resort in another. Consequently, finding a common template for energy assessment is challenging. But as we saw in Step 1, numerous building-energy measuring techniques are emerging worldwide. These differ in many respects, including name, but they all measure primary energy use relative to the floor area of the building and are independent of individual occupant behaviors. In other words, people's habits do not factor in the assessment. Perhaps a good analogy is the assessment of fuel economy in a car, rated in miles per gallon or litres per 100km. To continue the analogy, city driving versus motorway use influences cars' fuel economies, particularly as energy use changes in winter and summer. Moreover, a fast driver will use more fuel in the same car than a steady driver. Similarly, an occupant who overheats all the rooms in a building will use much more fuel than someone who doesn't.

Traditionally, measuring the energy performance of a building was the concern of specialist building-services engineers. Their role was to rate the building envelope in terms of heat flows and then calculate the size of heating and cooling equipment and hot water requirements. In residential properties, in particular, this was a repetition calculation process that adhered to standard parameters and only included occupant preferences insofar as they were manifested in the built environment by way of building orientation, window numbers, room sizes, specialist rooms, numbers of bathrooms, etc. The building was deemed thereafter to operate under standard conditions..

The concept of requiring buildings to have an energy rating gained ground after the oil shocks of the 1970s, but it was not until the early 1990s that the first mandatory rating system was launched in Denmark.

A decade later, the rest of Europe followed. The EU then introduced the Energy Performance of Buildings Directive (EPBD) in 2002, making it policy for member countries to have mandatory energy ratings on all buildings. Since then, many more countries, states, and cities worldwide have followed suit.

Although individual countries have implemented their own energy-measurement processes, the net result is the same insofar as building energy performance is a measure of the efficiency of the national building stock. Although the Kyoto Protocol does not currently have equal standing in all countries, accountability for carbon emissions and energy security places the onus on governments to establish a baseline from which energy improvements can be made.

The elements that determine a building's energy performance are universally described using similar, if not identical, terminology. For example, terms such as rating, label, score, certificate, and benchmark are effectively different ways of saying the same thing, and most countries favor "rating" when referring to energy standards. The important thing is consistency and standard practice within each country if not between countries. There are too many different issues, everything from building practices to cultural needs, that render impractical an exact comparison between countries. The components that make up an energy rating system include:

- **Building Type:** The building type to be assessed is the first question to be addressed because the measuring methodology may change considerably depending on the answer. There are generally three building-type classifications, new or existing, public or private, and nonresidential or single-unit residential. The distinction between new and existing is fundamental. New buildings obviously can't be measured from existing utility bills, so projection models are required. A similar distinction is made in the next category, public or private, because government buildings in many countries are subject to more stringent energy-efficiency standards than domestic structures and are often supposed to be exemplary. The third category effectively distinguishes between private homes and commercial buildings.

- **Method of Measurement:** Nearly all energy-rating systems measure primary energy. That is the amount of energy actually used in a building, but it also includes losses during the generation and transmission processes used to carry power to the site. These losses can be significant, particularly with regard to electricity, where they can be as high as 70%. As a result, the primary energy figure can be much greater than that actually used onsite. Most rating systems will credit renewable energy generated onsite based on the net meter readings.

- **There are two main ways of quantifying energy use:** Either record information from utility bills or calculate using computer modeling software. The first approach is more suited to existing buildings and the second to new builds or proposed alterations, but both make use of customized software to take account of such issues as localized climate conditions, building type and occupancy, and comparison points.

- **Building Fabric:** All rating systems take the building's thermal envelope into account by way of the major insulation details for floors, walls, roof, windows, and doors, etc. In many cases, the exact thermal values cannot be determined without expensive and detailed opening up-type inspections, so most rating systems default to average values depending on the age of the building and local traditions. So if you know that your building has higher than average thermal insulation or if you carry out insulation upgrades, it's important to keep records, receipts, certificates, etc. to allow an independent assessor to factor in the information.

- **Building Energy Use Components:** If there's a deviation from a norm in energy ratings, it occurs during the evaluation of activities that consume energy in buildings. Some rating systems ignore lighting; others ignore all plug loads for such appliances as cookers, washing machines, and TVs. However, with most systems, the focus is on the building's heating, cooling, and hot water demands, which generally includes all associated pumps, motors, and fans.

- **Comparison Points:** The purpose of most rating systems is to provide guidance on the performance of buildings relative to other similar buildings or to minimum standards, as may be defined by national building codes. To do this, two methods are generally adopted. The first is a basic absolute reference point, which is becoming very popular, particularly with zero-carbon emissions targets set to be introduced in many countries and across Europe by 2020. The absolute reference point of zero kWh per square meter is a popular comparison point adopted by many European countries. In the United States, the HERS rating system, or Home Energy Rating System index, places buildings on a number line representing relative performance

- **Reporting:** The primary goal of having an energy rating system is to reduce energy, so to be effective, an energy label needs a comprehensive and prioritized list of recommendations for energy-efficient upgrades. In most countries, the label is mandatory but implementing the associated recommendations is advised only. The more detailed the report, the more likely the recommendations will be implemented. For a report to be effective, it must contain details of potential cost savings and payback periods because these are the primary drivers of energy upgrades. The U.K.'s energy performance certificate (EPC), for instance, provides a report with full linkage to a number of national incentive schemes for accessing cash to implement energy-efficient upgrades. The scheme is referred to as the Green Deal.

- **Assessor's Qualifications:** Quality assurance is critical to the credibility and success of any building-rating scheme. It is necessary at all levels, from validated assessor training and qualifications to standardized methods of measuring and the software tools used to produce the label. Verification of the audit process itself is also an integral part of most successful energy rating system, where the outcomes actually affect real-estate values.

Establishing Your Energy Rating

In order to prepare energy-rating certificates, it is first necessary to undertake an energy performance assessment of the building. There are many software applications, some of which are noted below, that will provide such an assessment on a DIY basis, but they can only give an indicative rating value. A qualified assessor must carry out the validated energy rating, and the information from that survey is inputted into the country's authorized calculation model for assessing a building's energy consumption. The assessor then submits the results to an approved system, which formulates the actual certificate, normally in both digital and paper format. Different countries have adopted their own particular version of the building rating system, but they all follow the same basic format. Some of the more popular labels are displayed below.

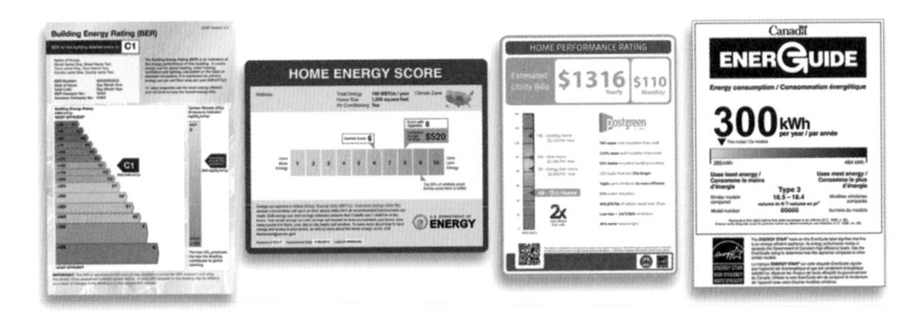

Whereas some countries have successfully implemented voluntary rating schemes, the most successful schemes are those that are mandatory and fully integrated for compliance with national codes and regulations. There are too many individual building energy rating schemes to detail all of them here. We will examine Ireland's building energy rating (BER) scheme because it is promoted by many global institutions such as the IEA as representing best practice in building energy rating schemes.

Building Energy Rating (BER)

A building energy rating, or BER, is Ireland's energy certification scheme, implemented under the European directive on Energy Performance of Buildings (EPBD). The certificate displays the calculated outputs from the energy assessment and provides visual evidence of the energy efficiency of the building to owners, tenants, sellers, and potential buyers. In diagrammatic form, the BER displays the energy band into which your building falls on a scale of A to G, where A is best and costs less to heat and G is very poor and costs more to heat. The BER is accompanied by an advisory report, which identifies potential energy performance improvements that could lead to better comfort levels and reduced energy use and costs.

Under Irish legislation, a building owner must provide a BER to prospective buyers or tenants when a building is offered for sale or rent and a BER must also be published for all new dwellings. Equally, all real-estate advertising must display the property's BER rating. The BER certificate itself contains such information as the building name and address, assessor registration number, validity dates, and BER rating A-G accompanied by the calculated energy value in kWh/m2/annum. The CO2 emissions for the building are also indicated, and the advisory report, which must identify potential energy performance improvements, is a mandatory attachment.

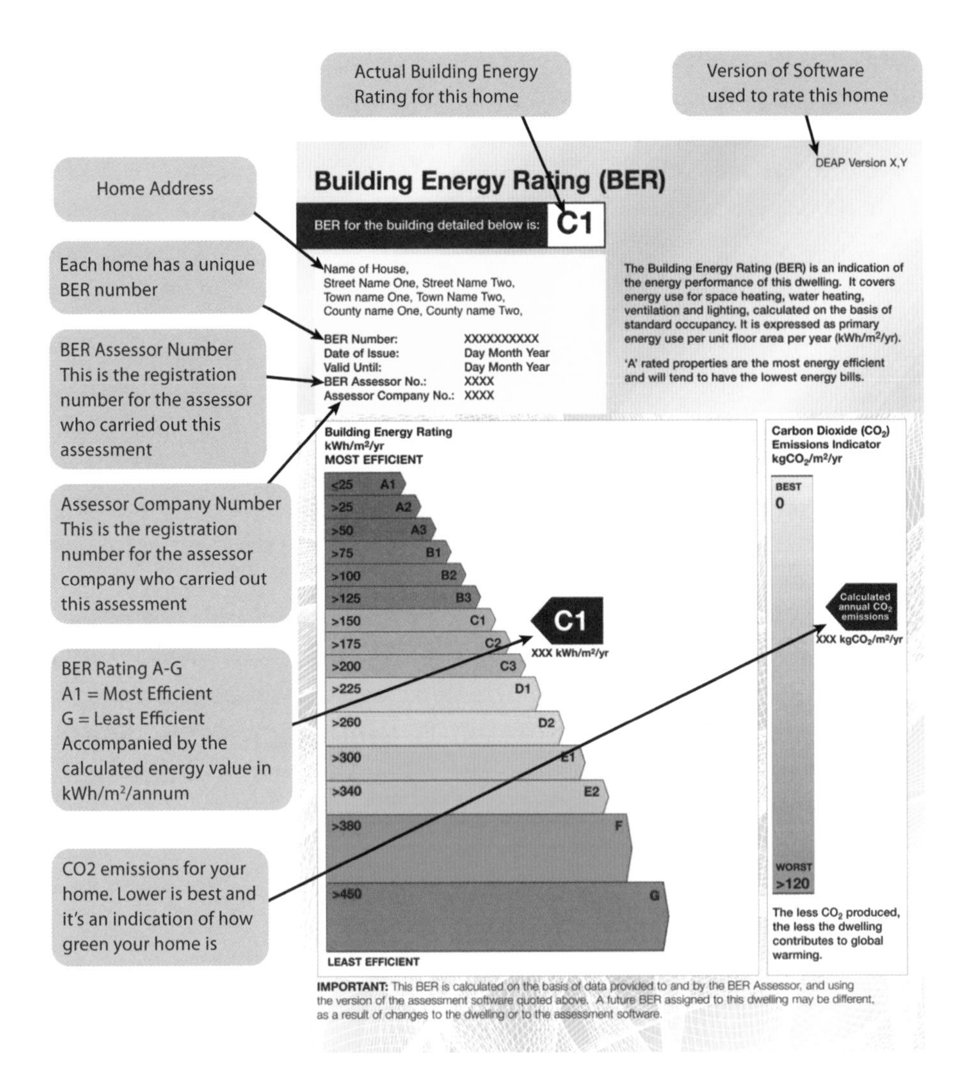

A BER is based on the calculated energy performance and associated carbon dioxide emissions in the provision of space heating, ventilation, water heating, and lighting under standardized operating conditions. Such factors as a home's dimensions, orientation, insulation, space, and hot water system efficiencies are used in the calculation. The BER is not dependent on current occupant behavior.

The energy performance is expressed as:

1) Primary energy use per unit floor area per year (kWh/m2/yr) represented on an A to G scale and
2) Associated Carbon Dioxide (CO2) emissions in kgCO2/m/yr

A BER does not include electricity used for purposes other than heating, lighting, pumps, and fans. Therefore, the energy used for electrical appliances such as cookers, refrigerators, washing machines, and TVs is excluded from direct analysis. However the software used to generate the BER does take into account passive secondary heating associated with such things as lighting, stored water heating, appliances, cooking and occupants.

Technology and web-based programs are making the job of enforcement very easy. This is particularly the case with regard to the design of buildings, where each country simply selects a software package and, thereafter, all designs must comply with the parameters set out in the package. The software used to calculate BERs for residential buildings in Ireland is called the Dwelling Energy Assessment Procedure (DEAP). Because minimum building energy performance measures are also mandatory under Irish building codes, the same software can be used to demonstrate compliance with these codes. For nonresidential buildings, the software used is the Nondomestic Energy Assessment Procedure (NEAP). It generates a BER for new and existing nondomestic buildings and demonstrates compliance with specific aspects of the building codes. Both DEAP and NEAP are freely available for use by the public but are not simple tools. Additionally, official BER certificates can only be lodged by an independent registered assessor.

Energy Modeling Tools

Energy modeling tools are used to design and model the energy performance of a building at an early stage. In the past, only experienced and trained professionals used them, but now, anyone can access some of the easy-to-use and free software packages used to predict energy usage for your home or any other building.

The data generated by such software should not override common-sense decisions, but it can be very useful in the decision-making process by analyzing multiple factors. There are new and more intuitive energy modeling programs on the market. The best software models have in-built compliance criteria with local building regulations and codes, so it is worth looking for a program that best suits your local climate. A quick Internet search for energy-design and energy-modeling tools will identify suitable programs. This is a fast growing and changing market, so here I have outlined just three of the better online free energy tools.

HEED

Home energy efficient design (HEED) is an easy-to-use, free online tool that shows you how much energy, carbon, and money you can save by making various design or remodeling changes to your home. The HEED software can be used to draw your floor plan, and you then click and drag to place your windows and doors in the correct location. The program features typical floor, wall, and roof construction types, along with lighting, heating, and cooling options from which you choose the best fit. HEED also has an option to input the rates for electricity and gas and will then simulate the annual energy consumption, energy cost, and CO2 emissions of your home.

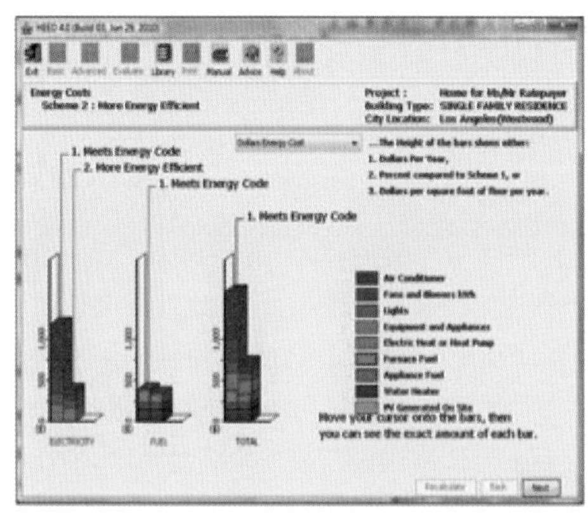

The software is specifically designed for the United States, but it can be adapted to suit any climate conditions. It will quickly compare costings for numerous design scenarios, and it is more than adequate to help you fine-tune your options to get the best performance strategy for home-energy upgrades. HEED makes it very easy for users to change any aspect of their design, and it recalculates the building's energy performance after each design change.

The HEED web site has a comprehensive tutorial for using the software for a residential building. It explains how to optimize the design to minimize energy use, and it has simplified graphics that show you how to save energy, CO2, and money.

RETScreen International

RETScreen is a government-led, free-to-use international building energy-modeling program, supplied and funded by the Canadian government. It is used in more than 200 countries and is part of the teaching curriculum in over 500 universities and colleges worldwide.

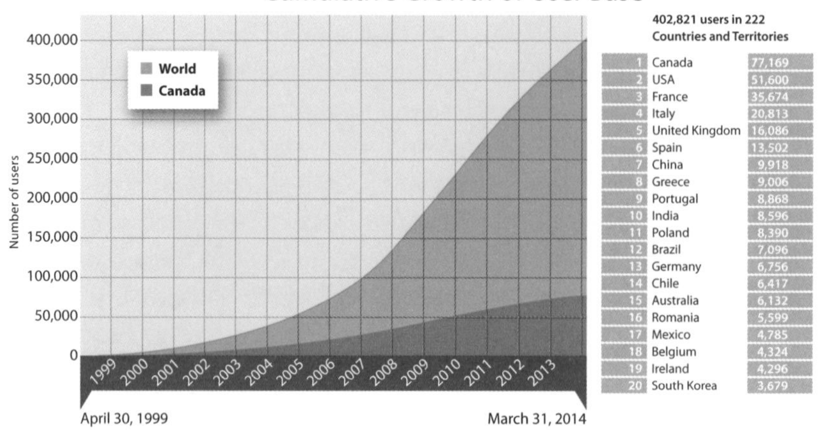

It is a powerful tool that enables architects, engineers, and financial planners to model and analyze energy-efficient projects. The software helps property owners to make decisions on the viability of their project based on energy, cost, carbon emissions, and financial payback. It also features case studies and sample project models that can be viewed online, from new houses and refurbishments to large industrial and commercial buildings. RETScreen is probably best suited for professional use, but it is free and can be downloaded with a full training suite. See Appendix.

There are numerous, freely available software packages that can take the difficult steps out of energy modeling our homes. If you are confident enough to use the simpler packages, that's great because you will learn so much about how your building reacts to various energy upgrades and the associated costs and payback periods. However, if you would prefer not to or feel you are unqualified to use this software, it is essential that your energy assessor uses such a package and demonstrates the various parameters and costs implications around your proposed energy works. If your advisor does not fully model the energy upgrades in this way, he/she should not be hired.

Pay as You Save (PAYS)

Pay as you save is a generic term commonly used to describe the process whereby investments in energy-saving installations can be recovered from the energy savings made by adding insulation, improving airtightness, replacing windows, upgrading boilers, or adding temperature controls, etc. For example, if a household's fuels costs are $2,000 per year and the installation of an energy-efficient boiler costing $1,000 reduces the fuel bill by $250, in simple terms, the boiler will pay for itself in four years out of the savings it makes. There are many ways that the basic principal of this approach can be integrated into the process of financing energy-efficient processes.

As financing often represents the most important obstacle when undertaking energy-efficient projects, some form of incentive is often needed. However, grants, tax rebates, FITs, and RHI can be costly to implement, so a pay as you save model is often favored. Many energy improvements pay for themselves over a period of a few years, so much so that most people will only approach an energy-efficient project on the basis of a short payback period.

Simple Pay Back

While it is interesting to know how much energy it takes to run an appliance, energy efficiency is about savings. Energy-efficient products tend to cost more than conventional energy technologies, prompting the question of how quickly it will take for the savings to cover a product's purchase price. Calculation of simple payback can determine at which point this will occur through realized electricity savings. Although simple payback does not take into account compounded savings, discount rates, inflation rates, or replacement costs, it is a very user-friendly, commonly used, and useful tool.

$$\text{Simple Payback} = \frac{\text{Cost of Energy Efficient Product}}{\text{Annual Electricity Savings}}$$

The quickest way to calculate savings is to insert the wattage difference between, for example, two lightbulbs, as follows:

$$\left.\begin{array}{c}\text{Annual}\\\text{Electricity}\\\text{Savings}\end{array}\right\} = \frac{(\text{Daily hours x 365 days/year}) \text{ x Watts saved}}{1000} \text{ x } \frac{\text{Cost}}{\text{kWh}}$$

For example, if a 100 watt incandescent bulb is replaced by a 5 watt LED bulb and used for four hours every day, if the cost electricity is \$0.08 per kW, then the savings would be:

$$\left.\begin{array}{c}\text{Annual}\\ \text{Electricity}\\ \text{Savings}\end{array}\right\} = \frac{(4\text{ hrs x }365)\text{ x }(100 - 5\text{ Watts saved})}{1000} \text{ x } \frac{\$0.08}{\text{kWh}} = \$11.09$$

Hence the annual electricity savings amounts to \$11.09. So if the energy-efficient LED costs \$16.75, and the annual electricity savings is \$11.09 as shown above, the simple payback is \$16.75/\$11.09 = 1.5 years.

$$\text{Simple Payback} = \frac{\$16.75}{\$11.09} = 1.5 \text{ years}$$

If you are replacing 100 of these light bulbs and the cost is the same, the payback is still 1.5 years.

The problem with evaluating energy-efficiency upgrades using simple payback is that it overly simplifies the investment, leaving out lots of valuable information. It only measures the energy-efficiency improvement until the investment reaches break-even point. There are many other equally valuable considerations that enhance the investment value but are less tangible to measure, including comfort, health, well-being, and energy and cost security. This latter point is important because investment in energy efficiency must increase, given the strong possibility that energy costs will rise in the future. Knowing what to measure and where savings can be made is the fundamental starting point on the road to greater energy efficiencies.

Step 2 Summary

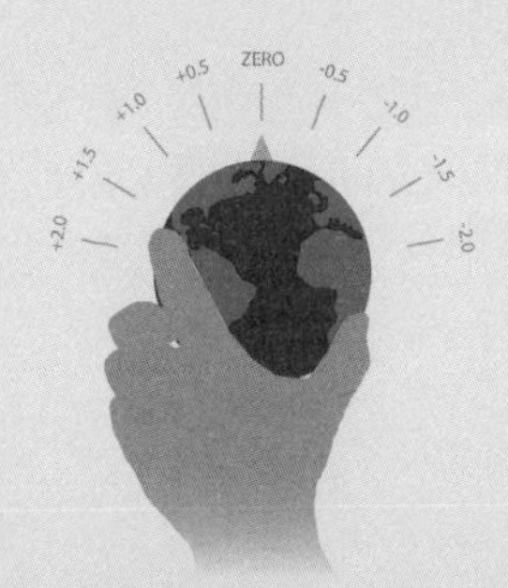

Twitter Summary
Step 2 is about energy measurement. What you can't measure you can't manage and combatting climate change is all about accountability.

Smart Citizen Summary
Every citizen in today's complex interconnected world has a role to play in reducing global carbon emissions. To do this the smart citizen must however:

- Understand the units of energy
- Know the difference between renewable and non- renewable energy
- Know the difference between energy and power and the key part that time plays in every energy bill
- Know how to measure energy and read energy bills
- Understand the concept of energy audit and energy balance
- Know how to read an energy label and building energy rating certificate
- Become familiar with the multitude of energy labels on products today
- Know the key factors in carrying out an energy audit of a building
- Know how to do a simple pay as you save calculation

Step 3: Airtightness

"A nation that destroys its soils destroys itself. Forests are the lungs of our land, purifying the air and giving fresh strength to our people."

Franklin D. Roosevelt

Why is Air Tightness so Important?

Surprisingly, airtightness is still not part of the everyday vocabulary associated with buildings and energy conservation. Its importance is very underrated in terms of measures that can minimize heat loss in a building. Insulation ranks as number one in most people's minds, probably correctly, but it is only wholly effective when there are pathways for heat to bypass the insulation. Try to heat even a fully insulated house with the windows open, and you won't get too far. The same principle applies to an insulated cavity wall when a cool breeze blows through the cavity from unsealed window reveals, air vents, poor soffit details, loose-fitting pipe outlets, etc. Here the insulation is rendered useless. The presence of cool air wipes out the good work done by the insulation material and provides an alternative route for the heated air to escape. Effective insulation slows down that movement of heated air outward.

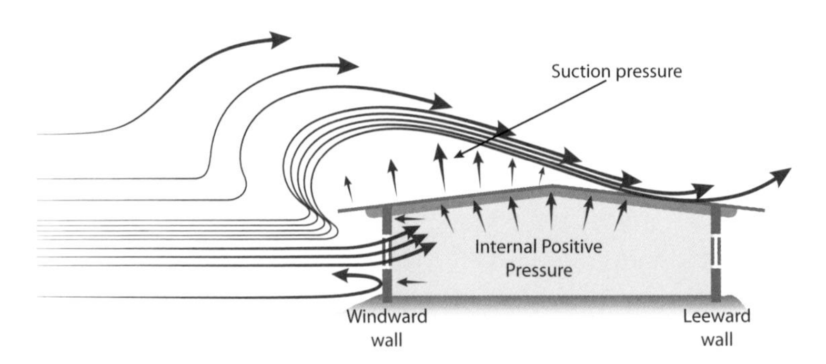

The first calculation a structural engineer will make when designing a large building is a wind-load analysis, which will determine stability. So large is the force of the wind that, if the engineer underestimates its strength, the building may collapse. This is the same force that lifts the wings of an airplane. Positive wind pressures on one side of an object, whether an airplane wing, boat sail, wind turbine blade, or building, results in an equal, negative (vacuum) on the other side, which effectively doubles the air pressure across the structure. Because most buildings are not airtight or sealed, the positive and negative pressure creates a multitude of smaller air paths (draughts) though the building. Have you ever gone into your attic on a windy day and felt like there was a window open in the roof, even when there are no windows? This is the case in probably 99% of buildings today. The force of wind pressure on our buildings and its effect on temperature and comfort are not factors that can be ignored if we are to take heat and energy efficiency seriously.

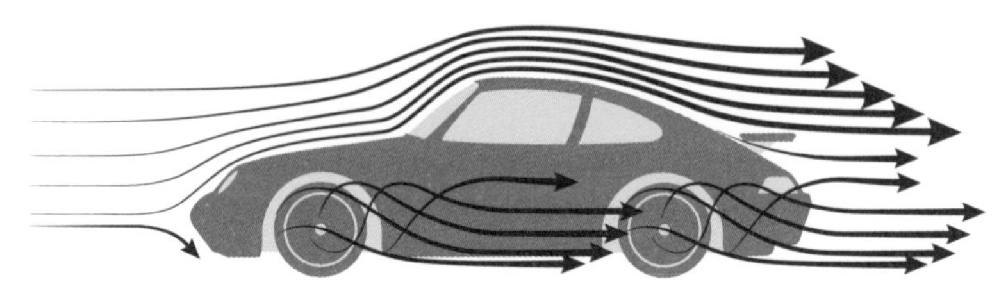

To better understand how we should model our buildings, picture what happens when, on a cold, windy day, you get into your automobile. There is an instant feeling of warmth when the door closes and you escape the wind. As you turn on the heating, the vehicle warms up pretty quickly, and as you drive off, the internal temperature remains constant even though the vehicle may be traveling into the wind at speeds of up to 100km/h. This is explained by the fact that the automobile is a precision piece of engineering specifically designed for this situation. Its body shape is aerodynamic to deflect the wind, and it is completely sealed inside. Air vents control the air intake, and the air-conditioning controls the temperature. We would never think of placing an opening the size of a flapping, loose letterbox in the front of a vehicle because of the discomfort it would cause. However, this is exactly the mistake we make with our homes, schools, offices, etc.

In the past, we ignored the effects wind has on internal temperatures, but more importantly we also ignored the effects of air leakage on the cost of maintaining comfortable indoor temperatures. Now, in response to climate change, there is a new raft of mandatory standards and building codes that demand precision airtight fabrication details.

Air Movement

Keeping our homes warm and comfortable is about preventing heated air from escaping to the outside. In summer and in warm climates, cooling systems can become very expensive to run if hot air from outside is drawn in through leaky walls, floors, roofs, windows, and doors. The way in which heat moves by conduction, convection, and radiation is discussed in more detail in Step 4. Here, we will just take a superficial look at air movement to better understand what happens when we try to control temperatures in draughty and loosely constructed buildings.

Modern building trends tend to be national and regional rather than local, even though a one-size-fits-all approach is inappropriate. People living on an exposed hilltop will not want to interact with their building in the same way as those living in sheltered urban areas, yet building codes and regulations treat them the same.

It's the luck of the draw in most developed countries whether your property faces north, south, east or west. Planning regulations will not take into account a building's orientation toward the sun or the prevailing winds but might insist that you simply line up, military fashion, with your neighbors and face the road. The priority for most planning departments is conformity with the existing built environment, but, as we saw in Step 1, this is beginning to change. Ironically, our ancestors would not have made this mistake. Ancient structures, although primitive in shape, were usually designed to rebuff the elements and had doors and windows on there sheltered faces only. Although it is not possible to relocate or reorient existing buildings, we can change our thinking to get the best from these structures. Often, some small changes to how a building is heated and used can to lead to a surprisingly large reduction in heating bills.

To achieve this, we need to have some basic understanding of the environmental effect of wind on buildings. First, we must dispel the myth that warm air must rise. In short, its movement is part of a cycle, and warm air can go nowhere until more dense cold air is introduced to replace it. Because most buildings are not airtight, cooler air will always be sucked in through the cracks and crevices, pushing warm air out. On a calm day, this would be the natural convection current moving through the building and warm air would then rise as it is replaced by colder incoming air.

But on a windy day and in an exposed location, warm air is flushed out and replaced by an endless supply of cooler air. When the heat mass of the fabric and structure is lost, the building will become difficult to heat and valuable heating energy will be wasted. What is more, when the volume of warm air in a building is being replaced by cold air, you need a very efficient heating system to keep the space warm.

Build Tight, Ventilate Right

There is a popular design statement used by architects and builders, which says "build tight, ventilate right." Let me explain the difference between draughty and well-ventilated buildings. Essentially, draughty structures have uncontrolled air changes, which is no substitute for well-controlled ventilation. Holes and gaps in floors, walls, roofs, doors, and windows allow outside air to be drawn in, and the extent of air changes is determined not by the inside environment's needs but by outside weather conditions. Even in a draughty building on a calm day in a temperate climate, there may be no air changes throughout the day. So when pollutant levels are high, as in sick building situations, draughts cannot be relied upon to cleanse the air. This can be an issue in open-plan offices and schools, which are are occupied by a large number of people throughout the day and the simple act of breathing creates high levels of carbon dioxide. For example, if there are no draughts to improve the air quality in a classroom, carbon dioxide build-up would create a stuffy atmosphere, in which students are more likely to fall asleep than to be alert, fresh, and amenable to learning. The opposite is also true on a cold, windy day; the inside warm air is flushed out and replaced by cold air from uncontrolled draughts, making for a very uncomfortable atmosphere.

In warmer climates, there is also a cost factor when using air-conditioning systems to cool leaky buildings. These units have to work very hard, cooling the inside air and treating a large amount of hot air that has been drawn in from the outside. This means that the units are more expensive to run. They are also poor at controlling moisture levels and can let in more outdoor noise. All of these factors make buildings uncomfortable and unhealthy places to occupy. So it is a myth that leaky buildings with gaps and holes are healthier and more comfortable than sealed, properly ventilated ones.

The "ventilate right" part is key to controlling energy costs and creating a healthy indoor environment. Ideally, an energy-efficient building controls ventilation by natural means, such as opening and closing windows, and through the natural stack effect of the building shape, which is discussed below. But in the real world, this is not always the case. It is possible to get the geometry in a new building design right to encourage natural ventilation, but when renovating an older property, the existing shape of the building rarely allows for full natural ventilation, so mechanically assisted ventilation is often required.

As the scientific evidence in support of climate change mounts, "build tight and ventilate right" is becoming part of the legislation for new and refurbished buildings, and the only variance from country to country is the level of airtightness and the degree of ventilation required.

Sick Building Syndrome

Reducing airtightness is worthwhile in terms of energy efficiency, but buildings still need an ample supply of fresh air if people are to live healthily inside. Unfortunately, the air inside our buildings is regularly of a poorer quality than that outside. Just consider the pollutants and toxins we bring in with us, including cleaning products, bleaches, detergents, perfumes, air fresheners, candles, and incense. We happily store these items in the home, in spite of the fact that they are harmful to the environment and cannot readily be disposed of. The same can be said of other household items such as batteries, printing inks, and deodorant sprays. Progress has been made in terms of our knowledge of the threat posed to food by harmful pesticides, but we still have some way to go before we fully appreciate the damage caused to our health by the multitude of chemicals that we allow and even bring into our buildings.

There are also some toxic materials in the fabric of our buildings, such as brickwork containing arsenic, windows and doors that contain vinyl chlorides, and fire-retardant chemicals and pesticides that are added to many popular insulation products. That's all before we start on building contents, everything from synthetic textiles, carpets, beds, and pillows to painted surfaces that can contain lead and carcinogenic elements.

There is an apparent lack of concern about this, and there is insufficient research on air quality in buildings. Building codes and regulations traditionally controlled only air quantity, not air quality, although this is now changing. Ironically, whereas building materials are not tested in our homes, rigorous analysis is always conducted for signs of toxic remnants in the soil and groundwater around the factories where these products are made.

According to United Retek, the leading provider of soil remediation services for industry, commerce, and government, nearly 100% of the company's workload comes from treating contaminated soils left behind by factories that manufactured housing materials such as bricks, treated timbers, PVC windows and doors, solvents, paints, adhesives, and dyes, or all the component parts of the buildings we live and work in. This does not bode well for the quality of the internal environment.

When occupants experience poor health that is in some way associated with time spent in certain buildings, the buildings in question are described has having sick building syndrome (SBS). The symptoms usually include headaches, dizziness, nausea, dry cough, asthma attacks, itchy skin, fatigue, flu-like symptoms, and many different combinations of these effects. Some people are more at risk and display acute symptoms, whereas others in the same building suffer no ill-effects. The causes of SBS are not fully understood, and very little research has been carried out on the problem to date. Suspects include toxins off-gassing from within the fabric of the building; biological sources such as pollen, dust mites, bacteria, molds, and Legionnaires' spores; or electromagnetic radiation from all the appliances and gadgets wired throughout the building (see also Step 6 on smart meters). External emissions from buildings are highly regulated, controlled, and tested by national environmental agencies, but not so internal emissions.

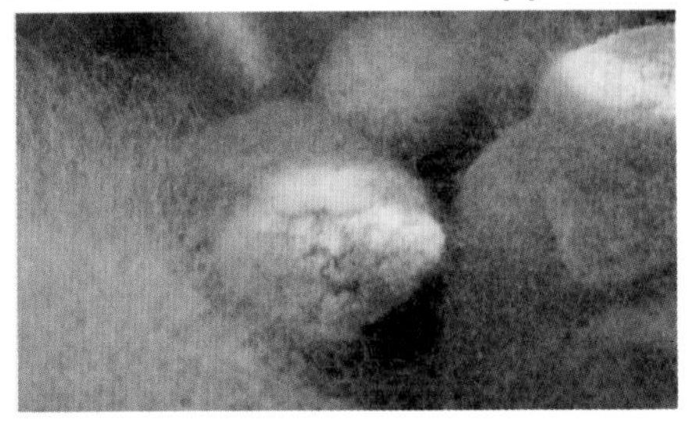

Airtightness can save energy and money, but unless a well-designed and well-managed process for introducing fresh air and removing harmful contaminants is introduced, buildings will increasingly become a health hazard. Well-managed airflow, not draughts, is the best way of ensuring that we live and breathe fresh air within our buildings. Thankfully, the technology for introducing controlled airflow through modern, nearly silent fans has improved greatly. The cost of heat exchangers, which exchange and balance the temperature of incoming air with that of the outgoing air so that the room temperature remains the same, has become less expensive.

As the opening quote of this step reminds us, it's worth remembering that our forests and plant life are like the lungs of the earth. So a simple way of improving a building's air quality, as well as the ambience of our surroundings, is to add some plants.

Measuring Airtightness

This is a relatively new concept for the building industry and involves much complexity. Not everybody agrees with the science behind the measurement of airtightness or the units used to best describe the process, but the practicalities of building airtight structures to new, scientific standards is a whole new ball game. Building regulation authorities in many countries have done a complete U-turn on this subject. In the old, carbon era, when fossils fuels were abundant and cheap, the accepted philosophy was that buildings needed to breathe. Getting fresh air into a building was seen as critical, so vents with minimum sizes were mandatory in habitable rooms, bathrooms, and kitchens. The structure and fabric also needed air supply, and areas such as under-floor voids and roof spaces were fitted with large air vents. In addition, any appliance that might have a health and safety perspective, including boilers, gas burners, cookers, and stoves, had great big holes inserted beside them. Instead of providing protective enclosed and sealed air ducts as integral parts of the heating and cooling equipment, the whole building was inefficiently ventilated.

What is ACH50?

In the low-carbon present, the word "minimum" has been replaced by "maximum" when it comes to airtightness. Modern building regulations specify maximum figures and methods of testing the airtightness of the building fabric. The colder countries of northern Europe and Canada have led the way in this regard, and air changes per hour (ACH) has become the standard unit for defining air leakage in or out of a building. For consistency, ACH is always measured at a pressure difference between inside and outside of 50 pascals. The universal testing method is known as a "blower door" test (see below), and the standard unit of measurement is referred to as ACH50. Other units of measurement are preferred by some specialists and regulatory authorities, and these are expressed in cubic meters per hour (m3/h/m2@50pa) or cubic feet per minute (cfm50) per area of building envelope. Although more accurate, they should probably be left to the specialists. The ACH50 unit is more easily understood, and while it may have different allowable values in different countries, regulations are all leading toward nearly zero leakage figures.

For example, in Canada, one of the first countries to regulate for airtightness, the mandatory figure is a maximum of 3 air changes per hour at 50 pascals (3 ACH50). In the United States, the figure varies from 3 to 7 ACH50, depending on where you live. Although a single piece of legislation governs all of Europe with regard to energy efficiency, each country can specify the most appropriate airtightness figure for its climate. In general, Europe has opted for more stringent targets of between 1 and 2 ACH50.

The Passive House standard, which is perhaps the most stringent standard of all, requires a maximum leakage rate of less than 0.5 ACH50. So you see there is a game change on here: The new language of airtightness figures will become second nature not just to builders, architects, and engineers but to the public at large as measure of a property's energy efficiency.

The challenge with these new standards is the almost military precision needed when addressing all of the sealing details. Every tradesperson onsite has to be fully trained in this new approach if sloppy workmanship and corner-cutting are to be avoided. During construction, it is possible to repair and reseal joints and details, but, as you can imagine, when a building is finished and decorated, an air leak can be virtually impossible to track down and fix.

I was recently involved in two school construction projects, built to Passive House standards at the same time but 100 miles apart. Schools are in the vanguard of the Passive House or near-zero energy revolution, in part for energy-efficiency reasons but also because controlled air quality and the removal of excess carbon dioxide can improve students' concentration and learning capacity.

The first school, which I will call school A for confidentiality purposes, had a well-coordinated design and building team. Every tradesperson coming onsite was briefed about the importance of airtightness and were encouraged to report any accidental slips, tears, or damage to the sealed building envelope that might occur or that they might have observed during the course of their work. Work at school B, on the other hand, followed a traditional approach to construction, with each trade working independently to meet high standards, as defined by previous building codes, while failing to fully embrace new airtightness standards.

When the day of testing for the schools finally arrived and with all the procedural issues in place, school A, to the delight of the full team, achieved a rating of 0.45, well below the target standard of 0.5 ACH50. In contrast, school B's test results were poor, coming in at over 2.2, and this was only the start of its problems. What followed were weeks and months of further testing. Newly completed finishes had to be stripped back to try to locate and repair air leaks, which were numerous, small, and difficult to find. The time involved in testing, retesting, and reopening "finished" elements looking for the elusive defects and then repairing the associated damage meant that the project came in over budget and missed completion deadlines.

Achieving the precision required to meet airtightness standards in new buildings or when renovating existing buildings demands an entirely new philosophy. It means that the building industry can no longer work as a series of loosely linked trades but must now move forward as a united team, trained, practised, and mentored in the skills required to deliver energy-efficient buildings. The results achieved by the two separate school building teams demonstrate that there must be a passion and commitment, followed by a coordinated approach by the team leader, builder, architect, or engineer. If the building owner wants energy efficiency, this vital issue cannot be left to chance.

Blower Door Test

The standard method of testing for air leakage or airtightness is the blower door test. This is performed by placing a fan with measuring devices attached to it in an exterior doorway and then sealing everything around it, including the entire door opening. The fan pressurizes the house to 50 pascals, or roughly the same as that exerted by a wind speed of 20 miles per hour. This is sufficient to identify the amount of air escaping from the building.

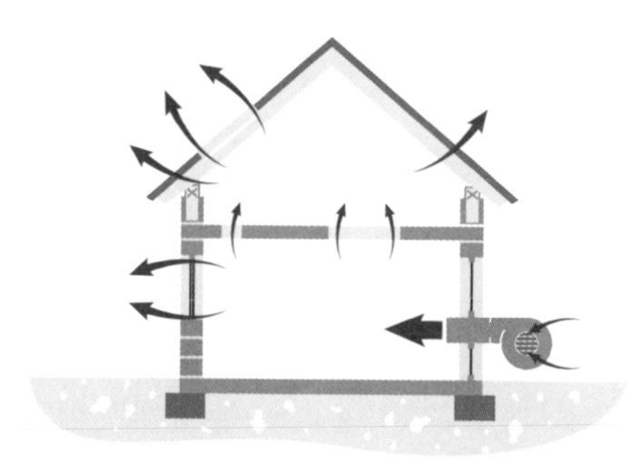

Once the building is pressurized, there are a number of ways in which air leaks can be identified. The simplest method is to use a handheld smoke pen. Because of the induced pressure difference between the interior and exterior, the smoke provides a visible means of pinpointing any gaps and cracks. These can then be marked and identified for immediate or later repair. There are other simple ways of testing for air leakage paths such as using a stick of incense and watching how the smoke fluctuates and disappears out through cracks and crevices. Carrying a candle will also reveal the location of mini draughts, indicated by the flickering of the flame.

Another way to identify elusive gaps and openings is to use a fog machine. This is a small device that creates white (or any color) smoke and is most often used in theatres and on stages to create special effects. It also has a role as a building diagnostic tool because it can very visibly pinpoint all breaches in the building envelope, particularly when viewed from outside.

The blower door test is now an essential part of the quality control mechanisms of building regulations in many places. It is particularly applicable to new buildings, but the nature of the test, insofar as the building must be fully finished, makes it equally appropriate for existing structures. While the regulations may not necessarily apply to refurbishments and upgrade works, the blower door test can tell how leaky the building is, which is a good place to start a refurbishment plan.

How to Seal Buildings

Most people think that windows and doors are the greatest source of leaks in buildings. While they are the most visible, they are generally not the biggest offenders. Some holes and openings have become such an intrinsic part of our building envelope that they are effectively overlooked in self-assessed audits. Blatantly obvious gaping holes, including chimneys, ducts, flues, and vents, seem to have a purpose so great that it justifies a major cavity in an otherwise enclosed building. The next serious offenders are gaps around floorboards and skirting boards, for example, which are often obvious. The greatest offenders are, however, the gaps that you can't see. These can be found under and behind cupboards, perhaps, around incoming services, and they are the result of interaction between different trades, poor work, and sloppy finishes. They are effectively ignored just because they will never be seen. Even when we do spot gaps, we often fail to associate them with the loss of expensive heated or cooled air.

For those who are conscious about airtightness and have sealed the obvious gaps, additional surprise air leaks can often be found around light fittings and switches on internal walls and ceilings. You may believe there is nowhere for the air to exit, but remember that every light fitting, switch, and socket has associated cables and trunking. These inevitably meander through the building structure and end up in an attic, service duct, or draughty cavity and eventually reach the point outside where the cable enters the building.

Roofs

The difference between ventilation and draughtiness is at its most critical in roof spaces. Ventilation is the controlled introduction and extraction of air and is part of the climate control needed to maintain the roof timbers and roof structure in good condition and free from rot and decay. Draughtiness, on the other hand, is uncontrolled and, while it may promote the health of the timbers, it will also cool the attic space and reduce the effectiveness of the insulation. The key here is to keep an airtight layer between the roof space and the rooms below. This is done by thoroughly checking that all gaps, cracks, joints, ducts, cable, and service openings are sealed. If the openings are small, simple sealants are adequate. However, larger, unseen holes are often found in cupboards and closets and may need to be built up with more a comprehensive assembly of suitable materials such as timber infill pieces and drywall boards.

Hatches and access doors can also be major offenders in roof spaces when it comes to uncontrolled draughts. Adding compression seals around a hatch and then a good quality catch should keep the cover tightly closed. Don't forget that the attic hatch needs exactly the same amount of insulation as the rest of the main attic.

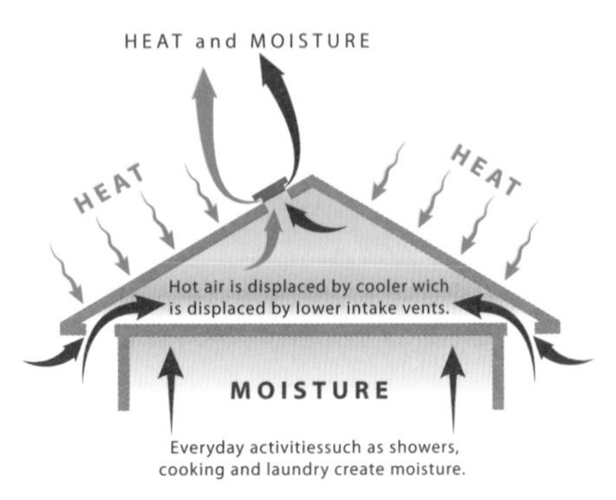

Walls

A close inspection of a building's exterior walls is a first step toward determining the extent of pathways for air infiltration. The usual culprits are gaps around windows, under sills, at pipe entry points, and around drain outlets. Structural cracks are also a leakage point; watch for weaker points in the wall structure such as above and below windows and doors and at junctions between different materials where settlement often leaves cracks. Sealing these cracks will obviously not mean the wall is structurally repaired, but it will protect the crack from adverse weathering and ingress of water and help to reduce air infiltration. An internal wall inspection is more complex. As already noted, offending gaps and holes are often hidden.

Chimneys, Flues, and Vents

Chimneys were designed for a completely different era and mind-set. Open fires gave out tremendous radiant heat, but 90% of the heat escaped through the chimney, which is only half the inefficiency story. A good chimney can extract an additional 90% of a building's other heat because of something we didn't previously understand, even if its effect was known, namely the "passive stack effect." This is a process for naturally ventilating a building by adding an opening at its highest point, channeling or piping it to a lower level, and then placing vents in the lower building. The warm interior air wants to rise, and the vents bringing in cooler air facilitate this. The net effect is a cycle of air through the building. This is exactly what takes place with a chimney, which pulls cold air through leaky doors and windows.

The solution is surprisingly simple if the fireplace is not in use. There are many DIY products for blocking up a chimney, including an inflatable balloon-type device that you insert inside and inflate until it seals the void. Another slightly more costly method, which probably requires a professional to install, is an adjustable cowl that sits on top of the chimney outlet and has a robust chain that extends to just above the open fireplace. This can be adjusted to open or close the cowl at a high level. The cowl solves another problem associated with unused fireplaces in that it keeps out the up to 30 liters of water that can pour down the chimney each year. Placing a cap or lid on an unused chimney is essential in a rain-intensive climate.

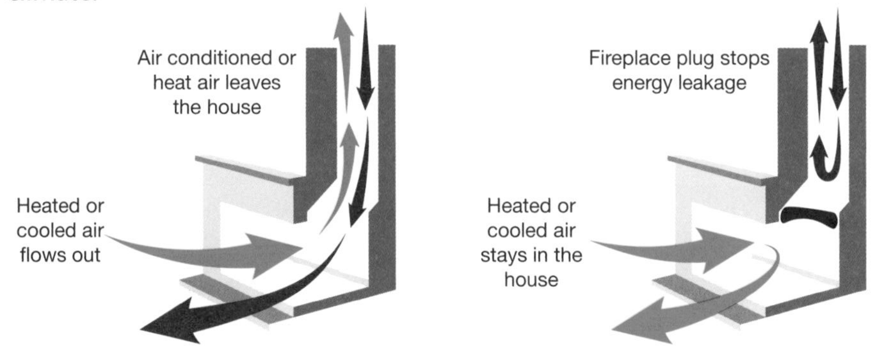

Sealing chimneys and closing off flues is the obvious way to go for those who don't want, need, or like open fires. But many people are very attached to their fires, attracted by the warmth and the comfortable cosy atmosphere they create. A simple way to reverse the 90/10 ratio and keep 90% of the heat within the room is to install a sealed flue, open-fire stove.

There are numerous attractive stoves on the market today, and they efficiently burn all varieties of fuels (see Step 5).

Other forms of flues and vents, including cooker hoods, bathroom extraction units, or simple wall vents, should all be checked to ensure that they have good fitting, self-closing covers. The covers should be of good quality, undamaged, and airtight when not in use, otherwise they will simply act as a hole in the wall. Also, vents should be checked for gaps and loose fitting around the edges to ensure there is no air leakage.

Floors

Older buildings are notorious for having draughty suspended timber floors. An uninsulated suspended timber floor can account for up to 50% of the heat loss from a room. This might seem like an extreme figure, but, in fact, some suspended timber floors are so well ventilated that outside weather conditions can effectively prevail immediately below a loose and ill-fitting floor inside. Cold and draughty floors create the most unpleasant and uncomfortable living space. So although draught-proofing our floors is usually the last job to be done, it should really be the first.

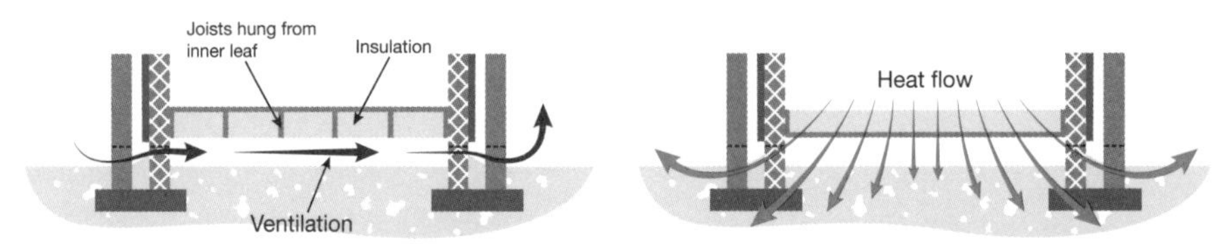

But before draught-proofing, it is important to understand what type of floor you have and what insulation, if any, already exists. Draught-proofing a floor is always a good idea and should be done before the floor is insulated. A good insulating refurbishment, as discussed in Step 4, will effectively make the floor airtight too.

There are really only two types of floor construction materials, timber or concrete, and two methods of construction, suspended or ground-bearing. There are many variations of these, but suspended floors are more likely to be draughty by their very design. However, sealing the floor can be the simplest and cheapest of jobs.

Draught-proofing floorboards depends on how large the gaps between boards are and whether the boards are tongued and grooved. Most importantly, the way in which the draught-proofing is executed will be determined by whether the floorboards are exposed as a decorative finish. In this case, the job is easier but the repair must be of a higher standard. There are plenty of filler materials and caulks of different colors to match the floor. Simply squeeze the filler into the gaps, pushing in slightly more than you need, and when it dries, shave off the excess. If the gap is larger, you might need narrow strips of wood that are glued and tapped into position. The slips can be stained to match the boards.

Gaps between the skirting board and the floor and wall should be sealed, as should air leakage around radiator pipes and other services. Suspended concrete floors are generally not as draughty but should be checked because slight structural movement or, more commonly, shrinkage cracks can provide air leakage paths.

If you are laying a floor covering, particularly carpet, you should still fill all gaps first because carpet has no airtightness properties. There are many good underlay products such as breathable membranes, soft felts, and foil-backed papers that enhance airtightness and improve the floor's insulation. Be careful not to use impermeable-type membranes, which will encourage rot in the timbers underneath.

Doors and Frames

Typically, most doors and their frames are at least in need of a resealing upgrade, if not complete draught-proofing. Draught sealing is not expensive, is easy to install, adds great comfort, and reduces fuel costs. External doors should be treated first to help seal the building envelope. The payback time for recouping the cost of a few seals and strips can be very short, if they are installed on a DIY basis.

Because doors are opened and closed continually, it is very important to consider the type and fixing of the seals. Most doors and frames fitted within the last 20 years will have a compressible strip, but with constant use, this may have worn thin and become defective. It is essential to assess the position of the door and the condition and type of any seals before planning to modernize the draught-proofing.

Door Bottom: Check to see if the door has a weather strip at the threshold on the outside. This is vital to stop rainwater blowing back under the door, but it also helps to provide a draught seal. The best solution is to fit a kit combining a solid weather trim made of timber/aluminum/plastic, which sheds the water, and a tubular draught excluder made from a more flexible material, rubber or soft plastic. It must be very durable because it will be continually trampled on. The trim is fixed to the outside face of the door and tight to the threshold, and it should fit snugly when the door is closed. There are many different types to choose from, and all of them do pretty much the same job and usually cost no more than $15. Additionally, nylon or rubber brushes can be fixed to the base, inside the door, to provide extra sealing where necessary.

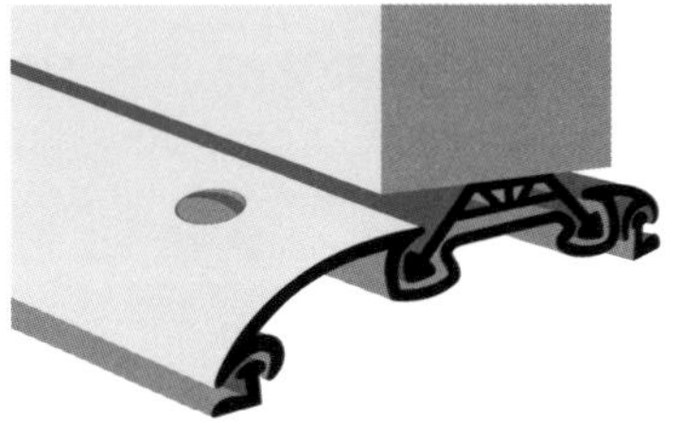

Flexible arch

Complete kit

Door Jambs: A well fitting door needs a gap at the sides and top so that it opens and closes easily. However, if the door is made from timber, it may swell when wet or damp and become difficult to close. Equally, in dry and windy conditions, it may shrink and the gaps at jambs will increase, leading to draughts. Getting the size of the sealants right is crucial. Draught sealants with an expandable range of up to 6mm and a compression allowance of 3mm will allow for seasonal changes in gap size and are ideal for these situations.

The cheapest way to draught sealing jambs is to affix self-adhesive compressible rubber or soft plastic strips; these may have to be replaced regularly depending on their durability. More durable, rigid strips consisting of a metal or plastic flange with tubular sections of foam or rubber can be fixed with nails or screws to the door jambs, with a receiving section fixed to the frame. This creates an airtight seal when the door is closed. An easier to fit but slightly less airtight method is to use V-strips. These are either glued or nailed to the frame and allow for good flexibility in all seasons without making the doors difficult to close. Prices for the different solutions can vary from $15 to $20, depending on the type.

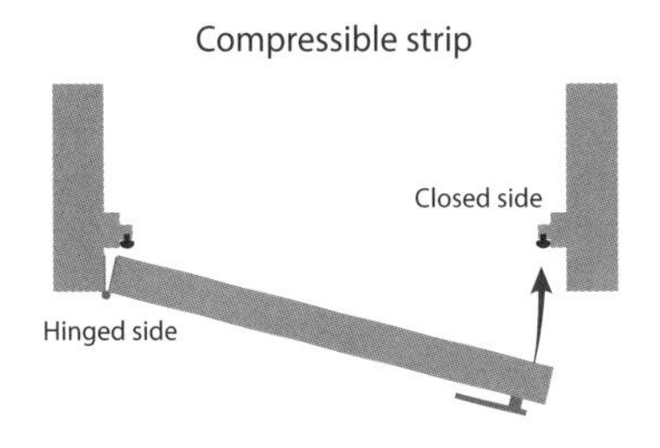

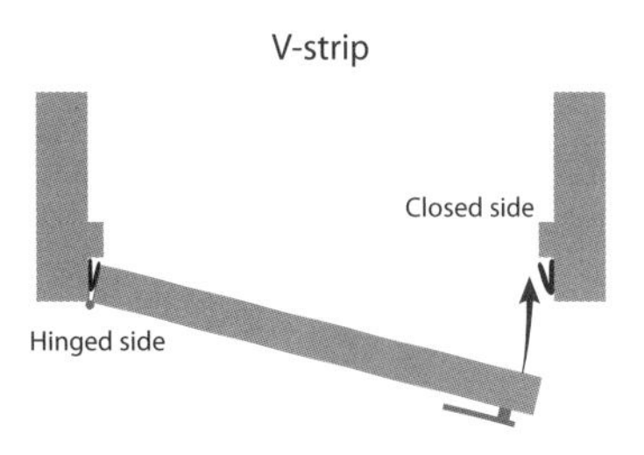

Mailboxes and Keyholes: Not only are doors commonly placed on the windward side of a house, but they generally have a mailbox opening cut into them. Although it might seem as if your mailbox is always closed, when external and internal pressure differences build on breezy and windy days, this thing could deliver not just the mail but up to four air changes per hour for the whole house. That sweeps out the expensively heated warm air, replacing it with cold air and in, hot climates, providing an endless source of air to be expensively cooled.

There are many solutions to the problem, including adding nylon bristles in a small frame that fits over the inside of the opening, which is not ideal. The best one is to fit a custom-designed cover, sometimes called an eco-flap, that is finely balanced to exclude air. These are a little expensive at about $25 but are worth installing if your door is exposed.

Another cause of significant air leaks is the simple keyhole. Companies carrying out air testing on buildings have demonstrated the immediate effect a closed keyhole cover has on the test meter results because this, more than anything, shows how such a seemingly small and insignificant gap can have major impact on air leakages. There is, however, an easy fix. There are plenty of keyhole covers on the market, from simple and cheap plastic ones to more decorative brass, copper, and silver types.

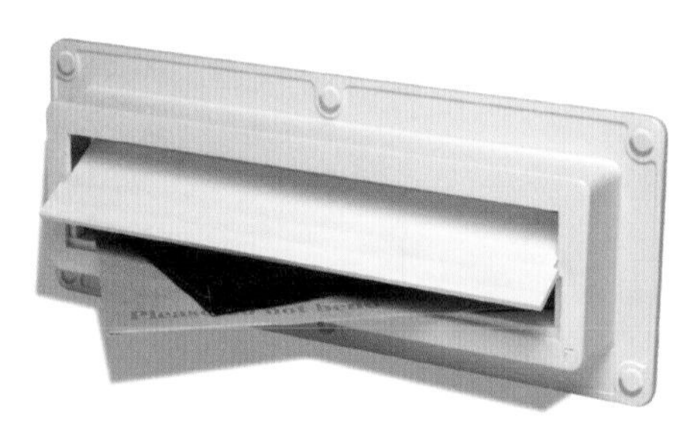

Internal Doors: Good closing mechanisms are essential on all internal doors, and defective ones should be replaced. A simple under-door draught excluder can be easily positioned to fill in gaps between the door and smooth surfaces such as wooden floors, linoleum, and laminates.

Windows: The simplest procedure for sealing around gaps in side-opening windows, sashes, and roof lights is to use adhesive-backed strips. This is a cost-effective DIY approach, but it may have to be repeated every few years depending on the resilience of the product used. For historic buildings or windows in conservation areas, it may be necessary to seek expert help to find effective solutions for draught-proofing more complex windows, including cutting grooves to hide seals and brushes. Externally, a frame sealant (usually silicone) can be used to fill the gaps between the window frame and the wall. If the gap is large, expandable foam filler may be needed. It will then have to be trimmed back when dry and finished with a frame sealant.

Secondary glazing, which usually consists of a secondary frame and glazing unit, is a great way of improving the draught-proofing of hard to treat windows. It has the added benefit of improving the overall insulation value of the window. This can be a very economical solution, and it can be undertaken on a DIY basis: You provide the measurements to the specialist who supplies the glazing unit for you to fit.

Porches and Windbreaks: Homeowners should be very wary of "belt and braces" insulation solutions that involve additions to buildings. Porches are a classic example of this, becoming places where insulation and airtightness standards can drop. Because the porch is seen as an extra windbreak, its mere presence is perceived as a design plus, and insulation and airtightness are secondary considerations. Consequently, many porches and conservatories are single glazed with loose fitting carpentry joints.

Having installed a porch, the next unfortunate line of thought is often to remove or at least leave open the doorway to the main building. What results is the exact opposite effect to that originally intended: an internal part of the building that is subject to external weather conditions. This applies equally to domestic and commercial buildings. Have you ever sat in the porch of a hotel, bundled up in warm clothing?

Ventilation

Getting the ventilation right in a building is about more than saving money; it's about protecting human health and comfort in the most energy-efficient way. The more we "build tight," the more we have to "ventilate right." Older homes, particularly in colder climates, rarely have mechanical ventilation equipment. At most, they may have bathroom and cooker extractor fans, which remove air from the house and rely on gaps and cracks to bring fresh air back in. This works from an air change per hour perspective but is costly in terms of extracting warmed air and replacing it with cooler air.

Solving the "build tight, ventilate right" conundrum is relatively straightforward with new buildings. Difficulties arise with older buildings where retrofitting measures can cause as many problems as they solve, if poorly executed. Balancing airtightness and ventilation in these buildings is probably the biggest challenge to energy efficiency.

Natural Ventilation

Within buildings, human comfort is not simply determined by room temperatures. Moving air has the effect of making us feel cooler, which is just what we need if temperatures are too warm. But if we are already cold, moving air or draughts cool us more and make us feel uncomfortable. Ventilation is all about getting the conditions right to promote good health and comfort. In the outside world, we can achieve this by wearing clothing to suit the prevailing climatic conditions, cold or warm.

We intuitively know what do. If there is a cold north wind blowing, we don't need a compass to tell us which side of a shelter will protect us from the wind-chill factor, we simply turn to the side or move to where there is no wind chill. On a hot humid day, we will intuitively seek out any small, cooling breeze. Indeed, we don't need to scientifically analyze why moving air has a comfort and cooling effect or why a coastal breeze is so refreshing. When we are not indoors, we exhibit more flexibility when it comes to ventilation and comfort levels.

Every building has natural ventilation, to a greater or lesser extent, depending on how it was designed and built. Ventilation was probably not optimized in the original design, but it is worth establishing the basic factors that will enhance the building's ability to provide fresh airflows by natural means.

- **Windows**. Opening and closing windows is such a basic form of ventilation that you might say it hardly needs mentioning. But the capacity of windows to provide natural ventilation is completely overlooked, and this is not always the fault of the homeowner. Too often, regulation gets in the way of common sense, and by the time the window manufacturer has complied with energy codes and health and safety standards, there is no accommodation for a small opening section of window. For example, fire safety regulations often require bedroom windows to be used as an escape route in the event of a fire. But if someone can get out the window, someone could get in, so for security reasons, these windows are rarely opened, hence they are effectively rendered useless for ventilation purposes. Modern house design, and window design in particular, favors clean lines, and architects and designers are reluctant to add clutter in the form of small window openings. In retrofit projects, when windows are being replaced, it is always worth considering adding small window openings at an easy to reach height, which is a practical solution. Small window sections that are easy to open also represent the most cost-effective way of removing excess moisture from inside a building.
- **Passive Stack Effect**. This is essentially the same as the chimney effect. Hot air is lighter than colder air and wants to rise. Hot air cannot actually rise until it draws in colder, denser air to replace it, making the airflow automatic or passive. On days when there is little or no breeze outside, the passive stack effect can be very successful, given the right conditions. A chimney will perform this role automatically, provided there is an air source or even a low-level air leak around the house, such as under doors. The effect can also be engineered easily by arranging a pattern of vent locations. If there is no existing chimney, it may be worth adding a roof vent with a closable damper as part of a passive strategy to ventilate the building.

Natural ventilation is always a bit intermittent because it completely depends on weather conditions. The real challenge with upgrading buildings for airtightness is to provide the right combination of natural and mechanical ventilation. Mechanical ventilation might vary from simple extraction fans to full-house ventilation with built-in heat recovery.

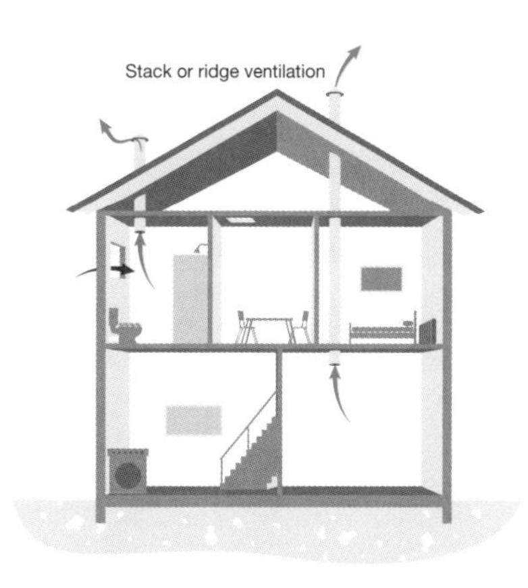

Mechanical Ventilation

Before installing any mechanical ventilation, whether a simple extractor fan or a full-building system, it is always important to work with the building's natural ventilation features. The easy part of this is the ventilation itself. It's usually just a combination of fans, extractors, motors, pumps, and ducting system, often with automatic controls and always run by electricity. Even if the fans and motors are working against each other or against the natural ventilation of the building, for instance when windows are open, this does not present a mechanical system problem. It just means the system has to work harder, but most modern ventilation systems are actually designed for these worst-case scenarios and operate at optimum capacity and efficiency at heavy loads. Ironically, the opposite also holds true, and mechanical ventilation systems work very inefficiently at smaller loads. None of this matters too much until you bring cost into the equation. Oversized systems are energy guzzlers and use just as much energy when operating at half load as they do at full load. Consideration should be given to turning mechanical ventilation systems off in summer and use natural ventilation where possible. With ventilation, it is not how much the system costs but how much it costs to run.

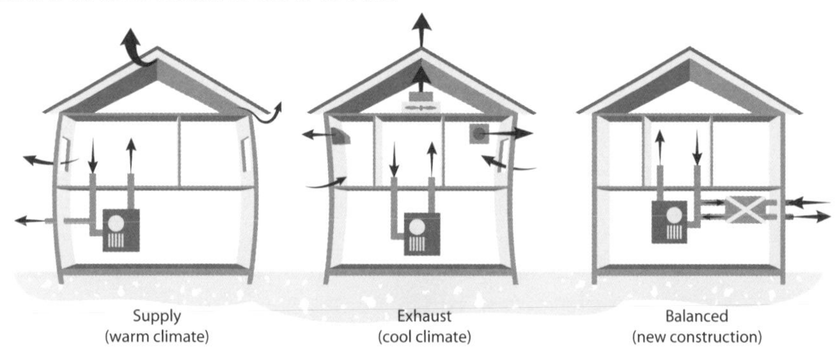

There are four general categories of ventilation systems: supply only, exhaust only, balanced systems, and heat recovery ventilation (HRV), which is usually associated with warmer climates.

Supply Only

Supply only ventilation is probably the least popular choice. It is best suited to warm climates because it can control moisture ingress into the building. Building control authorities also favored supply only in the past, when regulations were concerned with specifying maximum air changes in buildings. Today, by contrast, regulations specify minimum air changes. Supply ventilation uses a fan to draw clean outside air into the building. The fresh air combines with the indoor air, and the resulting air mix is at a slightly greater pressure than that outside. We have controlled the quality and amount of air intake, and because the building is under greater pressure, air will now only leak out, but not in, through the building's various cracks and crevices. Having the interior at a slightly greater pressure also keeps out other pollutants such as dust, pollen, mold spores, and moisture. Other benefits of supply only ventilation include:

- Cost-effectiveness, given that often only one fan is required
- Excess airflow is good for combustion appliances and minimizes the potential for back-drafting which is a situation whereby reduced air supply can force drag flames inward rather than outward
- Positive pressure reduces the likelihood of gas build-up inside buildings in areas of known high radon.

Placing a filter on the intake supply air vent is important, and regular maintenance here is critical to ensure the filter itself does not become a nest for pollutants. Another caution with supply only, particularly in colder climates, is when warm air is pressed out through cracks and crevices, it may carry moisture, which could condense on cooler structural elements, causing long-term damage such as interstitial condensation (discussed under Condensation below)

Exhaust Only

Exhaust only ventilation systems are very popular in colder climates, where they are traditionally used in wet room areas to get rid of excess moisture and odors. They are also popular in kitchens, over cookers, to extract steam and cooking smells. Unlike supply only systems, exhaust systems tend to depressurize the building. In hotter climates, this can encourage warm, moisture-laden air to be drawn into the building where it can cause problems. The humid air condenses on the colder internal structure, resulting in long-term structural damage, caused by interstitial condensation. Locally exhausting polluted air at the point where it is created, for instance at a cooker, bathroom, or shower location, is, however, the most efficient and cost-effective method. Sizing the fans correctly and installing energy-efficient motors with good sensors that minimize the running hours are critical steps from a cost perspective. It should be remembered that all the air extracted has to be replaced by air forced in through the cracks and crevices of the building structure. This air is unfiltered and likely to collect dust and mites as it works its way inside. Pollutants, particularly from a city environment, might need filtering. Of more importance, in older buildings, is the probable lack of a radon barrier, and too much negative pressure might, in certain areas, allow radon gas through the floor into the building.

Balanced Systems

A balanced ventilation system is a combination of the above two methods. With such systems, the quantity of indoor air extracted is matched by the outside intake supply. Although they are rarely exactly balanced, such system do not experience the extremes of pressure differences discussed above. The key to getting this right is to match both the size and time of use of the extraction and supply fans. For example, if 50 cubic feet per minute (50cfm) of ventilation is required, the system needs to be designed to exhaust 50cfm of stale air and then supply 50cfm of fresh outdoor air. The principal advantage of a balanced system is its capacity to control comfort levels with fresh air. Its downsides are cost and complexity. In most cases, people find it difficult to determine how to control and optimize single exhaust and supply systems; understanding and maintaining a balanced system is even more complex. Whole-house ventilation systems are also difficult to regulate in older houses because there are usually too many unknown leakage points within the building fabric, so getting the balance right without oversizing the motors and fans can be a challenge.

Heat Recovery Ventilation (HRV)

The difficulty with supply air ventilation is that the air it draws into the building is at outside temperatures. At some times of the year and in some climates, this might not matter. But these are the exceptions. More commonly, this air causes cold draughts and discomfort. Equally, in hotter climates, there are times when the air is too warm and needs to be cooled to maintain interior comfort levels. This is where heat recovery is used. This process takes the heat or cooling energy from the air being extracted and transfers it into the fresh air supply, and the heat is exchanged between the two. It works perfectly in both cold and warm climates because the process simply exchanges the heat from hot air to cold air. In HRV, it does this without direct contact between the two air sources, which meet through a series of coils or plates. Depending on the design, HRV can transfer up to 85% of heat with only a 15% loss in temperature.

- In colder climates, HRV preheats the incoming air with the outgoing warmer air
- In hotter climates, the reverse occurs, with colder outgoing air-cooling the incoming warmer air

Heat recovery units can be single-room or whole-house solutions, with ducts extending to all the principal rooms. In a new house, this is a relatively straightforward procedure and the required ductwork can be built in and planned for at the design stage. The HRV unit also needs to have a drainage outlet to carry away condensed moisture removed from the air. Whole-house, mechanical ventilation with heat recovery is popularly referred to as MVHR.

Retrofitting a HRV system is not a straightforward task because it won't work in an old, draughty building. Airtightness is a critical feature of a successful HRV system because, without it, not all of the air entering the building will pass through the heat exchanger. It is estimated that the energy benefits are only realized when the airtightness of a building is better than 5m3/hr/m2 at 50pa (5ACH), where nearly all of the air passes through the heat exchanger. To put this in context, an old, unused chimney could leak 5ACH. A popular and effective solution for retrofit situations is single-room heat recovery because it's easy to install and can often fit into the same opening as a passive room vent. It has the advantage of providing continuous ventilation without cooling the room. It also removes moisture, which can be very beneficial in wet rooms or rooms with condensation problems.

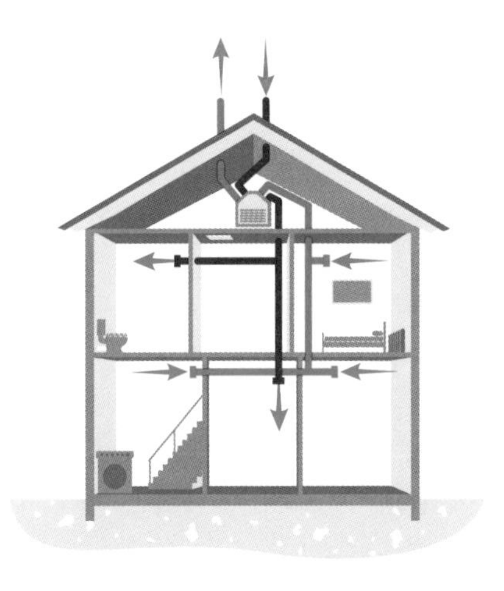

The optimum situation for heat recovery is in Passive House design. That philosophy is a "mixed mode" one, in which a mechanical ventilation system is used with heat recovery from the exhaust air and is balanced throughout the year with a natural ventilation system of openable windows and passive air movement methods. Passive House certification cannot be obtained until this mixed mode has been demonstrably achieved.

Moisture Control

Moisture should really be discussed under the "pollutants" heading. Water, in all its forms, must be treated with the utmost respect. Whether it is ice, water, steam, moisture, or vapor, water is mistreated at our peril. A top lawyer, who works for a large law firm specializing in building-defect law suits, tells me that 99% of the cases dealt with by his firm are water/ moisture related. Moisture is perhaps the least recognized indoor pollutant, affecting both the health and comfort of occupants and the integrity of the building fabric.

In bathrooms, in particular, excess moisture has tremendous potential to cause damage. During a bath or shower, humidity levels rise significantly, creating the perfect breeding ground for mold, mildew, and microorganisms that can negatively impact on health. In addition, long-term exposure to excess moisture and humidity can crack and peel paint and wallpaper, degrade wallboard, warp doors, and rust metal fixtures ad fittings. Good ventilation, therefore, protects both your health and your home. Moisture in bathrooms is, at least, visible, as is the damage it causes. However, it does travel, causing problems anywhere within a building where it finds the right temperature to condense.

Condensation

Condensation occurs when warm, moist air meets a cold surface and forms tiny droplets of water. It happens because warm air can carry much more moisture than cold air. So when warm, moist air meets a cold surface, it cools and loses its capacity to retain the moisture, and tiny droplets of water form. We are all familiar with how and when condensation occurs in our everyday lives. That might be a cold bottle of water from the refrigerator or the cold windscreen of an automobile, but the effect is the same. Something else most drivers are familiar with, particularly those with air-conditioning in their vehicles, is that it is no longer necessary to wipe down a fogged-up windscreen. Instead, simply press the AC button for a few moments and the windows are quickly demisted.

The capacity of the condensation process to literally form pools of water is very much misunderstood. I have frequently been asked to survey properties and report on the source of dampness. The type of dampness to which I refer mainly happens in new builds and refurbishments or where there is a change in tenants or heating systems. The builder will probably have made numerous repeat visits, each time adding some silicon sealant here and there in a desperate attempt to solve the apparent water ingress problem. Unfortunately, by the time it becomes apparent that there must be a condensation problem, the relationship between builder and occupant has deteriorated to the extent that the builder is no longer a trusted source of information.

Dry air, too, has its problems because it is an irritant and a source of discomfort for a building's occupants. It can cause sore eyes and respiratory ailments. Solutions to dry air problems can include what might be termed normal household activities: drying wet clothes inside, cooking, bathing, or washing. In excess, these things cause condensation problems, but in moderation, they add moisture to the air.

When it comes to ventilation and deciding on supply/extract/HRV systems, the first major decision relates to moisture control:

- What happens to the humidity levels within the building?
- Is condensation likely to occur?
- If so, where?

Unseen condensation, referred to as interstitial condensation, can occur behind fixtures and finishes and within the structure of a building and fester away for years, undetected, causing major damage. Interstitial condensation is also a potential problem associated with the introduction of internal insulation. Moisture naturally occurring within a property that is allowed to migrate to the cooler wall structure and condense into water droplets is called interstitial condensation. The difficulty is that this occurs within the wall structure and out of sight. While this might always have been happening, the old, uninsulated wall was able to expel the moisture and dry out naturally. If you change the way old buildings control moisture by adding insulation, there is a real chance that moisture may get trapped on the cold side of the insulation and condense, causing damp problems. Making a building more airtight and increasing the insulation levels, inside or out, will change how moisture migrates through the wall. The addition of new linings can lead to condensation problems if the materials are applied incorrectly. As we take structures and fabric all the way to Passive House standards, moisture becomes the primary threat we have to deal with. One golden rule to avoid interstitial condensation is to place a vapor check membrane on the warm side of the internal insulation to prevent moisture-laden air reaching and condensing on the cooler parts of the wall structure. On the other hand, because ventilation standards are becoming more prescriptive under today's building energy codes and the measurement, verification, and certification processes are more stringent, moisture management is more readily accounted for and controlled.

Step 3 Summary

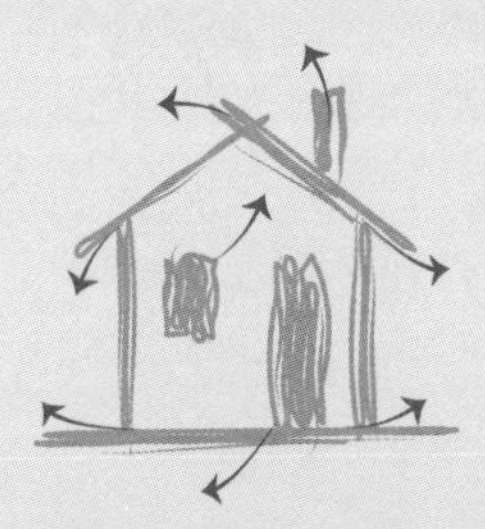

Twitter Summary
Airtightness needs to be part of the everyday vocabulary of energy efficient buildings. Airtightness can save energy and money, but it must be matched by well-designed fresh air ventilation systems.

Smart Citizen Summary
Step 3 is about understanding the relationship that heat flow, fresh air supply and moisture control have on a healthy and comfortable indoor environment. This understanding is also crucial, if energy savings are to be achieved, without degrading the internal living environment or the fabric and structure of the building. The smart citizen must understand the crucial role airtightness plays in achieving energy efficiency savings in our buildings by:

- Understanding why airtightness is so important in achieving truly low energy buildings
- Avoiding heat loss due to air leakage
- Avoiding drafts and discomfort
- Improved fresh air controlled ventilation
- Improved indoor air quality
- Avoidance of moisture related building fabric damage

Step 4: Insulation

"It doesn't make a difference what temperature a room is,
it's always room temperature"
Steven Wright (Comedian)

Insulation is one of the most important steps in energy conservation. When correctly installed, it can have the greatest impact on energy savings, in both new and existing buildings. So why, in this book, is insulation relegated to below airtightness in terms of energy steps? Insulation and airtightness go hand in hand; one without the other is useless. Most people understand that a property must be well insulated if it is to be kept warm, but not so many truly understand the importance of airtightness. All the insulation in the world won't keep you warm if there's a cool breeze gusting through your building or through the fabric of your building. Stopping draughts and uncontrolled air movements is essential if insulation is to do its job. The link between airtightness and insulation has all too often been missed, not just by the building industry but also by the majority of homeowners.

Picture yourself on a cold day wearing a warm coat. The coat is loose and unbuttoned and a light breeze is blowing. The effectiveness of the coat is diminished because it is unbuttoned. Instinctively, parents know to make sure children are zipped and buttoned up and that they have many "layers" of warm clothes. What might not be so obvious is that layers of clothing are an effective way of reducing the air pockets and air circulation associated with wearing loose-fitting clothing while serving as effective insulation. The principal is the same when it comes to insulating a building.

Understanding what insulation does is not difficult. It slows down the rate of heat movement through the fabric of the building. In cold weather, the heat is stubborn and wants to escape; in hot weather, heat contrives to enter the building. The more insulation you have, the harder it is for heat to get in or out. Unfortunately, the simplicity ends there and we need to investigate a little further in order to understand how heat is transferred and how insulation really works. Heat is sort of "hot-wired" to escape to cooler areas, even if they are outside a building. It seems to be much more clever than we previously thought, capable of moving in directions and using processes that were once unrecognized.

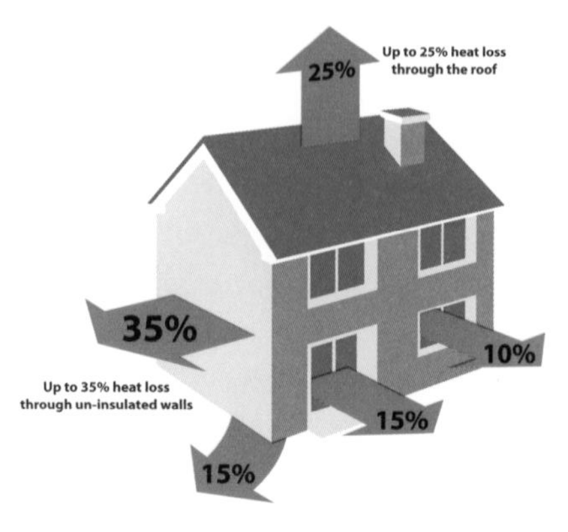

We're familiar with the theory that hot air rises. It follows, therefore, that the most important place to insulate is the attic, a space that is perceived as relatively easy and cheap to insulate. This is correct, but it doesn't tell the whole story. Heat is not restricted to vertical movement. It can move upward, downward, sideways, and by different methods, including convection, radiation, and conduction.

Heat movement is like the ebb and flow of the tides in that it is constantly gravitating from warm areas to cooler ones and will do so naturally, consistently, and persistently. This simplicity of movement disguises an underlying mission to succeed. Heat, just like the tides, is impossible to hold back and will eventually escape. The quality and thickness of a building's insulation will determine how slowly the heat passes through it. If there are weak points or thermal bridges such as joints, gaps, or areas that are impossible to get at, heat will pass through unrestricted. To meet the standards of today's compulsory building energy codes, along with even higher standards set by some of the voluntary codes such as Passive House, we need a better understanding of the best ways to insulate our buildings.

When we add insulation and set about controlling the movement of warm air, we also control the movement of moisture within the building. This is fine if we understand the process discussed in Step 3: that warm air and moisture can fall out when the temperature reaches a certain level, called the dew point. Moisture condenses and turns into water droplets, and this can happen anywhere within a building or building structure. It is, perhaps, the single most important issue to understand when insulating, given that moisture and damp can have detrimental effects on the structure and fabric of buildings.

Body Insulation

Our choice of clothing is key to determining how comfortably warm or cool we are, whether we are indoors or out. Some might view this is an unusual place to start when considering the details of building insulation.

The easiest way to control our own body temperature is to decide how much or how little clothing to wear, and we need to be reminded of this. In the developed world, people expect the environment in buildings to match their precise thermal comfort requirements. To say that we have become spoiled is an understatement. We have lost that intuitive ability to adapt to our indoor environment, apparently forgetting that we can regulate our own temperature and comfort levels with appropriate clothing. Our default position now seems to be to adjust the temperature controls or find someone in the building who can.

So much thinking currently goes into making new buildings and refurbishments more energy-efficient that automatic controls and intelligent sensors control our living and working environments, limiting the experienced range of conditions and temperatures. For example, there are thermostats that learn how you heat your home and forward set the temperature, predicting your future heating requirements. Unless we change our thinking, our ability to regulate indoor temperatures will be relegated to our capacity to complain and blame the smart thermostats. So as a reminder, here are three short lessons in how to dress for comfort.

Lesson 1: Remember the body has its own heating system.
We are warm-blooded animals, and as such our body temperature tries to remain constant, whether it's hot or cold outside. The human body continuously produces heat from two kinds of internal metabolic processes: biological, driven by food, and physical, from exercise such as moving, walking, running, and working. The deep body temperature is 37oC, and there is continuous transfer of heat to the skin where it is dissipated.

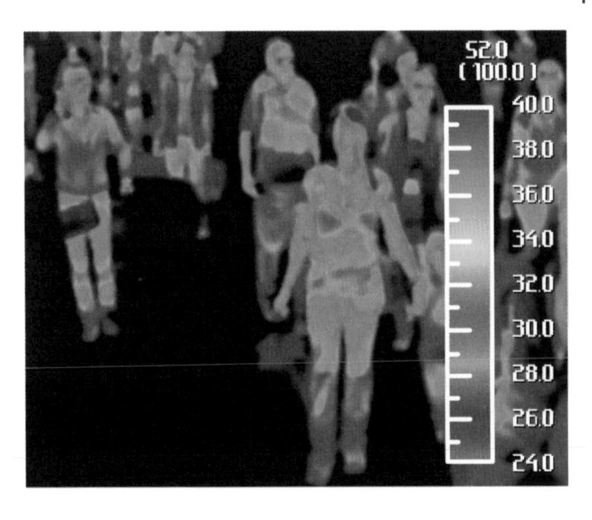

Lesson 2: The body has its own in-built heating and cooling controls.
There are numerous ways in which the body can control and dispel heat through the skin, including conduction, evaporation, convection, and radiation, which are discussed in detail below. When the body gets too hot, it can reduce the heat balance by evaporative cooling, otherwise known as sweating. If the body cannot reduce its temperature, heat stroke may develop and this can be fatal, particularly for the elderly during long stretches of hot weather. In cold conditions, the body also has a number of options to warm up. It reduces blood circulation to the skin, thereby lowering core temperature, which is often associated with goose bumps. The body's extremities are next, with fingers, toes, noses, and ears receiving less warm blood so that vital internal organs retain as much heat as possible. Shivering can also generate some heat but only for a short time and at the expense of depriving other areas of the body of much needed critical energy. If these temperature rebalancing mechanisms fail, hypothermia may follow and then, potentially, death.

Metabolic rates at different activities

Activity	met	W/m^2	W(av)
Sleeping	0.7	40	70
Reclining, lying in bed	0.8	46	80
Seated, at rest	1.0	58	100
Standing, sedentary work	1.2	70	120
Verylight work (shopping, cooking, light industry)	1.6	93	160
Medium light work (house~, machine tool~)	2.0	116	200
Steady medium work (jackhammer, social dancing)	3.0	175	300
Heavy work (sawing, planing by hand, tennis) up to	6.0	350	600
Very heavy work (squash, furnace work) up to	7.0	410	700

There's a quite a broad range of temperature differences over which the average human can exercise conscious control, from simply moving to a warmer/cooler location to increasing exercise levels to wearing more or less clothes to match environmental conditions.

Lesson 3: The Clo unit.
The Clo unit measures the thermal insulation of clothes, or the ability of clothes to keep us warm. It originally developed for military use, to determine the minimum clothing weight required to match maximum field performance. It is defined as the amount of clothing needed by a person resting to remain comfortably warm at normal room temperature and humidity. Another thermal measure used in Europe is the TOG unit, which mainly describes the insulation values of fabrics and quilts.

It is unlikely that people will start measuring the Clo value of clothes before wearing them, but there is a need to start taking back some individual control over temperature regulation. We should be able to adjust our clothing to account for a far greater range of indoor temperatures than we currently do. The greatest energy savings in all buildings are the human influences, and these should always outperform the technological ones.

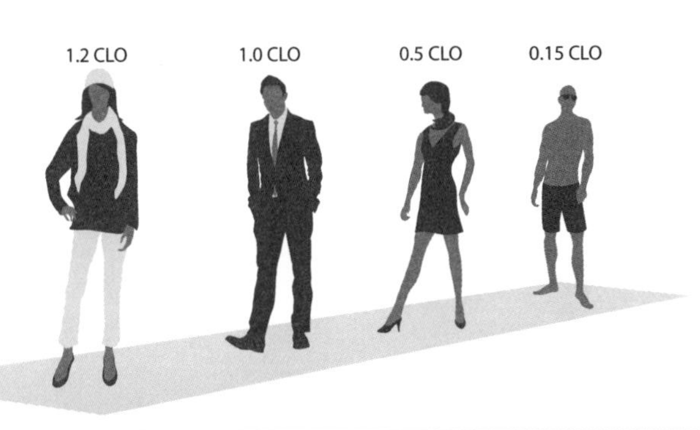

Insulating valeu of clothing elements

Man		clo	Women		clo
Underwear	Singlets	0.06	Underwear	Bra + panties	0.05
	T-shirt	0.09		Half slip	0.13
	Briefs	0.05		Full slip	0.19
	Long, upper	0.35		Long, upper	0.35
	Long, lower	0.35		Long, lower	0.35
Shirt	Light, short sleeve	0.14	Blouse	Light	0.20
	Light, long sleeve	0.22		Heavy	0.29
	Heavy, short sleeve	0.25	Dress	Light	0.22
	Heavy, long sleeve	0.29		Heavy	0.70
	(+5% for tie or turtle neck)		Skirt	Light	0.10
Vest	Light	0.15		Heavy	0.22
	Heavy	0.29	Slacks	Light	0.26
Trousers	Light	0.26		Heavy	0.44
	Heavy	0.32	Pullover	Light	0.17
Pullover	Light	0.20		Heavy	0.37
	Heavy	0.37	Jacket	Light	0.17
Jacket	Light	0.22		Heavy	0.37
	Heavy	0.49	Stockings	Any length	0.01
Socks	Ankle length	0.04		Panty-hose	0.01
	Knee length	0.10	Footwear	Sandals	0.02
Footwear	Sandals	0.02		Shoes	0.04
	Shoes	0.04		Boots	0.08
	Boots	0.08			

How Heat Moves

It is important to have a basic grasp of how heat and warm air move about a building before real progress can be made toward curtailing the escape of heat. Warm air rises and moves from warm to cold areas, which, in the past, was ample knowledge to allow builders and tradespeople to insulate properties. There was no monitoring, measuring, or compliance with regulation standards, and there were no energy certificates for display on buildings. Nobody wrote articles in technical journals on how to carry out energy-flow calculations and set performance criteria for insulation products. That has all changed, and a little effort is now required for us to be well enough informed to at least be able to shop competently for insulation materials: to ask the right questions and know whether the salesperson is knowledgeable. There are key issues to be determined, and these do not just relate to insulation performance but also other issues, including:

- Is the insulation reflecting or radiating heat?
- What glass should be used?
- Should the glass have low emissivity coatings to reflect the heat back in on a cold day or out on hot day?

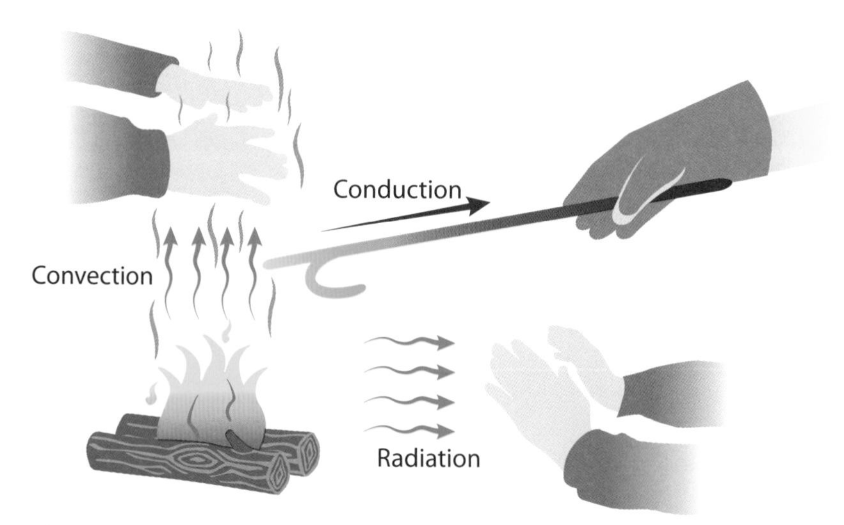

This is a relatively new industry, so the consumer needs to be careful because not all sales personnel will yet be experts. They might be selling a top-branded product but may still be new to the industry. You might be about to purchase a key product that will form an integral part of your property for upward of 50 years, and this might be on the advice of someone who has just completed a three-day certified training course.

I put an extension on my house almost ten years ago. Part of the structure included a glass wall and glass lean-to roof. The extension is south facing, designed to trap the midday sun, and the existing rear brick wall of the house was to act as a natural thermal mass, to store the heat collected during the day and release it slowly by evening. Key to getting this right was the quality and specification of the glass. As I was dealing with a reputable glass supplier, I hoped to tap into their superior knowledge of thermal values and glass emissive coatings, etc. Getting the emissivity, or low-e, glass coating locations wrong could result in the glass reflecting all the much-needed heat back outside. This might be fine in Dubai where keeping intense heat out is vital. In a more temperate climate, this valuable heat must be allowed in to heat the thermal store, in this case the brick wall, and then trapped so that the conservatory does not immediately cool down when the sun sets.

As I probed a little deeper in order to gain a better understanding of exactly how the composition of the glass wall and roof should work, it became abundantly clear that I was on my own. The specialist glazing company's expertise only extended as far as cutting and trimming the glazing products it sells. Beyond that, it was up to me to specify exactly what I needed. What is more, the little advice I did receive was not particular to my requirements and, had it been followed, the conservatory would have been too hot in summer and too cold in winter.

Given that energy conservation is a new and developing industry, there will be a knowledge gap while employees upskill and gain much needed experience in aspects of the business. In the meantime, the best way to avoid this limited knowledge loop is to equip yourself with enough knowledge.

Before exploring the mechanics of how heat moves, it is worth noting that this is not the same as how we can move heat. Without getting into too much detail here, it sufficient to observe that energy can neither be created nor destroyed, but it can change from one form to another. For instance, electric radiators convert electrical energy into heat energy; gas, oil, coal, and wood boilers burn energy-rich fossil fuels and release heat, which can be circulated via water or air; and heat pumps (see Step 5) work in a totally different way, picking up heat from one place and moving it to another. The way in which heat moves, on the other hand, is by convection, conduction, and radiation. Some detail is needed here because understanding this movement is fundamental to building modern, energy-efficient structures.

Convection

Convection is the process through which warm air rises and is replaced by denser, cooler air. It is an essential component in heating and cooling systems, in which the movement of warm and cool air is manipulated around buildings. It's also an important concern in a draughty building because warmed air is ready to move and will quickly escape through poorly sealed windows, gaps under doors, chimneys, or a multitude of other places.

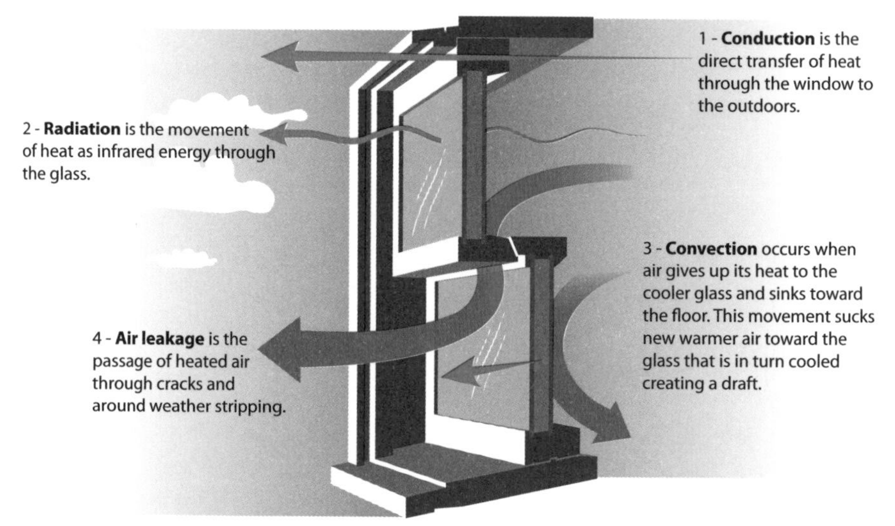

Significantly, insulation works best on the basis that the air cannot bypass the insulation with the warmer air on one side having to work hard to slowly make its way through to the colder air on the other and not get to take an easier route, through cracks and crevices.

Picture a hot air balloon, which would be an unattractive flight proposition if its fabric had a couple of air holes. It's simply one of the laws of nature that warm air will find its way to cooler air by the simplest route, whether we can see it or not. Strangely, something that seems to defy our logical sense of heat is the igloo. An igloo's inhabitants can remain relatively warm and sheltered from the outside elements because the structure is airtight and body heat is like a furnace, keeping the space warm. A little convection heat slightly melts the inside layer of the igloo, which refreezes, helping to improve the insulation properties of the ice.

Conduction

Conduction is the process whereby heat moves along a material that is often said to have thermal conductivity. It's similar to the way in which electricity runs through dense metal objects, or conductors. The same electricity cannot run through softer materials such as plastic or rubber (insulators), which is why you get plastic casings around electric cables. With conduction, the denser the material, the better the heat transfer, and the softer or more porous the material, the poorer the heat transfer. Unlike electricity, however, heat can actually travel through both hard and soft porous materials but at different rates. The denser the material, the faster the heat travels, which means that materials such as iron are great conductors. Brick is moderately effective, but it is neither a conductor nor an insulator. At the other end of the scale are materials such as glass fiber, mineral wool, and polystyrene, which are well-known insulators.

The thermal conductivity of materials increases when they are wet. Dry and wet bricks have completely different values, for example. A brick, a concrete block, and a plastered building have weaker thermal insulation values when they are wet. As well as weaker thermal conductivity values, there is also the problem of heat loss due to convection currents removing moisture and cooling down the surface.

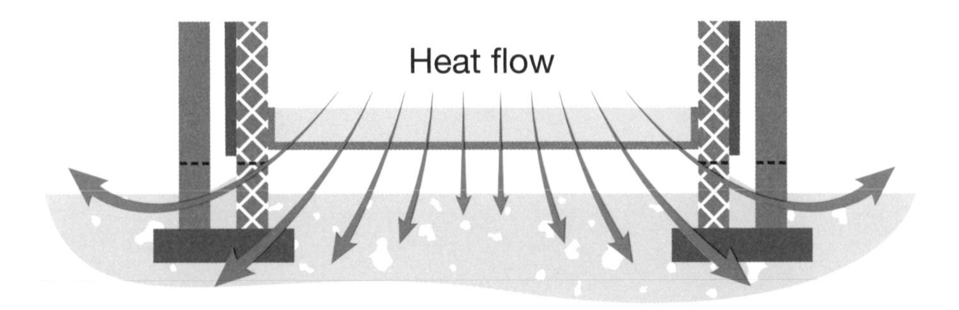

Another belief that can be dispelled relates to the insulation value of earth and that there is minimal heat loss through ground floors. First, heat can travel in any direction via conduction, so why wouldn't it travel downward through the great conductor that is concrete and then on to a probable layer of gravel through to the earth? Depending on where the water table is, the ground may be saturated, leading to an even greater acceleration of heat downward. Traditional thinking regarding ground floors has always underestimated the heat loss potential here. Another example of heat conduction in action is thermal bridging, and this is discussed in a little more detail below.

Radiation

Radiation is more difficult to understand and, unlike other forms of heat transfer, does not need air or a solid medium for heat to be exchanged. The heat travels or transmits from a hot or warm body to a cooler one. An open fire provides heat by radiation. Have you ever stood in front of a bonfire where the heat from the fire is intense but yet the air around it is cold? This is because the fire is radiating heat from a hot body to a colder one (yours) and not to the air around you. The greatest heat radiator of all is, of course, the sun.

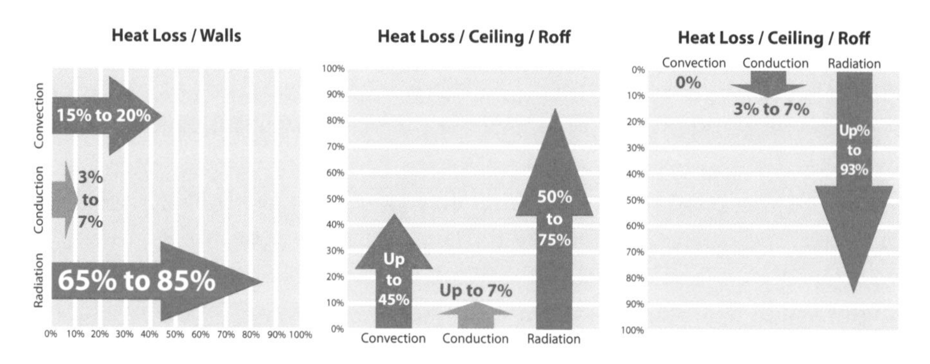

The quantity of heat transferred depends on the temperature of the material, so the hotter the surface, the more heat that will be radiated. Radiated heat loss or gain can therefore take place through walls, roofs, floor slabs, windows, and doors. Because heat transfer takes place between the surfaces of a hot and cold body, the surface material, type, and even color are important. Traditionally, very little is done to prevent radiated heat loss. It may not be as obvious as some other types of heat loss, and its prevention has to be treated a little differently. Did you ever ask yourself why someone rescued from the sea or a mountain suffering from hypothermia is not wrapped in blankets but in a very thin sheet of foil? This is because the foil will reflect the body's radiated heat, helping the individual to retain their own natural body heat.

Whereas heat can move in three different ways – conduction, convection, and radiation – within a building, it rarely moves in only one way but more likely in a combination of all three. Different types of insulation have different capacities to slow down the transfer of heat. It is worth examining how heat is measured in order to determine the best choice of insulation material.

How Thermal Insulation is Measured

There are a number of ways in which heat can be lost through the fabric of our buildings, but the same approach is used to quantify the thermal performance of insulation values. It is an approach that the whole building industry relies upon when planning, designing, specifying, and installing energy-efficient features. There are three main values that underpin the measurement of thermal insulation:

- K-Value
- R-Value
- U-Value

The U-value and the R-value are interrelated in that one is the reciprocal of other. This means that 1/R-value = U-value or 1/U-value = R-value. Therefore, a ceiling with an insulating R-value of R-25 would equate to a U-value of 0.04. The U-value is the preferred unit in Europe, and the R-value is preferred in the United States and Canada. However, certain products such as windows and doors only ever use the U-value figures in all countries. These universal values can make heat loss comparisons possible between such diverse components as walls, roofs, floors, doors, and windows across international boundaries.

K-Value

The K-value is a measurement in its own right, and it is the first concept to understand when considering the composition of the thermal resistance of a building's fabric. Thermal conductivity, or K-value, is independent of the thickness of the insulation material. Thermal conductivity measures the rate of heat loss (W) through one cubic meter of thickness (m) of the material with a one degree kelvin (K) difference in temperature between the warm and cold side giving a finished unit in watts per meter kelvin

W/mk. The lower this number is, the better the thermal performance of the material. Because different insulation materials may have different thicknesses, the K-value simplifies the process of making comparisons between different insulation products. The table below lists details of the thermal conductivity of some of the best and worst preforming building insulation materials.

Material	Density (kg/m3)	Thermal conductivity k (w/mk)
Vacuum insulated panels	25	0.005
Aerogel	20	0.013 - 0.014
Expanded polystyrene	15	0.033
Mineral wool	25	0.04
Sheep's wool	25	0.034 – 0.054
Hemp fibre	26	0.039
Wood fibre	115	0.039 – 0.061

R-Value

Referring to thermal resistance, R-value is a measure of how much heat loss there is through a specific thickness of material. It is a measure of the actual construction thickness and the thermal conductivity of the material. The relationship formula is:

R = L/K *where L is the material thickness & k is the K-value*

For example: Take the same thickness, say 50mm (0.05 m), of the best and worst performing insulation materials in the table above.

Vacuum insulated panel *0.05/0.005 = 10.00 m2K/W*
Wood fiber *0.05/0.039 = 1.28 m2K/W*

The higher the thermal resistance figure, the better the material is at preventing heat loss. From the above figures, it can be established that the vacuum panel is nearly eight times better than the wood fiber, or put another way, the insulation thickness could be eight times thinner and achieve the same thermal resistance. This is a vital factor when insulating areas with minimal space available to fit insulation.

Additionally, when there is a series of insulation materials together, the R-values can simply be combined to give an overall thermal resistance figure for all of the materials. The R-value, as discussed, earlier is also defined by its reciprocal relationship with the U-value.

U-Value

The U-value of a material or group of materials is a measure of the speed at which heat is lost through those materials by means of conduction, convection, and radiation. It is primarily based on the R-value but also takes into account losses through such things as air spaces or cavities (convection losses) and losses from wall and insulation material surfaces (radiated losses). The heat loss is measured in Watts (W) per square meter (m2) per degree of temperature difference across the material, usually measured in degrees kelvin (K) but can be degrees centigrade (C), giving a finished unit W/m2/K. The lower the U-value, the better because this means that there are fewer Watts of heat lost per square meter of building fabric.

In calculating the U-value a number of factors are taken into account:

- The value for all the materials through which the heat must pass before reaching the cold. For instance, in a wall it might be the sum of separate R-values for the plaster, brickwork, insulation, air cavity, and outer brick.
- The surface friction of the face of insulation exposed to air. If there are layers of air attached to the inside and outside faces, this will restrict the flow of heat. You can see here how the calculation, if carried out properly, will take account of breezy and draughty cavities in reducing the insulation value.
- The surface emissivity. Different surface finishes will limit the ability of the insulation material to radiate heat. A perfect example of this is foil-backed insulation, which is very effective in limiting the transfer of radiated heat. Another good example is the addition of a low e-coat to glazing units to prevent excessive heat gain in hot countries and heat loss in colder countries, according to which side the low e-coat is placed.
- The extent of known and repeating thermal bridging (discussed below). For instance, if a cavity wall has a series of wall ties that act as thermal bridges between the inside wall structure and the outside one, then these should be taken into account in the calculation.
- Building regulations and codes set down minimum U-values that must be achieved through the principal enclosures of a building such as roof, walls, floors, windows, and doors. For instance, a sheet of insulation has a particular U-value, but to determine the overall U-value of the wall containing that insulation, you have to add up

the individual U-values of all the other materials that make up the wall. In other words, the U-value calculation is expressed as U =1/Rt (W/m2K). Be careful when adding U-values. You don't simply add them, you must add the reciprocals (in other words you must convert them to K-values before adding them).

The calculation is not simple because Rt above is the addition of all the thermal resistances plus the surface resistances, emissive coatings, convection losses through cavities, and the effect of thermal bridging. In reality, nobody does this calculation without consulting tabled results for standard construction details or using one of the many free web-based tools.

Thermal Bridging

Thermal bridging, more often referred to as cold bridging, is conduction in action. The degree to which thermal bridging exists in buildings can vary from full-scale in solid brick walls to more localized occurrences such as around windows and doors, wall ties, bridging cavities, or gaps in insulation. Evidence of its effects can often be found around the inside or outside of a building. For example, after a frosty night, the location of supporting rafters on an insulated roof may be identified by melt lines because the timber supports act as a "bridge" for the internal heat to escape. Internally, thermal bridging can be seen around window reveals, when moisture condenses, often leading to damp stains and mold growth.

The ideal situation is, of course, where a full and complete layer of insulation is laid around the whole building without any cracks or reductions. This is feasible in a new building but requires great attention to detail and full cooperation from all tradespeople. Such a degree of insulation is more difficult in the refurbishment of an existing building. It is possible to reduce thermal bridging with internal upgrades, but special attention is required in some areas, notably hard to reach structural elements that protrude to the outside, including supporting joists, beams, and cantilevered slabs. The best opportunity to eliminate thermal bridging in an upgrade is to add a layer of continuous exterior insulation.

The quickest way to determine whether thermal bridging exists is to conduct a thermal survey using infra-red photography. As noted in Step 2, there is an app that enables smartphone cameras to take thermal images. There is also specialist software that models buildings, providing a thermal contour of all heat losses. As we move toward super-insulated buildings, the relevance of thermal bridging becomes even more important.

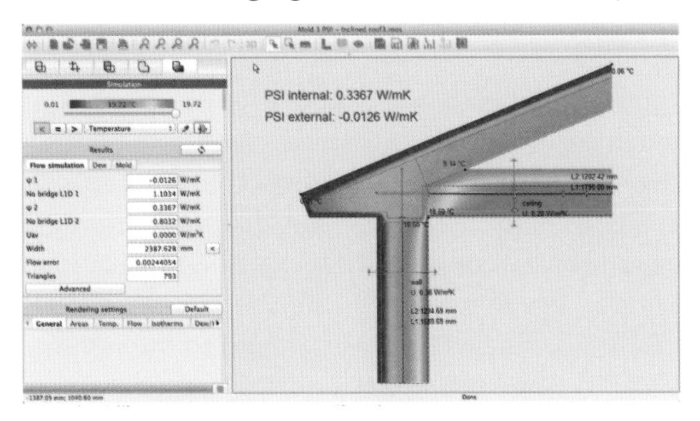

Choosing Insulation Materials

Insulation is probably one of the fastest growing sectors in the modern construction industry. There are numerous technical web sites with extensive data on everything you might ever need to know about U-values, R-values, emission ratings, installation details, embodied carbon, and carbon emissions. There is an abundance of information, some of it conflicting, but in the end, there is one principles-based decision to be made in terms of material choice: whether to select sustainable or nonsustainable materials. After that, all insulation must be properly detailed and installed.

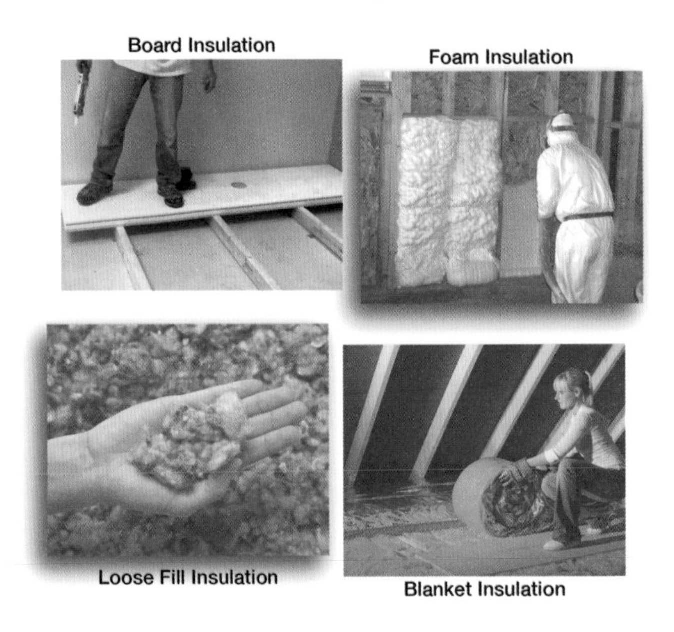

The decision on whether or not to use sustainable natural insulation material is often quickly arrived at, once costs are considered. Most people will initially aspire to using only natural materials, but more cost-effective, manmade compounds – mass produced and easily distributed – often win out, even for the more sustainability minded consumer.

Because insulation ranks so highly in the "must do" category, it is more important to insulate to the greatest thickness and detail possible, within the available budget, than to procrastinate over the multitude of alternatives. Different insulation materials are good at doing different jobs. Although heat flow is the primary concern, there are other insulation issues to be considered such as airtightness, moisture control, and drying capabilities. Special care must always be taken with regard to the potential toxicity of certain chemicals in some manmade insulation materials

Sustainable Natural Insulation

Sustainable and natural insulation materials come in all shapes and sizes. The main, readily available types are sheep's wool, wood fiber, cellulose fiber, and hemp. As demand for these products rises, so too will their availability and cost competitiveness. A house with sheep's wool insulation enclosing the floors, walls, and roof wouldn't need much marketing in terms of selling the image of a cozy, well insulated home. There are also other, not so apparent, advantages of natural insulation over some of their manmade counterparts such as better moisture control and reduced carbon emissions.

Moisture control in buildings is a one of the key issues, particularly as we move toward super-insulation in building design. Wool, cellulose fiber, wood fiber, and hemp are natural hygroscopic materials, which means they can absorb moisture and release it, allowing the surrounding structure as well as the insulation fabric to dry out naturally. Other advantages include the fact that these are natural, nontoxic materials that promote the health of the building's occupants and help to avoid sick building syndrome, and they have minimal embedded carbon unlike their nonsustainable alternatives. What is more, some of them, notably wood fiber, can serve as a heat sink or reservoir, absorbing heat from the sun if used in a roof space. This prevents the building from becoming too hot, and the heat is then slowly released at night, when the temperature drops.

One drawback of natural insulation is that some of these materials are relatively new to the building industry and their compatibility with other building products may yet have to be proven. In addition, some suppliers of natural insulation mix additives to enhance waterproofing and fire resistance and binders to provide stability. These additives are not necessarily a problem, but consumers should read all labels to ensure that no unwanted chemicals are introduced to an otherwise natural material.

Sheep's Wool

A number of companies are producing some very fine wool-insulation products. The wool is available in slabs, batts, and rolls of varying size and thickness, depending on requirements.

This is an ideal insulation material in retrofit refurbishments because it is flexible, easy to handle, and easy to trim and cut. It is particularly suitable for use in older buildings because of its breathability and moisture control capacity. In fact, it can absorb up to 40% of its weight in water without losing its thermal qualities or becoming degraded. The same cannot be said for any other popular building product.

Hemp

Hemp fiber is on a par with sheep's wool as one of the best natural insulation materials, and it has some excellent sustainable qualities. Unlike sheep's wool, hemp is not as widely used. It is believed to be one of the oldest domesticated plants, primarily grown for fiber and food. Today, its uses are numerous and diverse and it is found in everything from food products to cosmetic oils, textiles, building materials, and insulation. It is a fast growing, environmentally friendly crop, and it can be grown without the application of herbicides or pesticides.

The global hemp industry is undergoing a huge resurgence, in part because hemp has finally been able to shake off its bad reputation as marijuana's nearest cousin. The hemp crop is technically classified as Cannabis Sativa L, an association that led to a long-standing ban on its cultivation in many countries. Growing hemp is still prohibited in the United States, although it is legal to import it and it is readily sourced from Canada. In most other countries, including Britain, it is now legal and the crop's growth is actively encouraged because of its sustainability as an insulation material.

Hemp is slightly stiffer than other natural fibrous insulation materials and so has a greater variety of uses because it is less likely to slump behind wall panels or around pipework and openings. It is ideal for insulating attics and internal walls, which form part of a dry lining framework.

Wood Fiber

Wood fiber is a natural product usually made from sustainable material such as forestry thinnings, saw mill residues, and recycled timber shavings. The wood is usually pulped and made into boards by compressing the residue into various densities and thicknesses. The process is very successful, and wood insulation boards are very versatile and suitable for inclusion in standard construction or retrofitting works. Wood fiber insulation boards lend themselves to many different applications and can be used in wall construction, attic insulation, and under floors. With the addition of a latex type material, they can also be used for external cladding in association with a hardboard material or finishing coat of plaster. Like sheep's wool and hemp insulation, wood insulation may need to be treated with appropriate fire retardants. Full technical specifications for the many different wood fiber insulation products would need to be examined, given that cost, certification, and construction details and associated R and U-values will vary according to supplier.

Cellulose Fiber (Recycled Paper)

Cellulose fiber is made from recycled paper and is available in boards of various densities and thicknesses as well as in loose fill bags, and it can be pumped into position. Many people are concerned that paper is a potential fire hazard and are wary of using it in their attics. However, cellulose insulation can match the fire resistance standard of wood fiber and wool, and it is particularly good for soundproofing, airflow, and moisture control. Cellulose insulation is ideally suited to wood-framed construction and in situations where the building fabric needs to allow air in but keep moisture out. Cellulose is considered one of the greenest insulation products around, and it is very much preferred by those who are concerned about whole-product carbon footprint because of its low embedded energy and nontoxic features.

Manufactured Compounds

There are excellent fabricated insulation products on the market, and there is plenty of technical information available from the main market leaders, whose web sites contain more data and information than anyone could possibly digest. Fabricated insulation materials have two strategic advantages over their more environmentally sustainable competitors: cost and usability. Their thermal conductivity and U-value rating can match and surpass the natural materials, but they have the disadvantage of preventing walls and roofs from allowing air to pass out, and they don't have the natural hygroscopic qualities needed for moisture control. However, because they are engineered to very high standards and are precision made to suit construction requirements, their ability to dispel and keep out moisture in the first instance can be better than natural materials. Builders and tradespeople prefer them, not just in terms of cost, but also for buildability. The industry is more accustomed to using these products, and, performance notwithstanding, they must be installed to higher standards.

Some argue that many fabricated insulation sheeting and boarding materials have high embodied carbon and poor sustainability credentials and therefore should have no place in a near-zero, carbon-sustainable building. But the really significant carbon emissions take place during the heating and cooling lifetime of the building, and any steps to reduce these are good for the environment.

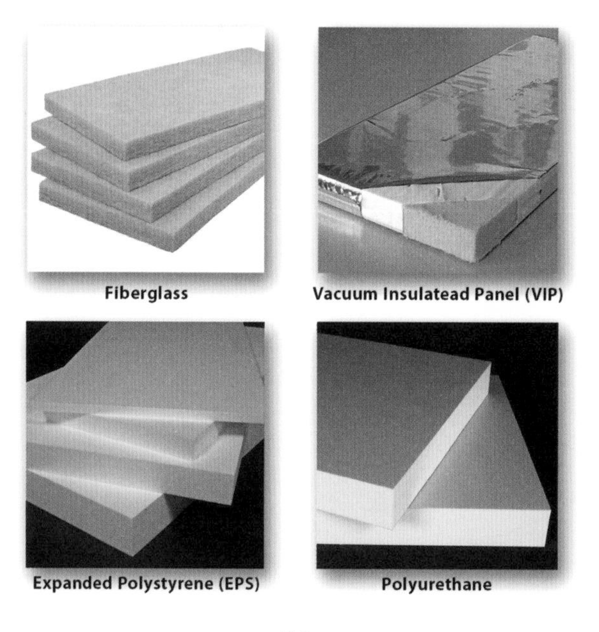

Fiberglass

Vacuum Insulatead Panel (VIP)

Expanded Polystyrene (EPS)

Polyurethane

External insulation, which is becoming increasingly popular, is best achieved using correctly specified, high-quality insulation, precision-made and engineered to meet demanding local weather conditions. Caution is necessary because each geographic climate is unique and external insulation cladding must be specifically designed. It doesn't always follow that imported solutions will be appropriate. For instance, the insulation materials best suited to the cold, dry temperature extremes of Canada do not automatically qualify for best use in Ireland or Britain, where there are more wet and windy conditions. In this example, extreme temperature differences are not as important as coping with extreme moisture and saturation levels as well as unpredictable weather patterns.

Spray Foam Insulation

Simple guidance is difficult to provide on this form of insulation. Pump-sprayed insulation ticks all the boxes in terms of best practice and thermal requirements. It can also represent a two-in-one solution for both insulation and airtightness, and it can serve as a semipermeable vapor barrier. It can fill wall cavities, fit into tight spaces, be applied in small quantities, and provide structural stability to rafters, joists, and battens. Its principal ingredients are no different to the best practice materials used in preformed fabricated panels. So what's the catch?

For one thing, foam insulation comes with a health and safety warning. So does everything, you might say! But spray foam insulation involves a complex chemical mix of two hazardous materials that combine to form an inert, nonhazardous solution that expands and hardens in its finished state. This chemical reaction does not take place in a controlled factory or laboratory setting but in your property. Occupants should be advised to leave during the spraying process, but vacating the property while "specialist" installers in safety clothing mix chemicals is only one of the critical items on the health and safety agenda. If the chemical components are poorly mixed, in the wrong ratios or at the wrong temperatures, the resulting foam might release irritating odors and lead to out-gassing, which may affect the health of the building's occupants. Other arguments against spray foam insulation include the high embodied carbon of its petrochemical ingredients. It is also nonrenewable, nonrecyclable, and difficult to remove, and it is expensive. What is more, it is not a job for amateurs. It's a highly specialized procedure that should only be undertaken by trained and experienced personnel.

How and Where to Insulate

Loft Insulation: This is the cheapest and often the easiest place to start when insulating a building. Most attic spaces have some level of insulation, from as little as 50mm to as much as 600mm in the best passive houses. So how much insulation should an attic space have? Clearly, 50mm is too little. A depth of 300mm is about today's average minimum regulation standard in most regions, but that could increase. Incremental increases have been the pattern of regulation changes over the past 30 years. The Passive House figure of 600mm thickness comes about from a requirement that the building is sufficiently insulated to obviate the need for primary heating systems. In other words, the building is heated and remains heated by passive means, so insulation levels beyond the Passive House standard would be wasteful and serve no purpose. Attic insulation should really aspire to match this optimum level set by the Passive House philosophy. Of course, it's rarely possible that this

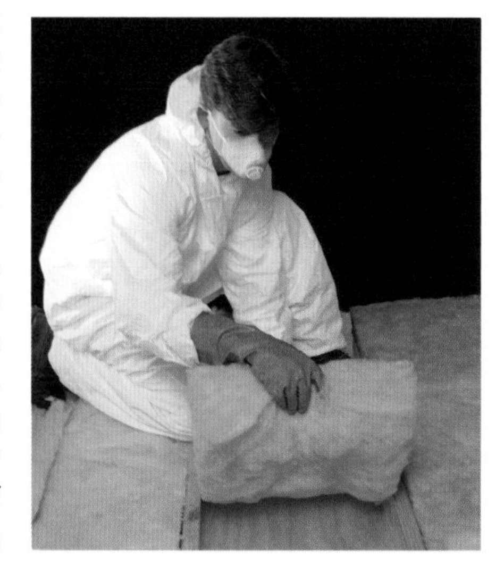

level of insulation can be achieved when retrofitting older properties, but it should be the benchmark to which to aspire.

How Much Could You Save?

If your loft is already insulated, the first step is to check the thickness of that insulation and how much space there is to increase it to a maximum. It is quite likely that a total thickness of 600mm will not be achievable in most existing attics, but, to future-proof the property, the absolute maximum overall thickness should be added, with a minimum of 300mm depth as a starting point. Insulating an attic space may not be the most expensive exercise, but it is a difficult and awkward job and not one you want to have to repeat.

How much could you save?

	Loft insulation (0 to 300mm)	Loft insulation (100 to 300mm)
Approximate saving per year	Up to $150	$30
Installation cost	$100 to $350	$100 to $350
Simple payback period	Up to two years	From four years
DIY cost	$50 to $350	$50 to $350
	Up to two years	From two years
Carbon dioxide saving per year	Around 720kg	Around 110kg

While insulating your attic yourself can be very cost-effective, there are some ground rules that must be adhered to, in order to avoid introducing faults in moisture control of the structure that could gradually develop into major problems in the future. Before insulating an attic or roof space, the following precautions must be taken:

- A full assessment of the loft with regard to health and safety should be carried out. There are many risks present, from electrical hazards to slips and falls.
- Check the depth of the existing joists and determine the maximum depth of insulation that can be placed between them and how much space remains available to insulate across them.
- Moisture control and ventilation are the two key issues that must be right to ensure the longevity of the roof timber frame structure. Hygroscopic insulation products (discussed above) are ideal for this, but it is essential that the manufacturer's instructions are carried out rigorously. Alternatively, allowing the roof space to have good natural cross ventilation is a simpler way of ensuring that moisture does not gather.

- If there is a room in the roof or attic, additional precautions must be taken to ensure that there is adequate ventilation across the pinch points where room structure and roof structure are one and the same.
- Electric cables should not be buried under insulation. They need to be left clear and visible. If there are any old heat-generating type recessed lights protruding into the attic space, these need to be replaced by low-energy, low-heat bulbs. Ideally, they should have light cans (discussed below) placed over them on the attic side, so that they can then be covered with insulation. In any case, fire-rated insulation must be used.
- After insulation, attic temperatures will be reduced in winter. Great care must be taken to ensure that all water pipes are lagged. The water storage tank also needs to be kept to the warm side of the insulation envelope. There should be no insulation under the tank but its sides and top need to be fully insulated.

There are two, often overlooked, places where attention to detail can be important. The first is the attic hatch or access point. Making sure that the hatch door is insulated and air-sealed is critical. The second is the cut-away hole in the ceiling and the insulation around recessed ceiling lights, more popularly referred to as light cans in the United States. A properly designed light can cover will keep the ceiling opening reasonably airtight and allow the insulation to be continuous over the light fixture.

Flat Roofs

Flat roof construction is the simplest roof type and, unquestionably, the most critical type to get right. Flat roofs normally consist of timber joists or concrete slabs spanning support walls. They are the most efficient structural form and particularly popular in warmer climates, where they are not subjected to persistent rainfall. Unlike a pitched roof, which is sloped to dispel rainwater and where cross-ventilation can be added to remove internal moisture, the flat roof must do both jobs within the limits of its own structural depth. The top surface needs to be watertight and durable, and the bottom layer must be impervious to moisture.

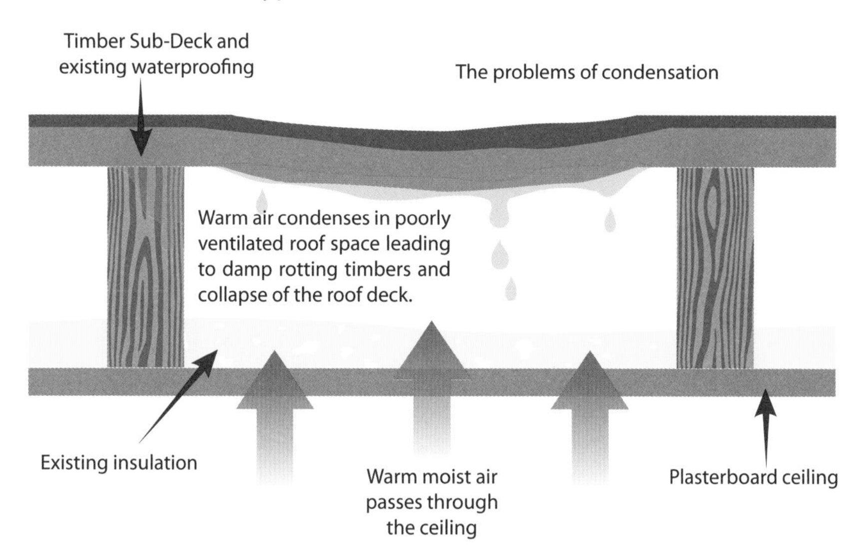

Flat roof construction is referred to as "warm roof" if the insulation is provided above the structure or on top of the roof, and "cold roof" if the insulation is provided below or internally. Positioning the insulation and the waterproof membranes is the most important detail of flat roof construction; get it wrong and the roof will either leak or be continually subject to interstitial condensation. Contrary to popular belief, flat roof dilapidation often starts inside the property, where trapped moisture condenses at a point below the sealed roof surface. Over time, this can cause the roof boarding supporting the sealed layers to sag, which can interfere with the designed slope of the roof, potentially leading to ponding, and this in turn degrades the surface layers. There is no room for error, particularly on timber structures, so flat roofs are best left to roofing experts.

Walls

Up to 35% of the heat lost from a building escapes through the walls, which is greater than the amount lost through the roof. Surprisingly, there has traditionally been more focus on attic and roof insulation than wall insulation, and the extent to which heat is lost through the walls has been regularly underestimated. It is important, therefore, to understand how heat travels through the fabric of the building, so that the most effective steps can be taken to minimize heat loss. If you add the heat losses from doors and windows to that from the walls, you have total losses of 60%. This demonstrates just how important the whole fabric of the vertical wall enclosure is in terms of the need to achieve maximum insulation values.

How much could you save?				
Measure	Annual Saving	Installation Cost	Payback Time	Carbon Dioxide saving per year
Cavity wall insulation	Up to $135	$100 - $350	Less than a year 3 years	Around 550kg

It seems bizarre by today's standards that the importance of treating and insulating external walls was not included in any meaningful way in building codes until after the 1970s oil shortage forced a rethink. In many places, the standard building method for external walls favored solid materials, whether brickwork, concrete, or timber, or a mixture of these materials. This creates an easy conductive pathway for heat to travel through, which presents a challenge, particularly in Europe where, for example, it is estimated that over 80% of the existing building stock will still be around in 2050.

The challenge is to correct the errors of the past and set about retrospectively insulating the external walls of these buildings. The numbers of properties involved compounds the task. In Britain alone, for instance, it is estimated that 70% of the 25 million existing houses need a wall insulation upgrade. This explains why an external wall insulation industry that didn't exist only a few years ago is flourishing today.

The challenge is not just about numbers but is also a technical and sensitivity one. The same issues arise in every country where older buildings form the vernacular built landscape. Buildings don't necessarily have to be protected, to be listed, or to be of historic importance for us to want to maintain their internal and external appearance. But whether wrapping a building in external insulation, dry-lining internal finishes, or achieving a nonvisible cavity fill-type solution, there are similar issues to contend with. A full understanding of the existing wall structural arrangement is essential before commencing any works. Upgrading the thermal aspects of the building stock is not a DIY job, and careful thought and planning must go into selecting the most appropriate, bespoke, solution for each building type in its climatic region.

Solid Walls or Cavity Walls

The amount of heat loss and the potential for energy savings depend primarily on the type of walls a building has. There are two main wall types: solid and cavity. It's then a matter of establishing the wall construction materials: brick, block, concrete, timber, or other composite material and the relationship between construction details insofar as this is economically and physically possible to determine. Because the internal structure of the wall is not visible, establishing the type of wall your building has is not always a straightforward proposition. There are, however, a few simple checks that you can perform. The first is to identify the date of the property. The building industry has always followed trends, and before the 1920s, building solid walls was the norm. From the 1920s onward, the trend changed with the introduction of cavity or split-wall construction i.e. two separate structural layers. The split was originally introduced to provide a moisture break, and latterly allows for the addition of insulation. Of course, the emergence of cavity construction was very influenced by geographic and climate. As a result of their cold damp climates, northern European countries were the first to introduce cavities to prevent driving rain and moisture from penetrating internal finishes. Colder, drier climates meant that Canada and some of the Scandinavian countries led the way in improving insulation standards.

Evolving building regulations and codes have influenced trends relating to cavity width and insulation. Construction methods have advanced, and the composition of external walls has become an exact engineering science. Leaving a cavity within a wall, whether for moisture or thermal break, is too inefficient, and cavity has fallen out of favor. Pinpointing the date of construction and, therefore, the particular building regulation that may have applied can, however, give a good indication of the likely internal wall makeup.

A second method is to measure the thickness of the wall, which can easily be done at window and door openings. It is possible to determine whether the wall is standard solid brick or block if you know the brick/block dimensions. For instance, a solid brick wall is 225mm (9 inches). If the width is greater than this and the brickwork is exposed, there is likely to be a cavity of width equal to the

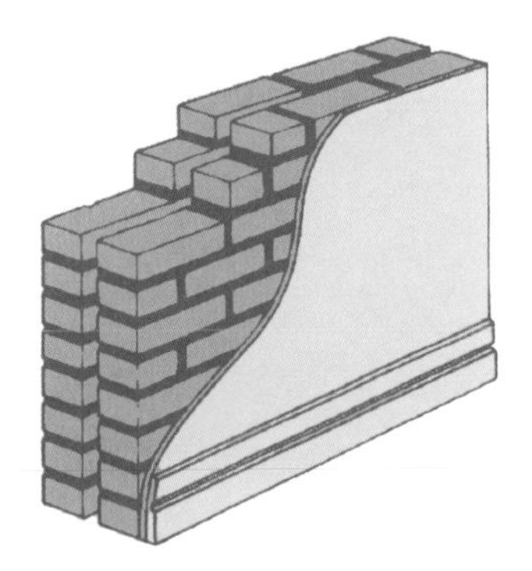

measured dimension less 225mm. So if the overall thickness of the wall measures, say, 315mm, then the cavity width is likely to be 90mm (315 – 225 = 90). However, if a solid wall is plastered inside and out, the overall dimension of the wall may extend to 265mm. With most other wall details, it is necessary to expose the original construction method by intrusive means, either by drilling holes or breaking out small openings to accurately determine the composition.

Cavity Walls

Traditionally, cavity walls consist of two construction layers that have a cavity between and are tied together for stability using special wall ties. The cavity wall came into fashion in the 1930s, though it was really only an upgrade of the original 225mm (9 inch) solid brick wall. The thinking behind the addition of the cavity was to prevent rain or moisture penetration across the wall. The thermal qualities were not part of the original rationale, so early cavities were minimal in thickness and merely served to break the moisture flow. It was not until the 1990s that building regulations and codes started to take wall insulation into account, and the obvious place to put the insulation at that time was inside the cavity. Over the intervening years, as regulation called for increased insulation, the cavities became bigger to accommodate more insulation. When planning a new build today, it is important to take account of the full efficiency of the wall.

U-values of typical upgraded existing cavity walls

Existing brick / cavity / brick wall	Thermal conductivity of insulation \ (W/mK) 0.025	0.035	0.045
Cavity width to be filled	**U-value of filled cavity wall (W/m²K)**		
50mm	0.46	0.58	0.67
75mm	0.35	0.44	0.52
100mm	0.22	0.29	0.36
Brick/50mm cavity/lightweight block wall	0.42	0.51	0.58

Materials used for cavity retrofit insulation include mineral wool, polystyrene beads, and cellulose fiber. Given that this is a specialist supply and installation process, it is vitally important to choose the right installer and ensure that the completed work is guaranteed. The installation company may not be around in ten years so it is important that the guarantee is provided by an independent, nationally accredited source.

Solid Walls

Solid wall construction was the traditional method for building houses up to the 1920s. Cob, solid stone, solid brick, and timber frame were typical building types of that time. Cob walls were normally 550mm wide, stone walls 500mm thick, and brick solid walls 225mm thick. The thickness does not, however, compensate for lack of insulation, and these walls simply conduct heat to the outside. Uninsulated solid walls can conduct twice as much heat to the outside as cavity walls. When these solid materials are wet, their ability to conduct heat can be even greater.

How much could you save?

Type of solid wall insulation	Saving per year	Total cost including installation	Carbon dioxide saved per year
Internal	Around $445	$5,500 to $8,500	1.8 tonnes
External	Around $475	$9,400 to $13,000	1.9 tonnes

Adding insulation to solid walls in a building can have the single most positive effect on reducing heating costs. There are just two ways to do this: adding insulation to the inside or the outside. Both methods are generally more costly than adding cavity wall insulation, but the savings achieved can be greater. Internal wall insulation involves adding insulation board to the inside face of the walls. External insulation is installed in a wraparound fashion to the outside of the building. A process of elimination usually helps one to make the choice between internal and external insulation. For instance, external insulation may not be an option for protected or historic buildings. In addition, the character of the building may be so significantly altered by external insulation that the planning authority may not grant permission. In circumstances where insulating a solid wall externally is not an option, internal insulation may then be the only solution. Internal insulation has the disadvantage of reducing the floor space available for habitable use and so may not be practical in smaller buildings.

Internal Insulation

Applying insulation to the inside of a solid wall can be quite disruptive to the occupants of the building because it is applied to the outside wall of each room. The most appropriate type and depth of new insulation must be decided, and it is usually applied in the form of dry boards or dry lining. Adding the insulation is perhaps the easy part. The preparatory work such as removing wall light fittings, sockets, radiators, pipework, skirting boards, window, and door architraves and repositioning them is time-consuming and costly. Some steps can be taken to ease disruption, including tackling the task room-by-room, which can add to the cost. If, however, the work is done in a coordinated and planned way, particularly if timed to coincide with internal redecorating on a phased basis, it can be cost-effective over time.

U-values of typical upgraded 220mm solid brick walls using thermal laminated plasterboard.			
Internal insulation thickness	Thermal conductivity of insulation \ (W/mK)		
	0.015 (Advanced insulation)	**0.025** (High performance insulation)	**0.035** (Typical insulation)
	U-value of insulated solid wall (W/m²K)		
25mm	0.42	0.59	0.71
50mm	0.25	0.37	0.47
75mm	0.18	0.27	0.35
100mm	0.14	0.21	0.28

Internal dry lining was traditionally the preferred method of adding insulation to an external wall because it allowed for a variety of insulation options such as mineral wool and other softer materials that are supported by a timber frame or stud wall. Mineral wool and some of the sustainable natural materials are not as effective in terms of depth as rigid boards, and this explains the need for more structural space. Because space is always at a premium, insulation solutions that keep the overall spatial reduction to a minimum are usually preferred. There are some new, engineered composite hardboard slabs on the market that offer neat, space-effective solutions.

The process of adding new insulation involves stripping back some of the existing plaster to obtain a flush fixing for the new timber frame that will support the insulation. A key aspect of this process is a close inspection of the prepared wall for signs of damp or moisture. A precondition survey to establish the exact condition of the wall, in particular to identify any damp problems, should be carried out prior to commencing the works. Any existing damp within the wall will likely be made worse by the addition of internal insulation because the damp will now be on the cold side of the new insulation, where it could fester and cause damage for many years before coming to light in the form of potential major structural defects.

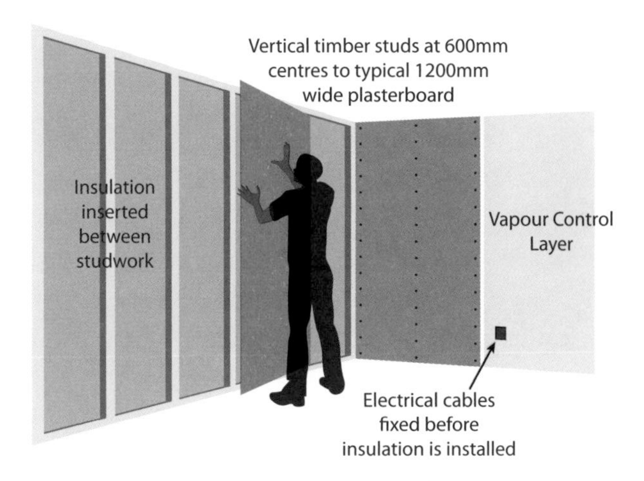

Interstitial condensation is another problem that can be associated with the addition of internal insulation. When naturally occurring moisture within a property is allowed to migrate to the cooler wall structure and condense into water droplets, the process is called interstitial condensation. The difficulty is that it occurs within the wall structure and out of sight. This might have always happened in the past, but an old, uninsulated wall was able to expel the moisture and dry out naturally. The introduction of linings to create a new wall configuration can lead to condensation problems if the materials are applied incorrectly. One golden rule to avoid interstitial condensation is to place a vapor check membrane on the warm side of the internal insulation to prevent moisture-laden air reaching and condensing on the cooler outer wall structure.

Summary of advantages/disadvantages with internal insulation:

Advantages:	Disadvantages:
Generally cheaper	Can lead to expensive redecoration
Usually only one wall per room	Can reduce floor area
Can be phased in room by room	Can be disruptive
Does not need planning permission	May need building regulation approval
Rooms quickly heat up	Thermal mass now on the outside

Key questions/issues to address with your specialist installer:

- Evidence of previous work
- What certification will be supplied?
- What U-values will be attained?
- What guarantees will be supplied, by whom, and for how long?
- How will dampness issues be approached and resolved?
- Take before and after photos

External Insulation

External insulation has many advantages over internal insulation. It can provide that much sought after "tea cozy" effect, and it solves moisture and cold bridging problems rather than creating them. The application of insulation to the outside of the wall leaves the whole wall on the warm side of the insulation. Consequently, the thermal mass of the wall remains on the inside, such that the internal space heating is stored in the solid wall construction. This can be particularly important in colder countries where the ever-changing external environment can be somewhat stabilized internally by the heat storage effect of the warmed solid walls. The opposite of this happens in hotter climates, where the walls are prevented from heating up in direct sunlight and storing the heat, such that internal air-cooling systems have to run constantly to maintain comfortable temperatures.

Insulation on the outside

The process involves attaching a layer of insulation using fixings or adhesives to the outside wall of the property, which is then covered by a hard-shell protective layer for durability and weatherproofing. The protective layer-type is usually chosen with a view to matching or blending in with the original façade finish. Planning permission may be needed if the building is a protected structure or changes are proposed to the external finish. Building code or regulation approval is, however, something that often gets forgotten; the builder assumes that the property owner is doing it, and the property owner knows nothing about such matters. Be aware that responsibility for compliance usually rests with the property owner.

The thermal performance of the external wall is dependent on the type and depth of the insulation. Similar decisions to those made before choosing internal insulation must be taken, namely identifying the thermal value of the wall (U-value and R-value) before the works and the optimum target value to be achieved. The optimum target value must meet today's building regulation standards and should actually exceed those levels to the maximum possible, given the available budget and any construction or planning constraints that may limit the scope of works. Normal finished depths of external insulation are 100mm-120mm, including all the layers of insulation, fixings, fabric, and finishes. Special care must be taken around openings for doors and windows because, in theory, the same thickness must be added to all window and door reveals. This is normally impractical in retrofit situations, particularly if the windows are not being replaced. The limiting factor is door and window frame thickness, and this regularly restricts the overall thickness of new insulation to 25mm-50mm. Poor insulation in these areas will lead to cold bridging on the inside at reveals, and this in turn can lead to unwanted condensation and damp problems.

A well-sealed and enclosed new insulation system should provide the property with superior weatherproofing and damp protection, but it is important that the new insulation does not bridge the damp-proof course (DPC) just above ground level in the building. At this point, a specialized detail is required to ensure that there is a weather break in the insulation to stop rising damp from passing through the building's DPC or membrane. Older buildings will not have a DPC, which might not have been a problem in the past, when the natural breathability of the walls may have dissipated all moisture. Adding new external insulation could entrap this rising moisture unless the correct details and materials are fitted.

Installing external insulation is certainly not a DIY job; companies undertaking this worked must employ trained and experienced personnel. The best place to find qualified and accredited installers is to check the local databases of national insulation associations and agencies such as NIA and CIGA. Every property is different, however, and each specialist installer tends to use a product range from a limited number of manufacturers. That range may not be the most appropriate for your particular building. It is important to obtain a list of previous works carried out by the installer, particularly those that are similar to the proposed works.

Summary of advantages/disadvantages of external insulation:

Advantages:	Disadvantages:
Can be added to the outside of the building	May need planning permission
Does not reduce internal floor space	Can be intermittent in terraces
Is weather-proof and seals old walls	Need access to all walls
Provides opportunity to strengthen old brick walls	Can be expensive
Freshens up and renews appearance	May need building regulation approval
Reduces condensation on inner walls	Can bridge damp proof courses

Floor Insulation

Floors are often another area of neglect when it comes to insulation, not necessarily because it's difficult to install insulation, but mainly because floors were not thought to account for a great deal of heat loss. Insulation in floors was only introduced into building codes around the 1980s. In the old school of thought, heat only rises and maybe travels horizontally through windows and doors but certainly not downward, particularly through a carpeted or timber floor. It is estimated that, 15% of heat generated in a house is lost through the floor. This is a whole-house average, but if you consider a suspended timber ground floor with cross ventilation underneath and no insulation, this heat loss figure could rise above 50%. In these circumstances, heat is stolen by the ventilated breeze blowing through the floorboards and working in opposition to the heating system. Light floorboards and perhaps a carpet finish have no thermal mass and cannot store heat. As a result, when the heating is off, there is no retained stored heat and rooms cool immediately. This is one of the classic heat loss situations that occur regularly in households afflicted by fuel poverty.

Finding out your floor type can be simpler than establishing wall types. There are two principal materials, timber and concrete, and two building methods, referred to as ground-bearing and suspended. Different periods of building also followed different trends. For practical reason, kitchens and utility rooms had concrete floors, while suspended timber floors were considered softer and more comfortable underfoot in bedrooms and living rooms. In the first instance, simply tapping on the floor will determine whether it is timber or concrete, but obviously care must be taken to distinguish between full timber construction and timber laminate or boarding fixed to a concrete slab. It may be necessary to lift a corner of the floor finish to have a closer look and see if the underlying structure is timber floor joists or concrete.

Ground-floor suspended timber construction should always feature a gap beneath the timber joists and the ground, and this must be ventilated to keep the timbers dry and prevent them from rotting. To facilitate cross-ventilation, air bricks or grilled openings in the external walls must be kept clean and free from obstruction at all times. Balancing the need for proper ventilation while keeping the room space airtight apparently presents something of a conundrum to those who lack the appropriate experience. By treating the two exercises as completely separate and by taking care and paying attention to detail, it is possible to achieve both on a DIY basis. This can be done by lifting floorboards and laying mineral wool or a natural insulation product such as sheep's wool, wood fiber, or hemp supported by netting or mesh, which can be found in any hardware store

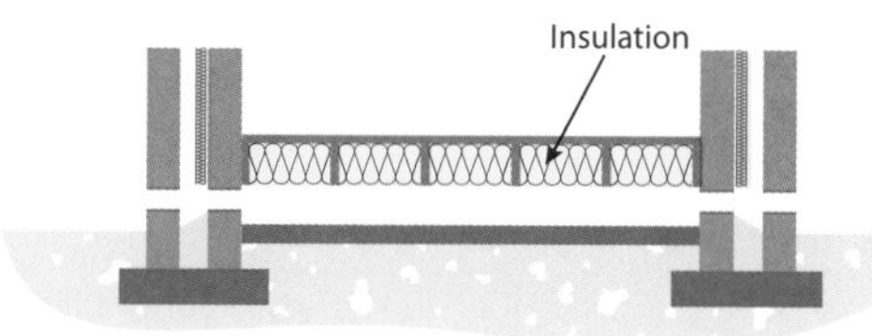

If there are no depth restrictions and cross-ventilation can be easily maintained, the maximum possible quantity of insulation should be installed. When the insulation is in place, all floorboards and skirting boards should be refitted to ensure that they are airtight and sealed. If the original floorboards are not tongued and grooved (T&G), it might be worth considering replacing them with T&G boards, which offer superior airtightness qualities. Suspended timber floors upstairs or over a heated room below do not need to be insulated. Upper rooms over lower, nonheated ones such as garages, passageways, and unheated lobbies should be insulated wherever possible.

Solid concrete floors are not so easy to retrofit with insulation. Taking up a concrete floor and adding new insulation underneath is something that could only be contemplated during major renovations. Otherwise, it would be cost-prohibitive. Adding insulation to the surface of the floor is often the only option, given limited budgets and taking into account the economics of reasonable payback periods. By stripping back existing floor finishes and allowing for minor adjustments to shorten doors and thresholds, most properties can accommodate up to 50mm of new floor overlay. Moreover, it is worth considering newer super-insulation materials such as vacuum insulation panels and Aerogel, which can provide a thermal value that is between five and ten times that of other products of similar thickness.

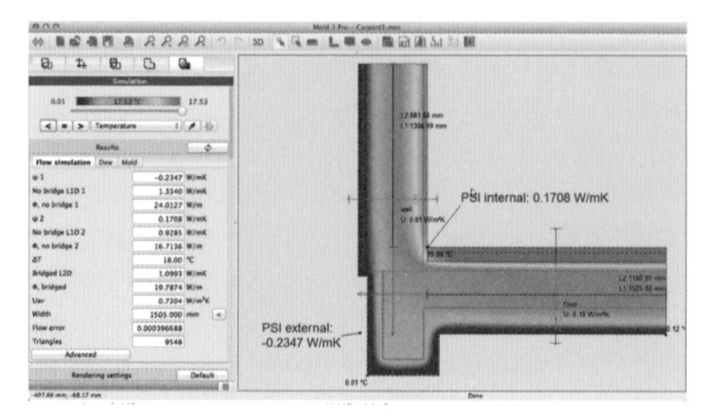

Key questions to consider before insulating a floor:

- Can renovation/redecoration incorporate increased floor insulation?
- Are there sufficient skills to upgrade insulation on a DIY basis?
- Is room-by-room redecoration an option?

Windows and Glazing

Windows have the potential to be the gemstones of the building envelope. Get them right, and they will be the jewels in the crown of the building façade, in terms both of their attractive appearance and their key role in regulating heat flow into and out of the building. Get them wrong, and they will leak valuable heat. The way in which we design and construct windows and glazing has changed dramatically over the last 20 years. Windows have become a precision-engineered piece of building technology with a number of interchangeable features that can add significantly to the overall energy efficiency of the building.

In order to buy the best performing windows, you need to know how windows work and what jobs they need to do to enhance a building's energy efficiency. Modern windows have a central role in controlling heat flowing into and out of a building. If this element is right, other benefits such as natural light and ventilation will follow. In most developed countries, windows are sold with an energy-rating label that lists the key essentials of their performance such as U-value, emission level or e-coatings, solar heat gains, and air leakage.t

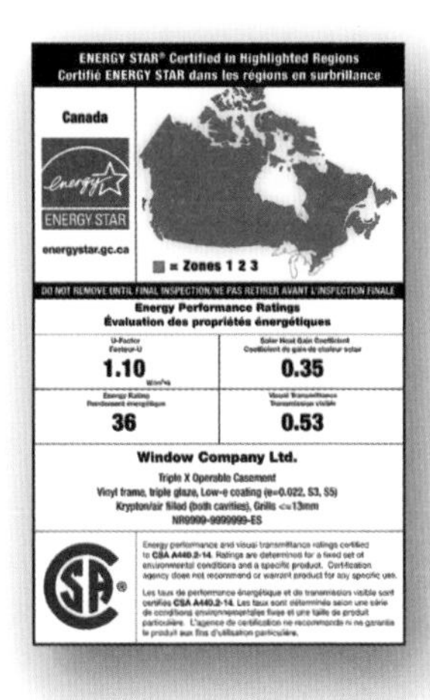

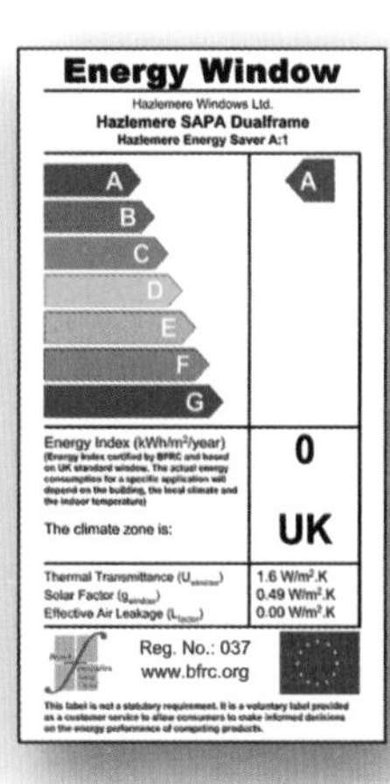

Window energy ratings are much the same the world over, and windows themselves are a very exportable commodity. Not surprisingly, colder countries such as Austria, Sweden, and Canada have a better reputation for producing better windows. If you are buying windows from abroad, the key issues to consider are:

Glazing

Good glazing is important because, among other things, it controls the amount of daylight, quality of light, and amount of solar heat gain entering a building. Glazing very much determines the thermal and visual comfort of a space. Appropriate values for glazing properties vary according to climate, size, and placement of the window. There is no one best kind of glazing, and requirements change depending on climate, size, orientation, and shading.

It's not unusual for a single building to have different types of glazing on each elevation. If you design to Passive House standards, you will more than likely be advised to take this approach. Increasing the number of panes of glass improves the insulation value of the window. Typically, double-glazed windows will provide twice as much thermal insulation as single-glazed units. Triple and quadruple layers further enhance the thermal resistance of the window. As layers of glass are added, however, the cost rises steeply, not just because of the price of the glass but also because the window is becoming more complex. The more layers of glass, the more opportunities there are for further enhancements, including improved frames, gas fill between panes, and emissions coatings to lower the heat transfer across the window. Extra layers of glass also reduce noise transfer and enhance comfort values. The usable space in a building is also increased because, quite simply, people won't sit or use the space beside a cold window surface.

Frames

The choice of frame type will have a large impact on the overall thermal performance of the window. Some materials are naturally more heat-conducting than others, and these are typically the most cost-effective. Aluminum is such a material. It is very popular because it is readily available, very economic, and easy to manufacture and form into window sections. It is durable and easy to maintain, but it is also a great conductor of heat. Have you ever felt the surface of an old aluminum window on a cold day? It is colder than the glass and often promotes condensation formation inside. The best modern frames have thermal breaks for eliminating cold spots, and these are built into the window section, meaning that the window frame's finishing material can be selected for durability or aesthetics and the body of the frame may be a mixture of materials selected for strength and thermal efficiency.

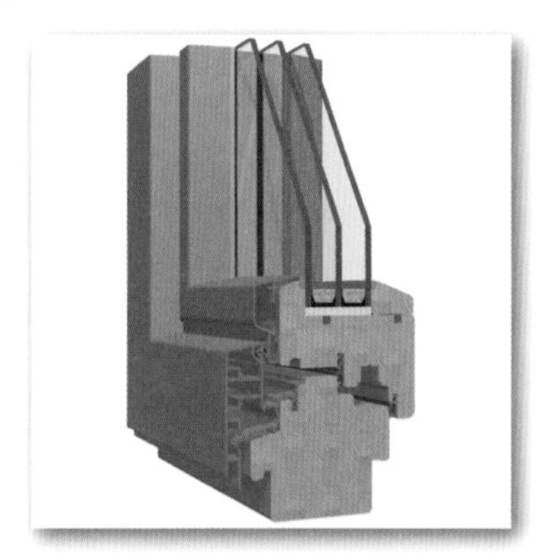

The most popular window frame materials include:

- Wood. If properly maintained, it can outlast most other building products.
- Aluminum. It is very versatile, durable, and suitable for making up composite sections.
- Plastic and composites. Popular from an economic perspective but not environmentally friendly.
- Fiberglass. Very popular in the United States and Canada and has many advantages over wood and aluminum due to its good insulation properties and durability.

Whatever materials are used, good thermal breaks are essential if the overall window is to achieve high energy-efficiency ratings.

Air Gap

In older double-glazed window units, the gap between panes of glass was simply air, which is a "good" insulator if static. "Good" is no longer enough to satisfy the high regulation standards that are now mandatory in the building sector throughout the developed world. Replacing the air with an inert gas such as argon, xenon, or krypton increases the thermal resistance of the window unit. It is standard practice in colder climates for all windows to have a 12mm gas-filled cavity with sealed spacers to prevent the gas from escaping. If for any reason the gas escapes, the efficiency of the window will be reduced. This may not be detectable unless moisture displaces the gas and the window unit fogs up. This can happen with any air- or gas-filled multiple glazing units and effectively represents a failure of the unit.

Low-E Glazing

This term refers to the application of an additional invisible metallic coating to the glazing units, which lowers the emissivity of the glass and, in turn, the U-value. The effect of low-e coating is to reflect heat back into the property, thereby keeping the building warmer in winter. Heat from the sun is shortwave radiation, and this can pass unobstructed through the coating, but heat that has built up in the building will not easily escape outward. There are two types of emissive layers, soft or hard coat, but the type applied is not important so long as both are correctly represented on their energy rating labels.

High Solar Gain

Windows are best described by the behavior of older single-glazing units, which excel at letting sunlight in but magnify the sun's heat in summer and lack insulation properties in winter. Today, things are much more sophisticated. The Passive House school of thought is that the glazing in buildings should add to the net heat gain throughout the four seasons. To do this in a cold country, the glazing must be highly insulated as well as appropriately positioned and sized to gain as much solar heat as possible without overheating in summer and losing heat in winter. In hot climates, the challenge is to restrict solar gain and reduce the workload of air-cooling systems.

The capacity of glass to allow or disallow solar gain is measured by its g-value (Europe) or SHGC value (United States and Canada). Both values range between zero and 1. The closer to zero, the greater the ability of the glass to shade unwanted solar heat, and the nearer to 1 the more magnified the solar gain through the glass.

Insulated Doors

Doors seem to be the forgotten element in the building fabric when it comes to insulation requirements. Even the Passive House standard certifies overall compliance without a Passive House door. The average single-panel timber or uPVC door hung at the front or rear entrance of 95% of properties has a U-value of 5.0W/m2 K. When you consider that windows can have a U-value as low as 0.25W/m2K, with a little bit of thought and not too much cost, doors should at least reach 1.0 W/m2K. Insulated doors tend to be very heavy and require well-anchored hinges to ensure that they swing smoothly as they open and close. Newer models, made from glass fiber and laminates, have insulated cores, are considerably lighter, and can be hung using normal fixing mechanisms. Key elements to consider when insulating doors are their airtight seals and the way in which their mailboxes and keyholes are detailed (see Step 3).

Step 4 Summary

Twitter Summary
Heat flow like water flow follows the path of least resistance. For Insulation to be fully effective, it must be all enclosing, because heat will flow- not through its strongest sections -but through its weakest links.

Smart Citizen Summary
Step 4 is about understanding heat, so that we can slow down its movement through the structure and fabric of our buildings. The smart citizen must also appreciate that the thermal envelope of a building needs to be enclosed to the highest standards before any renewable energy options should be considered. This is because wasting energy whether its renewable or non-renewable is not an option for the smart citizen. Additionally To achieve the smart citizen must:

- Understand how heat moves and how heat is measured.
- Become more intuitive about the simplest ways of keeping the body regulated at comfortable temperatures, which might not necessarily involve heating systems, but the right choice of clothing.
- Understand the labels and specifications that constitute good quality sustainable insulation materials.
- Know how and where to insulate to achieve the best results
- Appreciate that the correct location and specification of windows in todays building represent a tremendous opportunity to both promote and preserve comfort temperature levels at near zero operating costs

Step 5: Temperature Control

"I'd put my money on the sun and solar energy. What a source of power!
I hope we don't have to wait 'til oil and coal run out before we tackle that."

Thomas Edison (1847-1931)

Perhaps the greatest impact we can have on climate change is to lower carbon emissions through the systems we use to heat and cool our buildings. A new language of energy has taken center stage of late; out go old terms such as gas burners, oil boilers and open fires, and in come some new terms, including condensing boilers, air and ground source heat pumps, solar thermal and solar mass, combined heat and power (CHP), district heating systems, and many more. If concepts such as these are not part of the fabric of a new building or the retrofit of an existing one, projects won't comply with tomorrow's building codes and will not be eligible for funding under many of the popular government schemes set up to encourage energy efficiency and reduce carbon/fossil fuel dependency.

Energy expended on heating and cooling amounts to a staggering 50% of total energy used in housing, which explains why governments have targeted the building sector in their drive for energy efficiency.

Energy use in homes largely follows the same pattern in all developed countries, as discussed in Step 2. The highest energy usage goes on space heating and cooling, depending on local climate conditions. In the colder regions, the highest demand for energy is for heating to keep buildings warm. In warmer regions, cooling and air-conditioning accounts for most energy usage. In more temperate areas, a combination of heating in winter and cooling in summer makes for balanced energy usage.

Where Does my Money Go?

Annual Energy Bill for a typical Single Family Home.

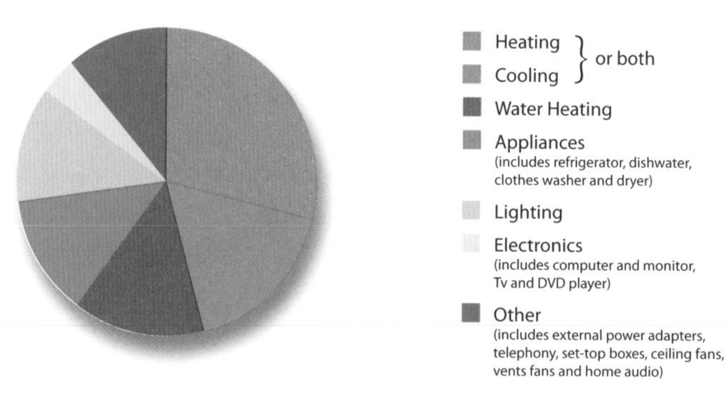

Figuring out how much heat or cooling energy we need is not a simple task, however. There are a wide range of factors at play, not least of which is human comfort, which is different for everyone. Today, the key to effective and efficient future heating and cooling is to first establish a good thermal envelope, as set out in Steps 3 and 4. The optimum heating system can then be designed without wastage, a topic we will return to later. Before a heating and/or cooling system is designed, it is worth investigating the comfort needs of a building's occupants and identifying the best thermostatic controls to suit their everyday needs.

Comfort

The factors influencing human heat requirements are more sensitive than those affecting our cooling needs. A chilling breeze on a cold day is very uncomfortable, whereas a warm breeze on a hot day can be soothing and comforting. Other factors impacting on specific temperature needs include gender, age, fitness, diet, habits and moods. Such diverse considerations mean that building engineers couldn't possibly design a one-size-fits-all solution.

At the same time, the basic human requirement is for buildings that are comfortable to live in, work in or visit. When it comes to the fundamentals of building, thermal comfort in the 21st century demands that we maintain consistent, narrow temperature ranges in our buildings as though the occupants, like exotic plants, would not survive otherwise.

In extreme climates, the weakest links in the building fabric are the windows and doors. In response to this, the igloo, for example, dispenses with windows and blocks up the door. This, along with its small size, allows human body heat to maintain comfortable temperature levels. By contrast, the desert tent remains fully open to allow cooling breezes to circulate throughout. Similarly, the Antarctic explorer doesn't carry electric heating systems but wears many layers of insulated clothing, zipped up for airtightness, appropriate to the climate, and the nomadic Arab wears loose clothing to keep cool.

Our ability to adapt and acclimatize to any region, is certainly counterbalanced by an apparent inability to adjust the heating controls. Numerous studies have found that the more we control and regularize our indoor environment, the less capable we are of making adjustments to simple heating controls such as thermostats. Technology has had to advance to the point where heating controls become intelligent and can independently decide what our appropriate temperatures should be.

Design for Climate

"Climate is what you expect, weather is what you get"

Robert A. Heinlein

Globally, the built environment accounts for over up to 40% of today's carbon emissions, with transport and industry/griculture accounting for 60%. It might be easy to conclude that there is little that we can do about climate and, in particular, its influence on our existing stock of buildings. But that overlooks a fundamental criterion of building design. Our ancestors instinctively knew what this was. For them, the functionality of design was always more important than pure aesthetics.

Throughout history and long before the advent of planning laws and building regulations, people built with a more innate and natural response toward the local environment. They were much more intuitive about how to orientate their homes to suit the local environment. As discussed in Step 3, they would have sought out sheltered locations to build and would never have placed a door on the windward side of their home. In warmer climates, shade was sought where possible, whether under trees or on the cool side of mountains or rock faces. The city of Petra, deep in the Jordanian desert, is a classic example of how ancient people carved out buildings from rock to create a living city in the cool canyons and cliff faces of the mountainside. Similarly, the Anasazi, meaning "the ancient ones," occupied an area of the southwestern United States from about the 13th century CE. They built their houses and often entire villages into cliff edges, remote locations that were difficult to access and offered protection againt the harsh climate and maurading intruders.

In an age of mass produced buildings, much of this intuition seems to have been forgotten, at least in the West. Indeed, when it comes to purchasing a new home, most people's awareness of these considerations is limited to the orientation of the property - which part of the plot receives the most sunlight at different times of day.

Nonetheless, there are ,many examples of good design in modern buildings, particularly with the advent of Passive House standards and the desire to create A-rated and net-zero buildings. Architects, builders, and homeowners are becoming more aware of the need to maximize available energy through solar gain and to minimize energy loss using overhangs and shading techniques. Although it is simpler to design and orient a new building to maximize energy gains, it is also possible to refurbish existing structures to make equal gains, a process often referred to as a deep energy retrofits.

If we are to break the spiral of dependence on fossil fuels, particularly with respect to existing buildings, we must look again at how climate and local weather patterns can positively influence energy use. Designing new buildings, with low energy requirements and low carbon emissions, is relatively easy if a few basic fundamentals are understood.

Passive Solar Design

The truest form of renewable heat available is undoubtedly from the sun, which delivers average radiated heat to the value of 1,350W per square metre per year, or infinitely more heat/energy than we could possibly consume. Harnessing just a small fraction of this will fulfil all our needs. In this book, I have focused on three different forms of solar energy, namely solar thermal, solar photovoltaic (PV) and passive solar. Quantifying the solar resource is the same exercise for each type and is dependent on understanding the relationship between the sun and earth.

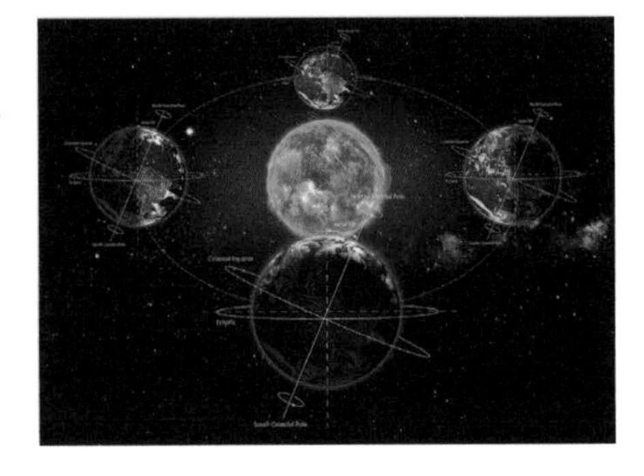

As the sun shines, the radiated heat provides solar gain to all parts of a building directly in the path of its rays. The strength of the solar gain varies according to the time of year, the sun's angle in the sky, and the type of surface the rays strike. There is a misconception that solar gain is only achieved through windows and glass. This might be the case with newer construction where there is a highly-insulated building envelope, but older buildings with poor insulation details can radiate heat into the building as well as out. Ever entered an attic-space on a hot summer's afternoon? You will find it very warm, heated by the sun's radiation on the roof tiles. Although heat is lost through a poorly insulated building's wall, roof, windows, and doors, there is also radiated heat gain in the opposite direction. Significantly, heat gain and loss, though similar, follow different rules. Understanding these is the key to successfully designing a building to optimize its energy efficiency.

With refurbishment, it may not be possible to obtain full passive solar benefits because many of the main solar passive design features relate to the building's orientation toward the sun. Consequently, options are somewhat limited with existing buildings. At the same time, many solar passive upgrades can be made. Central to this process is maximizing solar gain in winter and minimizing or controlling it in summer.

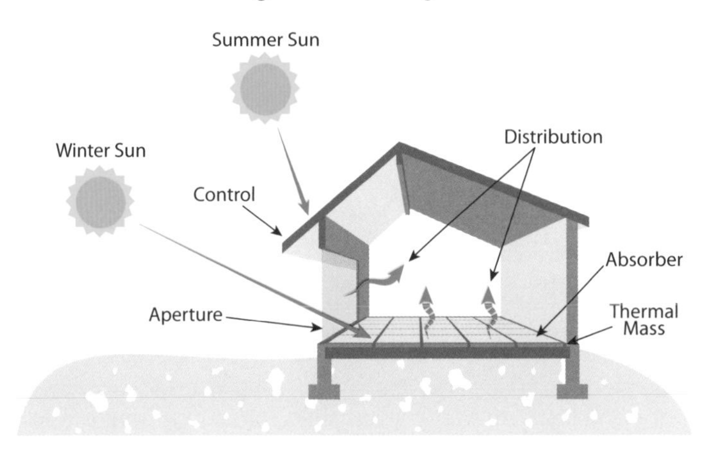

In warmer climates, the primary concern is to keep the strong heat out during hot days. In colder northern climates, things become more challenging because there is need to achieve an intricate balance between heating, cooling, and lighting. Given the resources spent on heating in cooler regions, it goes against the grain to block out the occasional and exceptional blast of solar heat because we are aware that the heat will dissipate all too soon. In commercial properties, offices, schools, or buildings that are unoccupied at night, saving or storing daytime heat is not perceived as important, but, if handled properly, the heat thus gathered inside a building can be maintained overnight to leave the building warm in the morning. To maximize solar gain, the following principles can be followed. They more readily apply to new buildings but can also be introduced in existing buildings, in some cases.

- Choose room-to-use locations guided by the rising, setting and midday sun. Some rooms occupied only occasionally and needing little heat such as stores, bathrooms, corridors, and stairs could be located on the colder northern side of the building.
- Orientate the geometry of the building along an east-west axis, and if possible the main façade (with the most windows) should face the sun. Paradoxically it is easier to control solar gains and shade south-facing windows because the sun is at a higher elevation.
- Choice of window size, location, and materials is probably the most critical decision that can be made in terms of optimising solar passive design. In relation to existing buildings, a good architect can with even a small budget work wonders, effectively re-orienting a building by simply manipulating the size and location of the windows.
- Careful design of window overhangs and their colors can play an important role in managing both light and solar heat through windows and doors. Particularly in existing buildings where scope for physical alteration may be limited, well designed shading can reduce unwanted heat gain in summer and provide valuable reflected light in winter months.
- Thermal mass is important when considering how best to optimize passive solar design. New or existing solid concrete floors or block walls are perfect materials. If located properly, they can absorb daytime heat and slowly release it in the evening when the air has cooled.
- Landscaping can do more than provide shelter from wind and rain to the garden. Judiciously chosen planting can provide shade in summer and facilitate winter solar gains. Deciduous trees can block

90% of the sun's radiated heat in summer and allow up to 75% of the sun's energy to pass through when they shed their leaves in winter.
- Solar collectors for generating electricity and/or heat are the essential final ingredient in passive solar design.

Other Sources of Heat

Combinations of the factors listed above can be deployed where, for example, central heating is supplemented by additional heating sources. Because we super-insulate our buildings, secondary heating sources contribute to the overall heating:

- 90% of energy from an incandescent light bulb is heat.
- Heat is generated from cookers, toasters, and kettles and is radiated from hot food and water, making sense of the popular maxim "If you can't stand the heat get out of the kitchen."
- Refrigerators perform an inner cooling function 24/7, but to do so they must continuously pump "waste" heat outward into the surrounding space.
- Dishwashers not only heat water to clean the dishes but also contain large fans, which explains how dishes come out so hot and so dry at the end of the wash-cycle.
- Washing machines have long heating cycles and heat a lot of water. If you observe the outlet pipe from a washing machine in full cycle, you can see that waste heat is often discharged as steam.
- Clothes driers are probably more easily recognized as heat generators, given their function and the noise they create.
- Hot water systems generate heat. Every time a hot tap is run, a mini heat distribution system is created as hot water meanders through the pipe network from tank to tap.
- Stored hot water always loses its heat over time, no matter how well-insulated (lagged) the cylinder is. That is why the location is known as the Electric showers and baths. A long, relaxing hot shower has the potential to heat the whole waste pipe distribution all the way to the public sewers, and a good bath can match that too.
- Televisions, radios, computers, phone chargers, etc., all dissipate heat on a 24/7 basis when left plugged in.
- Finally, we often miss the obvious point that our bodies are one of the greatest heat radiators in the house. In Passive House design, body heat is an integral part of the temperature control calculations.

The number of mechanisms and technologies available to us to control the temperature of buildings has greatly increased. Today, the building energy industry is alive with new ideas and new inventions to do just this. Building energy must be managed efficiently and intelligently, so as to conserve our cash, meet government building regulations, and conserve scarce resources.

Degree Days

The level of insulation and type of structural details needed to maintain comfort levels in a building varies according to temperature and prevailing wind conditions. If/once the building is basically watertight and reasonably airtight, the main determinant of comfort level is temperature. Thereafter, the size of the heating/cooling system required to maintain the building at a comfortable temperature is directly related to the outside climatic conditions.

The effect of external temperatures on heating or cooling energy is defined by what's referred to as degree days. Figures vary, but it is generally accepted that no heating or cooling is required within a building when outside temperatures are between 15.5 and 21o C (60–70F). It is assumed that the heating system will be turned on once the outside temperature drops below the base figure of 15.5o C. When the outside temperature rises above 21o C, some form of inside cooling will be needed. The greater the temperature difference between inside and outside, the greater the rate of potential heat loss through the fabric and structure of the building.

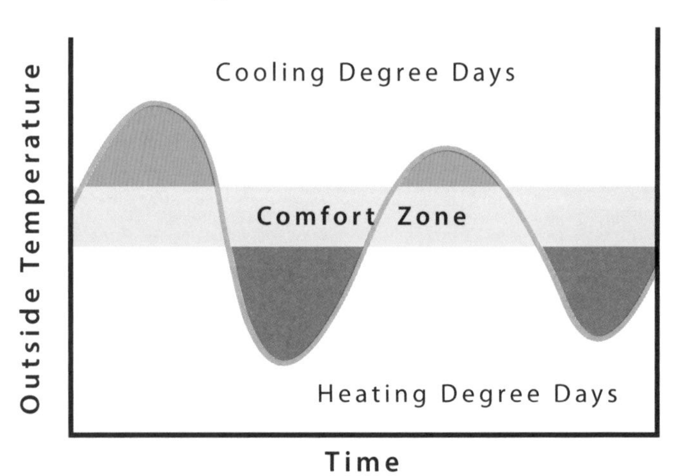

Heating degree days are calculated by adding together every degree the outside temperature drops below 15.5o C over a full year. Conversely, cooling degree days are calculated from the sum of every degree the temperature rises above 21o C over the year. For example, if the outside temperature falls to 14.5o C for a total of 144 hours over a year, this is equivalent to 6 degree days (1o C drop x 144/24 = 6). Cooling degree days are worked out in the same way, by multiplying the total number of days by the average number of degrees above 21o C in the year.

Most countries have prepared degree day maps called isopleths, which detail historic average degree day values. Isopleths and degree days are important reference points when sizing heating systems for buildings in different temperature zones. They are also key when you are purchasing or importing insulation products from areas outside your building's zone to ensure that the energy ratings on all products comply with relevant regulations.

Most people don't need to know how to calculate degree days, but it is vital that the system's designer ensures heating and cooling requirements match the local region's degree day profile. It is also important to understand degree days when comparing energy bills on a year to year basis, as a high degree day profile in a particular year will alert you to expect higher heating bills.

Heating/Cooling Systems

The majority of buildings are heated and cooled by a centralized system. In cooler climates, such as northern Europe, Alaska, and Canada, a gas, oil, or biomass-fired boiler, which heats and distributes hot water via an array of pipes to radiators, is the preferred system. In areas where both heating and cooling are required, such as most parts of the United States, one finds centralized furnace or burner systems that distribute hot or cool air around the building through a series of large ducts. The boilers and burners were traditionally fed by oil or gas but, today, biomass – in the form of wood pellets, fibers, and logs – is becoming a popular renewable energy source.

Next up in the centralized system is the storage radiator heated by electricity, often on a reduced nightly charge rate. This is very popular in multistory buildings because of the ease of installation and the elimination of the need for boiler houses and complex networks of pumps and pipes. Rarely appreciated by residents is the difficulty associated with regulating the heat output in these systems. In most cases, you have to predict the previous night what heat will be required the following day. Get it wrong and there is no secondary adjustments except on a hotter than expected day, when windows can be opened to let the heat out, or on a cooler day, when one can only wrap up to stay warm. A good retrofit solution for old and inefficient electric storage heaters is to simply replace them with infrared (IR) electric heaters. These can deliver up to 70% energy savings and supply the same level of personal comfort as traditional electric storage heaters.

How to Size the System

How we choose to heat and cool our buildings will dictate the level of savings that can be made from implementing the changes set out in Steps 2, 3, and 4. If monitors are in place, the buildings made airtight, and the insulation correctly installed, it is likely that the original heating and cooling system will be oversized and, therefore, ineffiient. Replacing the system with a smaller, more efficient one could mean greater than a 50% reduction in bills.

The size of the heating, cooling, or air-conditioning system needed for a building depends on a number of basic factors, including local climate conditions, building size, the speed of heat gained or lost, and the fine-tuning of the system to match the occupant's needs. There is little we can do about the first factor, unless, like some birds, we can migrate seasonally. The other factors are, however, very much in our control, albeit at a potential cost. At the same time, it is important to remember that the savings associated with energy efficiency measures are all about potential future reductions in terms of cost, energy, and carbon emissions.

Most people who choose a new kitchen for their home do so for aesthetic reasons, but the same people do not add thermostatic controls or a new condensing boiler in the belief that it will enhance the look of the heating system. Decisions about when and whether to replace heating systems tend to be more about function, more practical. Maybe the existing system is about to collapse and there is no option but to replace it, or the capital costs of a new system will have a short payback period based on tangible, measurable results prepared by an energy assessor or supplier. A new heating system is likely to be one of the biggest expenses for a building owner; it should be a near once-in-a-lifetime investment. Not only will it consume more energy than anything else on a day-to-day basis, its purchase cost can pale in comparison to its fuel costs over its lifetime.

The first rule of sizing a new heating system is never to base it on the size of the old one. Why? Because the old one will most likely have been oversized in a previous generation when buildings were poorly insulated and fossil fuel was abundant and cheap. A system that is too big for the work it performs will never run at its optimum design capacity. It will be inefficient, wasting money and fuel, and will produce noxious emissions as a result. The second important factor when sizing a system is energy conservation: shading of unwanted heat gains, reduction of heat loss, etc.

The essential question to ask is how much you want to spend on fuel in the future. If the answer is very little, which it probably is, then it is essential to size the system correctly and choose the best possible and most readily available fuel. In practice, sizing the system will be down to the trade and specialist heat suppliers but with one critical caveat: as building owner, you should have a basic understanding of the information upon which the specialists base their heat system requirements. They issues are discussed in Steps 2, 3 and 4:

- Outside temperature ranges (degree days)
- Heat loss/gain of the building fabric (U-values)
- Air leakage (Ach 50)
- Area to be heated/cooled (ft^2 or m2)
- Hot water requirements (see also Step 7)
- Fuel type (price variable or fixed)
- System efficiency (COP factor)

How much heat you need is also related to how big your building is and how you intend to control the heat, whether through room thermostats, heating zones, or timing switches. If you are replacing a system, it is important to check the local building regulations and codes because these also set down mandatory requirements for energy-efficiency levels on heating/cooling equipment. Those levels vary depending on where your property is located. Moreover, modern system efficiencies are much better than older system values.

Fuel Choice

The easy option when it comes to fuel choice, if you are upgrading your heating system, is to stick with the original fuel type. But an upgrade should really be viewed as an opportunity to take a step back and reconsider what fuel best suits your property in terms of cost and security of supply for the future. In Step 1, the differences between renewable and non-renewable energy were discussed, and because governments worldwide are starting to tax the one and incentivize the other, careful consideration should be given to opting for some form of renewable energy, that is, non–fossil-based fuel. This may not always be feasible or economical in the very short term, so optimizing efficiencies is critical. Unfortunately, switching fuels is not yet as simple as switching energy suppliers because the efficiency of most heating/cooling systems is specifically designed for single fuel types. The principal fuel types are set out in the table below and, depending on location and availability, they all have different price structures (the table below shows tipical UK costings in sterling.)

Running Cost Comparison

Fuel	Equipment	Efficiency	Price per KWh	Annual Cost
Natural Gas	Condensing Boiler	85%	5.2p	£1,223
Air Source Heat Pump		COP 3	15p	£1,176
Oil	Condensing Boiler	85%	4.8p	£1,129
LPG	Condensing Boiler	85%	4.7p	£1,106
Ground Source Heat Pump	Horizontal Array	COP 4	15p	£ 882
Wood Pellet	Boiler	90%	4.8p	£ 844
Water Source Heat Pump	From Borehole	COP 5	15p	£ 706
Wood Chip	Boiler	80%	2.8p	£ 550

Mains gas is probably the most cost-effective fuel type for many buildings. Depending on local price regimes, there can often be up to 20% saving in running costs when compared to LPG or diesel fuels. The key factor when considering this energy option is the cost of upgrading or changing an existing boiler system and of the associated builder's works to pipe in the natural gas. Dividing the capital cost of the works by the annual savings will give you the simple payback in years

Traditional Sources of Heat

In the 21st century there has been a resurgence in traditional and historic heating methods. For example, biomass is far from being a recent invention, our ancestors used wood chip and brambles from the forests to light fires. Before that, they relied on the heat of the sun (solar thermal) by day to stay warm, and, at night, they retreated to caves (geo-thermal) to keep warm.

The main heat sources considered to be renewable are solar thermal, biomass, heat pumps and combined heat and power (CHP), which were discussed in Step 1. Of these, solar thermal has a readily accepted place in the renewable technology

category, but a number of issues need to be addressed before some of the others are similarly accepted. Biomass generally refers to a renewable fuel, but it very much depends on where the biomass is sourced for it to be termed renewable. For instance, forestry thinnings, saw mill residues, and recycled waste wood products are sustainable sources, as discussed earlier. However, chopping down mature oak trees for fuel is neither sustainable nor renewable. Heat pumps are accepted by definition because they can be very efficient, often to a multiple of 4 or 5 (referred to as COP factor, below), but they are bespoke and property-specific. Getting this element of the design wrong happens all too often. A poorly designed and operated heat pump should never be classed as renewable because it can waste more kilowatts of electricity than it generates in heat. CHP can be accepted if its fuel comes from a renewable source such as biogas.

Where we have to or choose to use fossil fuels, the emphasis is on increased efficiencies. In practice, changing to renewable technologies on a mass-market basis will only be phased in gradually over many years. Most governments that have set targets for low-carbon economies have done so in time lines that stretch to 2020 and 2050 for strategic planning purposes. While there have been tremendous advances in this area, there is still a long way to go before technology, training, and mind-set are ready for full changeover to a zero-carbon economy. This might not satisfy climate change purists, but it is our reality. Combinations of renewable and non-renewable energy, as defined in Step 2, will be a fact of life in making progress toward our goals.

Open Fires

Perhaps one of the greatest symbols of warmth and comfort is the open fire, and in many places, particularly homes, they are simply lit for that cozy effect. They are, however, incredibly inefficient. Most people lighting an open fire do so in the full knowledge that it is solely for a comfort effect and realize that most of the heat travels directly up the chimney.

Another important but less well-known consideration is the capacity of open fires to vacuum up heat from other rooms and discharge it, also, through the chimney. Although there is radiant heat gain in the room with a fire, there is a large penalty in terms of overall

heat loss throughout the rest of the building. An open fire is a sure way to achieve a poor building rating certificate. If you need an open fire, it is worth investing in a system to provide an outside air supply, piped directly to the fire, thereby avoiding dependency on the whole building for air supply.

There are many renewable fuels available today to generate heat in an open fire, including traditional timber logs, pellet logs, and various combinations of fabricated fuel sources from fast-growing plants such as hemp and miscanthus grass. The use of fossil fuel sources such as coal and peat logs in open fires, irrespective of the impact on global warming, represents poor value for money and will substantially reduce a property's rating in terms of energy certification. This is a vital consideration because it's the law today in many countries that every property – house, office, shop, factory, etc. – must have an energy display label when it is being let or sold. Solid-fuel open fires can de-value properties by many tens of thousands. The days of open fires are therefore very much numbered. However, all is not lost. If the occupants insist on the "look and feel" of a fire in the house, the solution is to achieve greater efficiency by use of a stove. The key to an efficient stove is a sealed door arrangement where air supply can be controlled, thereby eliminating the inefficiency associated with the open chimney vacuum. There are many excellent stove models on the market that dramatically reduce inefficiency while retaining the open fire effect.

Most houses built prior to the 1970s would have had at least one open fireplace. Central heating systems subsequently became popular, principally because of the superior all-round warmth they supplied. Any refurbishment around this time would have favored central heating over fireplaces, which, in many cases, were blocked up. The fuel used in open fires was mainly coal, but bans on the burning of coal, considered the main cause of smog in major towns and cities, spelled the end of the traditional open fire and the loss of the iconic rooftop chimneys.

Stoves

The advent of modern stoves, which fit nicely into the opening left following the redundancy of a traditional open fireplace, was timely. The stove can also sit proud of the wall, with its flue exiting from the rear and bending through 90° to connect to the existing chimney. Most people who install stoves are motivated by a desire for increased fuel efficiency, but there are other important, secondary considerations, including aesthetic appeal, ease of use, convenience, comfort, and the desire to have something approximating an open fire. Stoves may also include built-in back boilers that will supply hot water, and some provide supplementary space heating. Stove fuel types include the full range of carbon-neutral products such as natural wood logs, wood chip logs, and hemp logs. Wood pellet stoves are also very popular and are chosen principally for their ease of use, convenience, and fuel efficiency. Aesthetics is not the only factor, and both stove and fuel supply are often located in an out-house or garage, with an automated shute for delivering the pellets to the stove at an adjustable rate dictated by heating requirements.

The king of all stoves is, of course, the kitchen range. These are primarily designed for cooking but can also contain very efficient back boilers for space and water heating. The overall efficiency of kitchen ranges is, however, poor because heat output is compromised by the need to provide for overheated cooking plates and ovens.

What is more, larger kitchen ranges usually need to be kept running continuously, chiefly because they are difficult to start up from cold, which has an obvious downside in terms of continual and unnecessary fuel feed.

The ideal location for such ranges is in rural homes where a supply of local natural raw material (wood) for fuel may be available. When large ranges are located in urban settings, the fuel source is more likely to be natural gas. Although these are not as carbon friendly as their rural counterparts, they can be switched on and off, helping to reduce fuel wastage.

Condensing Boilers

Previously, the gas or oil burner was the heat engine in most buildings, hidden away in a shed or boiler room and rarely visited unless it broke down. In most developed countries, it is now policy to replace all boilers older than 15 years and enforce minimum efficiency standards when specifying new boilers. Generally, current policy dictates in favor of condensing boilers with a minimum of 90% efficiency. However, the principal drawback of the condensing boiler is that it is a fossil fuel-fed system with associated carbon emissions. Consequently, future government policies will have to favor more carbon-neutral technologies such as the solar and micro-CHP hydrogen fuel-cell systems discussed below.

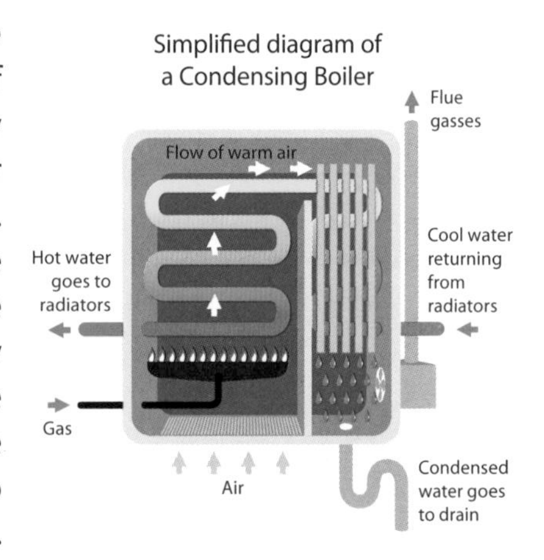

Condensing boilers look just the same as any other gas or oil boiler of the past 40 years. They are currently the most used technology for domestic heat generation in Europe. The only physical difference and the point to note when trying to determine whether or not a boiler is potentially an energy efficient condensing type or an older standard boiler is the presence of a drain valve and pipe to discharge the liquid water condensate. Condensing boilers work on the same principles as the standard boiler, with one exception: They efficiently recycle and recover heat energy that is normally discharged into the atmosphere through the exhaust flue. A properly installed condensing boiler should be running at over 90% efficiency. At this peak efficiency, the water vapor produced by the burning gas or oil condenses back and a heat exchanger extracts this heat for beneficial use. There is added efficiency in that this heat exchanger helps to cool the exhaust gases, allowing the system to operate at the optimum running temperature.

Solar Thermal

Solar thermal is the general term used to describe active space and water heating from solar panels. Solar thermal is not to be confused with solar PV, which is the process of generating electricity from solar panels (see Step 6). It is also worth noting that the most common type of solar thermal system installed today heats water only. Hot water, unlike space heating, is required in all climates, all year round for domestic usage. The solar thermal process is at its simplest for water heating; however, that's not to say that solar thermal cannot be extended to provide space heating. Solar panel design along with integrated system tanks can provide a contribution to valuable whole-house space heating. As temperature control technologies become more developed, the ability of solar thermal panels to provide whole house heating solutions will become more economically viable.

Given current energy awareness, it is important to distinguish the need for space heating from the need for hot water. The production of hot water as a by-product of an oversized heating system might have been common practice in the past, but today the efficient production of hot water must be considered in isolation. (See also Step 6 on electrical efficiency and Step 7 on water efficiency).

The basic technology behind solar thermal is very simple. The solar panel itself is essentially a glass system that traps direct sunlight in order to heat the enclosed air/water/liquid, depending on the particular design. There are two basic forms of solar panels: flat panels and a series of evacuated glass tubes containing a liquid that is heated and passed through a system of pipes to an insulated water cylinder. The heat is then transferred to the water in the cylinder by conduction and convection before being passed back through the solar panel for reheating. The final energy output is wholly dependent on the quality of the technology and the level of detail applied to the process, from insulation of the glass collecter coatings (such as low-e glass discussed in Step 4) piping materials, sensors, and controls.

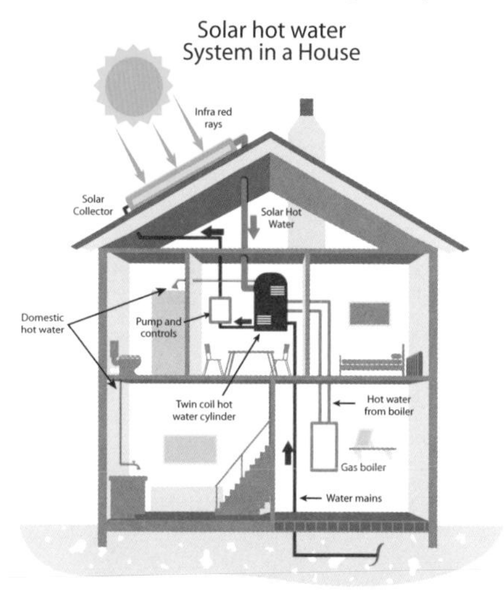

Solar heating is one of the most sensible additions to any property and, where possible, should be first on the list for consideration in a low-carbon, economical retrofit. Solar thermal units harness the heat from the sun to supply hot water and space heating. In summer, it can successfully supply 100% of a building's hot water needs, and in winter it can supplement an existing heating system. In simple terms, 50% to 60% of the average house's annual demand for hot water can be met by a 4-metre-square solar collector, with 100% supplied in summer.

In larger offices, schools and commercial buildings, solar panels can supply 30% to 40% of the annual hot water supply. This percentage rises considerably when all water saving devices and techniques are implemented, as discussed in Step 7.

An important factor when considering any solar thermal system is to determine whether it is direct or indirect. The direct system also known as an open loop is the simpler of the two. With this system, the water that is heated is transferred directly to the storage tank, then used as required. Because antifreeze cannot be used, this system type is best suited to sunnier

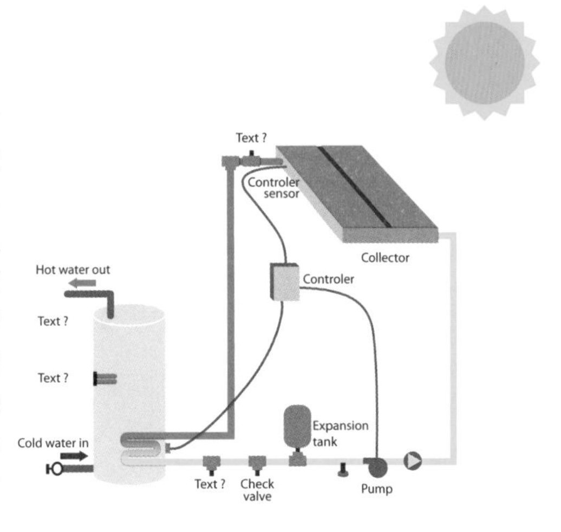

climates where night-time and winter freezing are unlikely. The indirect or closed loop type is more complex, allowing for a greater diversity of uses. It contains an antifreeze solution and is therefore suitable for use in colder climates. The transfer of heat from the solution takes place in a heat exchange coil in the storage cylinder.

There are two basic types of solar panels for harnessing heat energy: flat panels and evacuated tubes. Both types have to be designed and built robustly to withstand varying outdoor temperatures in extremely exposed locations. They also have to perform the dual function of harvesting the maximum amount of heat from the sun and minimizing heat loss. This is particularly the case in winter, when the sun has the potential to maximize heat gains in the panel, but colder air temperatures could quickly steal the heat if there's a technical flaw in the insulation mechanism.

Flat Panel

Flat panel solar thermal units are the more popular of the two panel types, mainly because they are a simpler design and cheaper to make and install. They feature a collection surface, black-coated for maximum solar absorption, and a group of embedded flow pipes. The liquid running through the pipes is either water (direct systems) or an antifreeze solution (indirect systems). The pipes and insulation are contained in a steel or aluminium rectangular box frame, which also holds the outer glazed unit. The glass type itself is key because it facilitates the essential greenhouse effect, allowing solar radiation in to heat the fluid in the pipes while trapping the heat and preventing it from being radiated out due to a low-emissivity (low-e) coating.

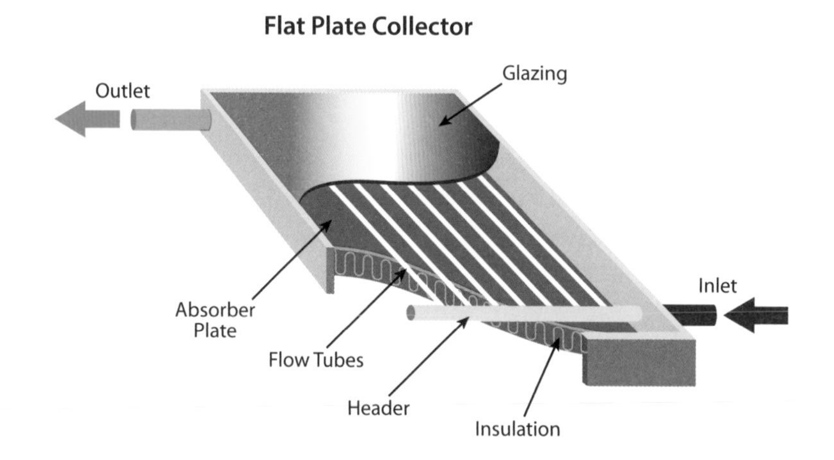

Evacuated Tubes

Evacuated tubes harness the sun's energy in a similar way to flat tubes but are slightly more efficient. They consist of a series of glass tubes enclosing a vacuum and flow pipe. The glass coating has high absorbance with low emissivity, and this, coupled with the vacuum, makes the tubes very efficient in terms of heat retention. The evacuated tubes also provide more focused heat, allowing the system to make better use of diffuse solar radiation on more cloudy days and for longer, including in the colder, darker winter months. Other advantages include greater flexibility in terms of orientation and location because their curved profile allows greater deviation from south-facing roofs. They can also be used on vertical walls. Evacuated tubes are always preferred when there is a need for greater temperatures and/or a requirement to supplement hot water with space heating systems. Because they require a more complex piping arrangement, they don't scale up as readily as flat plates and they are also more expensive.

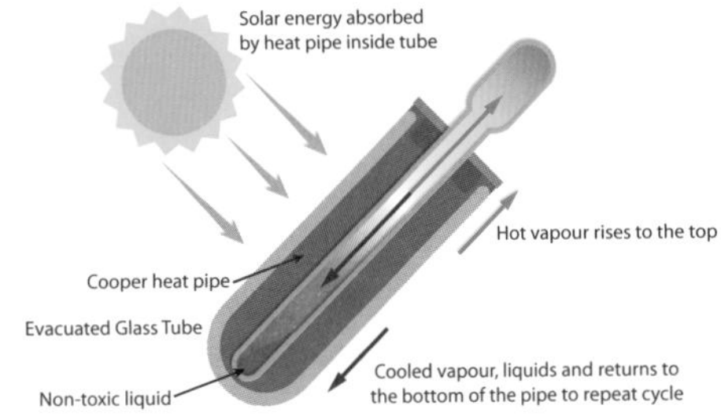

Heat Pumps

At its simplest, a heat pump is an electrical device that moves heat from one location to another by using a small amount of energy. It works on the same principle as a refrigerator but in reverse. A sequence of compression and evaporation cycles takes the heat from outside air, ground, or water and leverages it up using the compression/evaporation cycle before delivering it to the inside of the building. The reason heat pumps work so efficiently is because they simply transfer heat rather than having to create it from first principles such as through the burning of fossil fuels. Modern heat pumps are very effectively and efficiently used for space heating and cooling and water heating. The main task of a heat pump is to move heat energy in the opposite direction to its natural flow such as from a cooler to a hotter place but energy is required to achieve this.

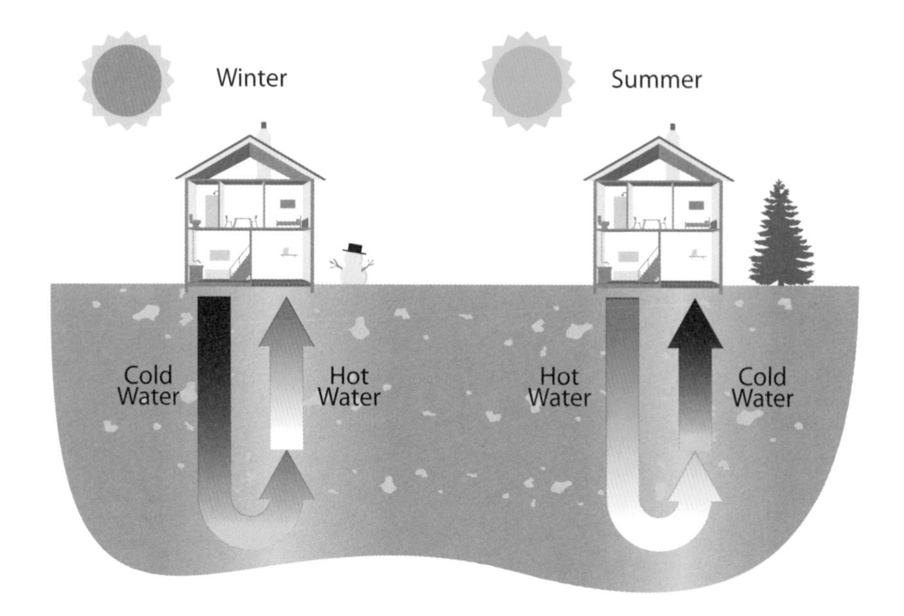

To most people, this process is counterintuitive. It is easy to grasp that heat flows from a warm area to a cold area, but the reverse flow takes some explaining. In fact, the process wasn't figured out on a commercial scale until the 1850s, before which refrigeration, which is based on the heat pump, was unknown. Until then, the only way to preserve large quantities of food at cold temperatures was to use ice, which fell out of favor as a mass-market commodity as refrigeration came of age. While the technology is proven, tried, and tested, it's use for heating and cooling buildings is less understood particularly by those who matter most, the building's users.

The Heating and Cooling Process

Anyone considering installing a heat pump in a new or retrofit property would benefit from taking a few moments to understand how the process works in order to maintain and use this unique form of heating efficiently. Because the heat pump uses the same technology as the domestic refrigerator, this is a good place to start. The principle behind the refrigeration process is knowing that certain gases and liquids (called refrigerants or coolants) absorb heat upon compression and dissipate heat upon expansion. There is a requirement for a temperature difference between an area to be cooled and an area to be heated and vice versa. In the refrigeration cycle, there are then five basic steps to what is essentially a heat pump process.

1. The process starts with a small compressor located at the back of the fridge. The compressor squeezes the liquid refrigerant, raising its temperature and pressure. The coolant is now a hot, high-pressured gas. In a similar way, you may have noticed the heat generated by a bicycle pump as it compresses air and pumps it into a tyre.
2. The pressure difference pushes the coolant through the thin radiator pipes on the back of the refrigerator where it loses its heat into the room and cools down into a liquid.
3. The refrigerant then enters the expansion valve. As it passes through the restrictive pipes and into the greater area, there is a drop in pressure, which allows it to expand, and as it expands it cools. In the same way, an aerosol spray cools down as it leaves the confined space of the can.
4. The cooled refrigerant now flows through the evaporator coils hidden inside the refrigeration compartment. Here it absorbs all available heat in the refrigerator's air and contents.
5. The warmed refrigerant then evaporates to a gas and flows back to the compressor where the cycle starts over again.

Because heat is transferred from the warmer to the cooler area, this makes heat pumps very suitable for controlling temperatures: In winter, they can heat, and in summer, they can cool a building. The heat source from which the thermal energy is taken determines the type of heat pump needed. The heat pump is a renewable low-carbon heat source. Or is it? There are mixed opinions on its low-carbon credentials, and many experts have substantial doubts about the merits of heat pumps.

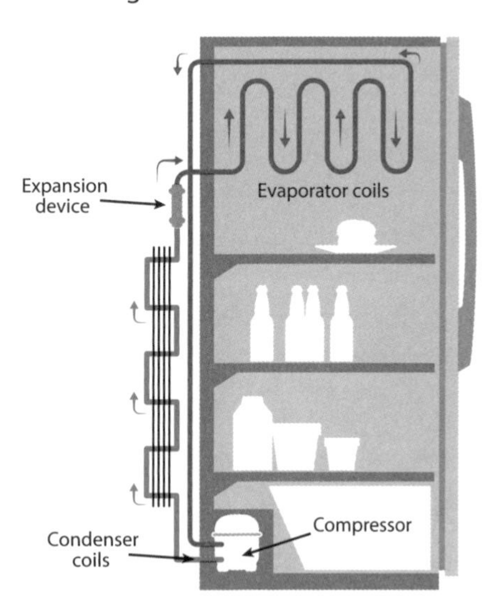

Ground Source Heat Pumps (GSHP)

Ground source heat pumps draw heat from the ground via a series of pipes just below the soil's vegetation layer to a minimum depth, depending on the temperature of the ground and its soil type. There are three main types of collector systems to extract heat from the ground (or to release heat into the ground for cooling purposes). They are vertical loop, horizontal loop, and slinky loop, and which one to use on the available ground area and soil conditions. Wet or moist soil is more efficient than dry soil for heat transfer to and from the collector systems. Deep vertical pipes are more expensive to install but may be the only feasible solution where a larger open area is not available for shallow laid horizontal systems.

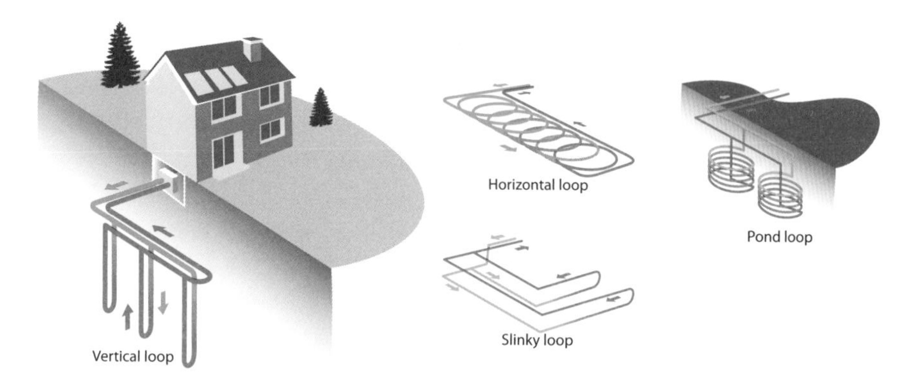

Water Source Heat Pumps

Water source heat pumps are similar in principle to ground source pumps but take heat from a water source such as a river, lake, or well. A key difference is that the loop collecting the heat can be open. In other words, it takes the actual water in the pipe and, after extracting the heat, discharges the water downstream. The open loop system can be very efficient because it simply takes in water at one temperature and discharges it at another. However, there can be environmental problems if the discharge temperature is vastly different to the ambient temperature of the surrounding waters at the discharge point. This could have a detrimental effect on the ecosystem in the waters at the discharge area and may need a separate environmental assessment.

Air Source Heat Pumps

Air source heat pumps simply extract heat from the air outside the building, just like an air-conditioning unit but in reverse. They can do this even in the coldest months, but their efficiencies diminish as the temperature difference between inside and outside rises. The colder the air temperature, the harder the heat pump must work to lift the temperature up to what is required for heating. Their efficiency, or COP, can reduce to 1 in extreme conditions, which is the same as a standard electric heater. In these circumstances, they are not considered "renewable" because they are now generating heat as opposed to harnessing heat. For this reason, air source heat pumps are slightly less efficient than their ground and water source counterparts, but this slight loss of efficiency is reflected in costs they are typically less expensive to install.

The most common type of air source heat pump used in dwellings is an air to water heat pump – the water referring to the method of heat distribution, i.e. through an under-floor heating system (which uses water). Other types of air source heat pumps include exhaust air heat pumps, which are usually fitted to ventilation systems to provide hot water/hot water and heating, and air-to-air heat pumps, which use the ventilation system instead of water systems such as under floor heating or radiators.

These heat pump systems are generally reliant on electricity as a prime motive energy source. In spite of impressive COP ratings, e.g. 4:1, it should be understood that heat pumps of all sorts use electricity as the denominator (the "1" above) AND the other number is the number of heat units delivered (the "4"). Depending upon the precise market for electricity and heat at a point in time, the relative cost of each type of energy, electricity, and heat can commonly vary by a factor of between 1.5 to 3.0 or even more, with electricity being consistently the more expensive.

Micro-CHP

Micro combined heat and power (micro-CHP) refers to a group of technologies that generate heat and electricity simultaneously from a single source in individual homes or buildings. It is also sometimes referred to as co-generation. When cooling is added to the mix, the technology is referred to as tri-generation, although, to date, this is generally only available for larger scale projects. This technology has been rapidly developing in recent years, notably in Japan, where more than 50,000 micro-CHP fuel cell systems were installed in 2013. Japan, the world's third biggest economy, has oriented its energy policy toward micro-CHP. This move to a more sustainable, localized energy resource is a direct policy response to the failures of centralized energy production exposed by the Fukushima-Daiichi nuclear plant disaster in 2011.

Micro-CHP is not a renewable energy source, but with the right technology and application, it can be a relatively energy-efficient and low-carbon source of power. Moreover, with a renewable fuel source such as biogas, the CHP unit can be an integral part of a zero-carbon energy solution and so can be deemed renewable. This is true for larger anaerobic digesters (ADs) that are fitted with a CHP unit at the back end, powered by the biogas from the digesters (see Step 6). An important aspect of the effectiveness of CHP is that electricity generated is used at the source plant and hence there are almost no distribution losses, as compared with centralized electricity generation. Currently, in most countries, centralized electricity is generated mainly from carbon-intensive gas and coal, so considerable carbon savings can be made by opting for micro-CHP. By contrast, in countries where energy is derived from less carbon-intensive sources, e.g. where central electricity is produced from nuclear power, hydro, or wind-generation units, micro-CHP may not result in any significant carbon savings. Carbon savings are at the heart of government policies on energy efficiency, and each national government has its unique mix of concerns and opportunities. A number of factors need to be taken into account before choosing CHP, notably the availability and form of government incentives for carbon reduction.

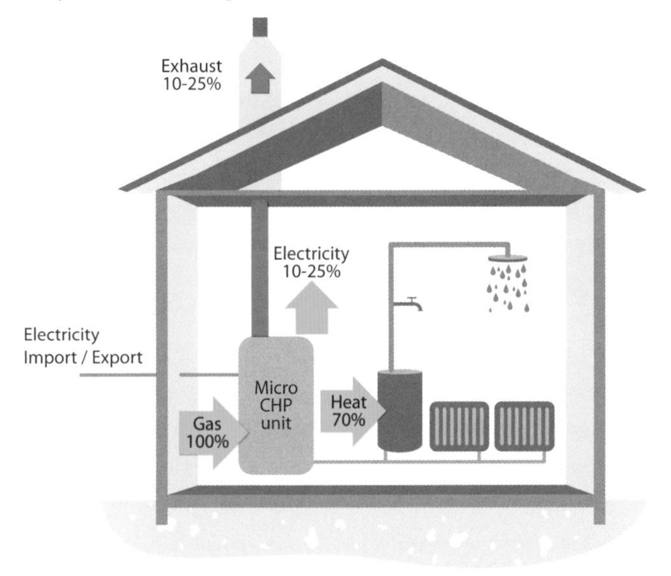

The biggest advantage of a micro-CHP unit is that it can directly replace a condensing boiler, heating a home in the same way by providing hot water to a central heating system. Although the efficiency of a micro-CHP unit is the same as that of a condensing boiler, it is the generation of electricity that gives the CHP unit the economic advantage and helps finance the capital cost of the investment. That economic advantage to generating your own electricity by the CHP process can be even greater in areas where the price of grid electricity is more expensive.

The key factors to take into account when considering micro-CHP are typical of those for all clean energy sources, including fuel type, technology efficiency, government support systems, and local availability. But because CHP units supply both heat and electricity, the exact amounts of these and the sequencing throughout the year are essential first questions to be answered. For instance, electricity generated may have a value and use all year round, but the heat generated may have zero value and may actually have to be dumped if there is no specific need for it during summer. The ratio of heat to electricity produced by the CHP unit must be a good fit with the heat and electricity requirements of the building on an all-year basis. The ratio of heat to electricity on older units is often in the 6:1 range, that is, six times as much heat as electricity, both measured in kilowatts. However, emerging technologies with greater efficiencies are moving toward 1:1, balanced heat and electricity output. When the CHP unit is producing electricity, it is also producing heat. The energy efficiency of a micro-CHP unit is usually dictated by maximizing the beneficial use of the heat first. There will always be a use for the electricity, particularly if the unit is connected to the grid. The ability of the unit to stop/start and only run when there is a need for heat is a critical issue. Some CHP units are good at this, but others need to run continuously for maximum efficiency. So before looking at energy-efficiency issues, it is necessary to understand the different types of technology that generate heat and electricity such as CHP engines, generators, and fuel cells.

Engine and Generator

Consisting of an engine that drives a generator to produce electricity, this is the most proven technology for micro-CHP. The heat is taken from the engine's cooling waters and exhaust system. The most popular type of engine is an internal combustion engine, although diesel engines are also used. To understand how the CHP process work, it is best to consider how a car's engine operates. Instead of driving car wheels, the CHP engine's primary function is to generate electricity. A by-product of the internal combustion engine process is the generation of heat, albeit unwanted in the car mechanisms. The engine cooling process works by allowing a coolant to pass through the engine, where it extracts heat and then passes it through the radiator to cool. In a car, the radiator's key function is to dissipate this heat to the atmosphere, thereby allowing the engine to operate at an optimum, cooler temperature. The process is continuous, and if it stops, the engine will overheat and the car will come to a shuddering halt.

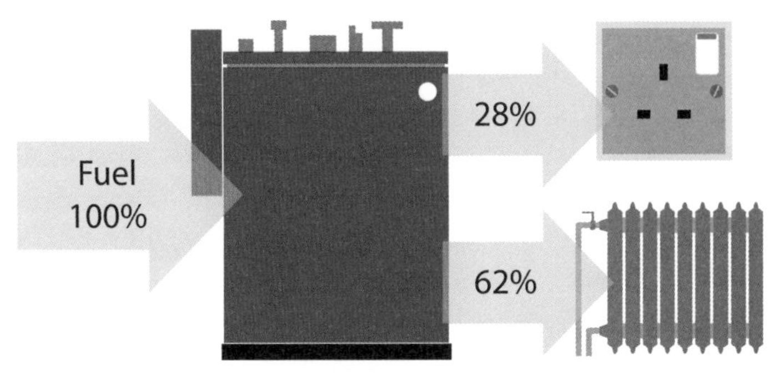

The efficiency of a CHP unit centers on harnessing the heat generated from the engine. Instead of passing the coolant through the radiator, a heat exchanger is used to extract the heat, which can then be used for a central heating system or to generate hot water for storage or usage. More advanced micro-CHP units (such as the type described above) also extract heat from the engine's manifold and exhaust systems.

Stirling Engine

The Stirling engine is very suitable for use in a micro-CHP process. It is not yet widely used, although the technology is well established. The Stirling engine differs from the standard gas or diesel engine insofar as it is a completely sealed unit, which has lower emissions and is much quieter than a standard engine, making it ideal for use inside a building. Unlike the internal combustion engine, which requires a fuel to ignite, the Stirling engine needs a heat source to expand and contract an enclosed gas, just like a heat pump. For this reason, the it can work very well in renewable systems where the heat source can be any fuel, including biomass and solar.

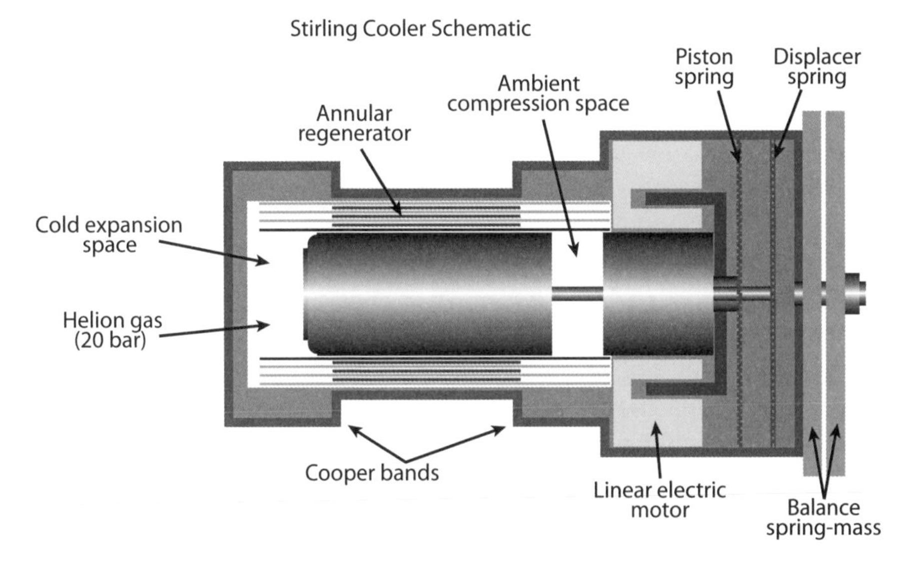

Stirling engines are more often used in larger CHP processes, where bespoke designs are more justifiable in financial terms. In fact, the Stirling engine is much more efficient than the traditional combustion engine, with a lower power to heat ratio, and supports a wide range of sizes, from under 1kW to upward of 100kW. As the micro-CHP market expands, the commercial viability of smaller Stirling engines driving the CHP process will become more attractive.

Fuel Cells

As a result of advances made largely in Japan, fuel cell technology now offers huge potential for heat and power generation in small buildings and homes. Micro-CHP fuel cells are over 30% more efficient than the nearest alternatives, making them a favorable economic option for future energy savings. The technology operates on a similar principle to that of a battery but, unlike a battery, is a self-generating energy source. Provided that fuel is available, fuel cells will not run down or require recharging. They use an electrochemical process to produce heat and electricity from the oxidation of hydrogen, with only pure water as a by-product. The process is even quieter than that of the Stirling engine, and because there are no fossil fuels involved, it is a low-carbon emissions technology. While many combinations of fuel and oxidant are possible, most fuel cells now use hydrogen and oxygen to convert chemical energy to electrical energy.

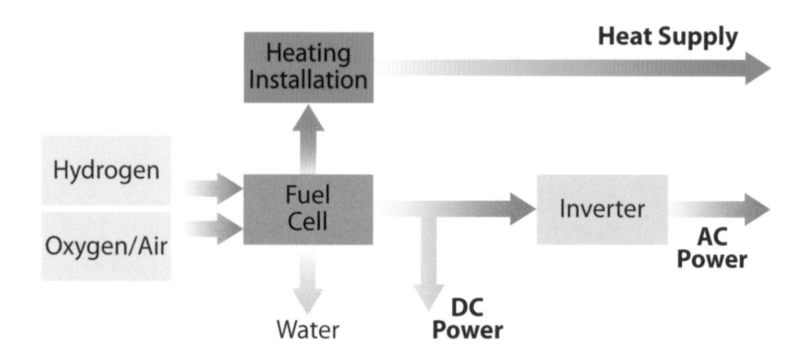

There are many different fuel cell types, but they all generate electricity through an electrochemical process. The cell types are usually only referred to in the industry by their acronyms, which can make understanding the design and technology even more complex. Hydrogen fuel cells will unquestionably become mainstream, and the language of their operation and design will become more commonplace. Until then, some definitions of the principal types, set out below, will help to improve understanding. (Fuel cells are generally distinguished by the electrolyte and operating temperature range, hence the terms such as alkaline, proton exchange membrane, molten carbonate, solid oxide fuel cells, etc.).

- **PEMFC** – proton exchange membrane fuel cells operate at low temperatures and can vary power output quickly to meet demand. They are principally suited to the automobile industry for this reason but also have application in buildings where there is no heat demand and the unit regularly needs to be turned on/off.
- **DMFC** – direct methanol fuel cell is similar to PEMFC and also operates at low temperatures. DMFCs are suitable for smaller power requirements and are regularly used in such products as laptops, cell phones, and consumer electronics.
- **PAFC** – phosphoric acid fuel cells operate at higher temperatures and can use a greater mix of source fuels such as biogas and methanol.
- **SOFC** – solid oxide fuel cells also operate at higher temperatures, allowing a greater mix of source fuels, from natural bio-fuels to heavy hydrocarbons. SOFCs are suitable for larger commercial buildings where continuous energy needs arise.
- **AFC** – alkaline fuel cells are one of the original fuel cells developed by NASA to power hydrogen-fueled space missions. The by-product of the process is water, which was beneficial in space missions.

In most countries, micro-CHP qualifies for feed-in tariffs and government support grants. The technology is still not mature and so, in many cases, is still not commercially viable without some financial supports. However, costs are reducing as more general appeal helps to begin introducing economies of scale.

Why Building Temperature Control is so Important

A djusting the thermostat can have the single biggest effect on the amount of energy we use, yet we rarely do this with cost savings in mind. During my numerous energy audits on commercial buildings, the biggest complaint most occupants have is either too much heat or an air-conditioning system that makes the building too cool. There seems to be a disconnection between extreme temperature settings on the one hand and our ability to recognise and take responsibility for the associated wasted money on the other. Equally ridiculous is observing staff opening windows to cool particular rooms in a building, while the heating system struggles to provide heat to the rest of the building.

Climate control is the new catch-all terminology for heat, temperature, and thermostatic controls. If you are looking to upgrade your heating system's controls, there are three main categories:

- Manual controls are the basic type placed on heating systems or radiators, and they require human input to adjust them to change set point temperatures or timings and setbacks.
- Programmable controls allow users to define a series of temperature settings for various times of the day/week/year. These can have two-way communication features that allow remote access to the controls.
- Programmable communication controls can carry out the same functions as above but offer additional multiple communication via web site, smartphone or cloud-based remote access with automatic complex algorithms integrating occupancy habits and the capacity to set climate control.

When it comes to saving energy and money, it's not about how sophisticated your climate controls are, it's more about having the ability to exercise control and strike a balance between thermal comfort and energy use. Manual thermostats are perfect if you just want to set the base-line temperature. The most common and easiest energy saving is achieved by slightly lowering the heating temperature and raising the cooling temperature set points. This doesn't have to mean sacrificing comfort for energy saving, but it does mean taking a level of control over your comfort zone and perhaps dressing accordingly, as discussed earlier.

Climate control is made easier with programmable thermostats. That's not to say that energy savings will always be achieved by setting a time schedule of set temperatures into the future. There are still too many variables, such as outside temperatures and changed occupancy levels. What is more, because programmable thermostats are more complex to adjust than manual ones, they tend to get set once and left, making optimum temperature control arbitrary at best. However, there are many two-way communication, programmable heating controls that allow you turn on/off and reprogram heating times from a smartphone. These allow real-time adjustment to your heating requirements from anywhere.

Manual thermostat | climote remote programmable | Nest

The most sophisticated level of climate controls involve multiple communications with all sorts of hardware and software that integrate with such things as HVAC systems, windows, doors, blinds, and home security. Climate programs can also optimize set points from hybrid systems, including back-up energy from solar, heat pumps, and micro-CHP. Comfort levels are optimized based on preset conditions, coupled with occupancy detectors with complex software packages that can analyze past habits and predict future behavior. When this information is integrated with smart meters, the utility companies interpret future grid demand response and create attractive cost regimes that will help co-ordinate time of energy usage. This may sound a little intimidating, but it is merely a by-product of today's smart era.

Maintenance

Maintenance usually only takes place where there is an emergency or breakdown, but how you manage heating controls and maintain heating equipment can have a large effect on the energy efficiency of the system and the size of the heating bills. Maintenance of heating equipment should be carried out at least once a year, and thermostats and heating controls should be regularly checked to ensure they are correctly set.

A typical maintenance check-up should include the following steps:

- Have a professional tradesperson carry out an annual health check on the heating and cooling system. It is very important that you get a full checklist with before and after values recorded for all items. This record will be very useful, particularly when it comes to repair/ replace decisions. Your professional should also check the accuracy and location of all thermostats with some simple tests to verify all calibrations are reasonably correct.
- Check thermostat setting and controls to ensure that the optimum settings are in place to suit short-term needs without sacrificing

comfort levels. This needs to be done regularly so that the control adjustment and desired response are fully understood. Correctly adjusted temperature set points can have the largest single effect on cost control.

- Check to ensure that there are no leaks and spillages in and around the boiler or furnace, including a check to see that all vents are free and unobstructed.
- If there are air filters, these need to be cleaned or replaced every three months. Clogged filters don't just affect the efficiency of the system but may also reduce air quality to the point of posing a health risk.
- In a water-based heating system, it is advisable to bleed trapped air from hot water radiators. Trapped air, which can be a persistent problem in a poorly designed system, will restrict flow and may leave cold spots is some radiators. A full purge of the water should also be carried out if it is found to be discoloured or dirty. It is worth adding a magnetic filter to the pipe network to help remove impurities from the water.
- Excessive noise from the boiler or other heating/cooling equipment is a sign that the equipment is not running efficiently. Vibrations and hammering sounds in pipework are also a sign of a fault in the system and should be checked and eliminated.
- Check for unusual smells, notably gas. Apart from gas smells, any unusual smell could indicate electrical faults or excessive moisture resting on heated surfaces.

If your heating bills show unexpected increases, it might the result of a simple fault in the heating system or an indicator that an old system needs replacing. Remember, of course, if your heating/cooling system needs replacing, always take the opportunity to reassess your overall heating/cooling needs.

Step 5 Summary

Twitter Summary
How we choose to heat and cool our buildings and where we source our fuel energy will have the greatest impact on climate change. But ultimately how we use technology and integrate renewables into our buildings will determine how successful we will be.

Smart Citizen Summary
Step 5 is about seeking a deeper appreciation of the factors that determine the energy demands of our homes and buildings. Taking a lesson from the more intutitive understanding our ancestors seem to have about how to intergrate their homes into the surrounding environment, should help us reduce our dependency on finite natural resources. To do this the smart citizen must: the structure and fabric of our buildings. The smart citizen must also appreciate that the thermal envelope of a building needs to be enclosed to the highest standards before any renewable energy options should be considered. This is because wasting energy whether its renewable or non-renewable is not an option for the smart citizen. Additionally To achieve the smart citizen must:

- Understand why temperature control is so important
- Become conscious of the part simple clothes selection can play in regulating body temperature
- Recoginize the basic role passive solar heating and cooling plays in regulating the temperature of our buildings
- Recognize that, while we don't all need to be engineers, we do need a basic grasp of the principal factors that determine how much energy we need for heating and cooling buildings

Step 6: Electrical Demand

"A nation that can't control its energy sources can't control its future"

Barack Obama

Over time, electricity meters have become more like speedometers: always moving and always measuring. The difficulty is finding anybody who seems to know how to interpret them, let alone how to slow things down. Understanding and taking back control of our electricity usage is what Step 6 is about.

Because we shy away from trying to understand matters electrical, we allow power companies to do our thinking for us. Most people don't know how to read an electricity bill and never query meter readings. Leaving that control to the suppliers is costing us dearly, not just in oversized bills but in terms of being denied many opportunities for generating our own electricity and making some real, tax-free income from government green incentive schemes. More importantly, new smart meters have arrived that use clever algorithims to record every minute of energy usage and learn from past habits to predict future energy use.

The multitude of appliances that support our lifestyle at home and work and in our places of leisure keep the electricity meters in our buildings in continuous motion. There is no downtime. There is always a refrigerator, a computer, or some other appliance on a standby setting, charging or running unnoticed in the corner. Our interconnected IT world would dissolve like the morning mist if users weren't continuously connected to a regular power supply. Whether connected to the grid for mains electricity or a generator run from off-grid power, you won't survive in today's appliance- and gadget-strewn world without electricity.

However, some of the most straightforward savings can be made by simply paying attention to the electricity "speedometer" appropriately named until such time as we learn to control our meters.

Electricity

The success of the low-carbon era is will depend on our understanding of electrical energy. Electricity is the form of energy used to power virtually every building. Other energy forms may also be used for heating, including gas, oil, coal, and wood, but when the electricity stops flowing, so too do most heating systems, which depend on some form of electric supply to keep going.

Most of the electricity generated worldwide today is from fossil fuels. Coal-fired electricity generation stations were the principal source of power from the 19th century onward and have begun to be augmented. Some are being replaced by mainly oil and gas powered plants. Nuclear power stations have also played their role to this point. Electricity generation has generally followed the local availability of fossil fuel resources. Not surprisingly, renewable energy technologies follow the availability of natural resources. Successful wind farms are located on exposed hills, on mountainsides, and in coastal regions with good prevailing wind-speeds. Equally important, they are situated in regions where governments have set out policies to encourage and incubate renewable technologies. A classic example of this is cloudy Germany, which has, until recently, led the world in solar technology. More than 20 years ago, the government there introduced policies to encourage the installation of solar photovoltaic panels on roofs. Initially known as the Thousand Roofs scheme, it was highly successful in its uptake and has led to the introduction of a feed-in tariff (FIT) scheme, discussed in Step 1, that is now emulated the world over. Frequent travelers in Europe in 2015 can determine which country they are in just by noting the concentration of solar rooftop installations.

Whether it's saving money on reduced electricity usage or generating electricity from your own building and feeding it into the grid by way of a FIT scheme, it is important to understand how electricity is made so it can be measured. You might feel like skipping this section, but having a basic grasp of this concept will go a long way toward helping you to better tackle its measurement. Electricity is a form of energy found in nature. Lightning is a fine example of electricity in action, but it doesn't occur regularly enough for it to be harnessed for power.

We need to go back to basics, to physics 101. For those who never studied physics, what we are discussing here merely summarizes natural processes in the world around us that we rarely bother to appreciate. It is the model that powers our world. All matter is made up of positive and negative charges. Positively charged particles are called protons and negatively charged ones are known as electrons, and they spend their time spinning around a nucleus in that smallest particle of matter, the atom. Because opposites attract, these particles stick together to form larger molecules, and this in turn forms matter. In our world, all positive and negative charges appear balanced, so all matter around about us is stable, relative to our perception. I say relative because the out-of-balance force of gravity pulls all matter to the earth's core. But because gravity is constant, our perception is one of balance.

Scientists discovered how negatively charged electrons flow to positively charged protons and how some materials such as copper facilitate that process better than others. They found that electrons are much smaller than protons and that they move around within a material, called a conductor. Inside the conductor, the electrons bounce around in a random fashion as they follow the positively charged protons.

It was subsequently discovered that placing a magnetic charge across the conducting material changed this unpredictable pattern, making all the electrons spin in the same direction. The electrons will continue to spin as long as the magnetic force is present. Moreover, if the magnetized material or conductor is arranged in a loop, the electrons will flow around in the direction of the magnetic charge. In effect, this

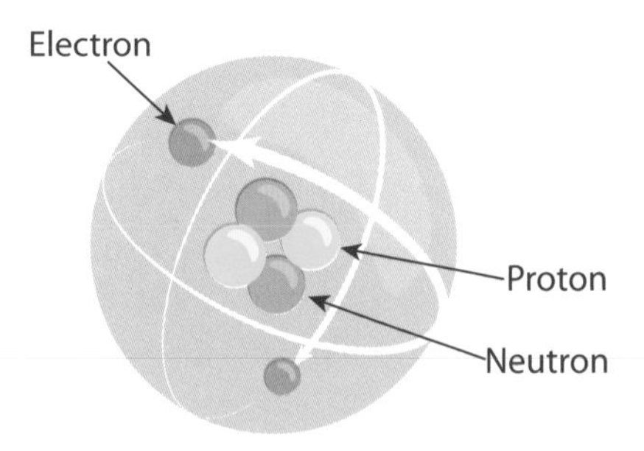

was the invention of what we call electricity. It wasn't until the 19th century that electricity was generated and formally harnessed by man.

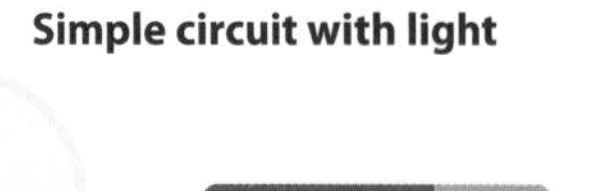

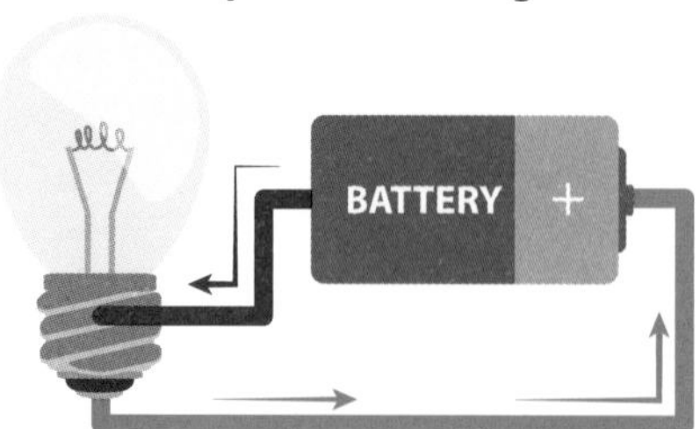

Given that electricity was so convenient for consumers, efficiency was never part of the calculation in terms of supply. Traditionally, a central grid supply, on average, wastes more electricity than it generates, through inefficient power generation plant and distribution losses. The problem for locally generated electricity, on the other hand, particularly that derived from renewable sources, has always been that times of supply rarely match times of demand. In other words, electricity generated during the day from, say, a solar PV unit may not be needed until later in the evening. All of this is now changing, and companies such as U.S. electric car manufacturer Tesla have developed innovative new battery systems. The advent of batteries for electricity storage has the potential to revolutionize how we generate electricity in and around our buildings and can help to balance household electricity usage. However, before discussing the various options for generating renewable electricity and maximizing efficiencies, it is important to understand the role that smart grids and smart meters will play in controlling our use of electricity.

Smart Grids

The electricity network required to run today's interconnected world has become very sophisticated. The popular term "smart grid" is so-called because the network must be responsive to the multiple demands of modern economies. Computer and other electronic equipment is so finely designed that inconsistencies in electricity supply in terms of voltage, harmonics (power balance), and power surges can irreparably damage equipment or lead to data loss. We are creatures of habit, and our interconnectedness via social media and even TV means that we are potentially, be it locally, regionally, or globally, all doing the same things simultaneously. That's fantastic for global communications, but the driving power behind that communication is centralized electricity generation. Everyone is communicating and sharing similar daily routines, rising, eating, working, networking online, watching TV, and sleeping. As a result, time zones across countries become less relevant as power-generating companies have to be responsive to the peaks and troughs of electricity supply in unision across the globe.

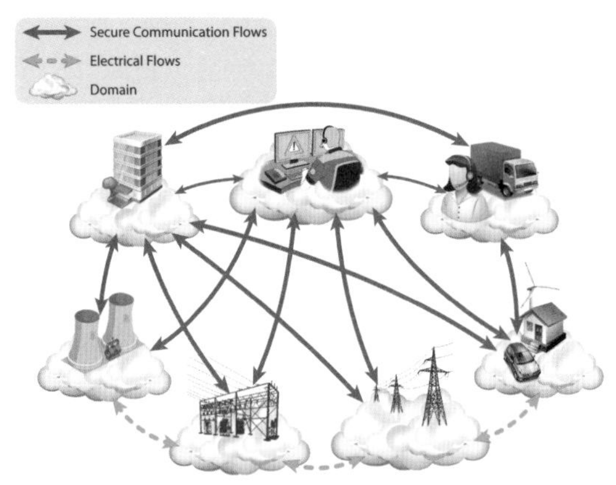

Utility power generation companies keep a close eye on peak television viewing hours, between 5pm and 7pm, when popular shows and sitcoms can play havoc with the national electricity supply. The power companies monitor the shows' expected ratings, some have many millions of viewers their start times, end times, and the timing of ad breaks. They have to prepare for the possibility that a large percentage of viewers may decide to boil the kettle or begin cooking the evening meal during the ads or immediately after a show. If each viewer boiled a kettle at the same time, this could lead to a 4 minute demand-surge of 25 Terawatts (or 250,000,000 Watts): 10 million kettles @ 2.5kWs per kettle is enough to power a large city. The energy suppliers have to anticipate these loads and supply electricity during this peak period, otherwise there could be a blackout. That would be catastrophic in terms of electricity supply.

In the event that a power company anticipates a load surge that it cannot meet, it resorts to what is known as demand-side reduction. This is only possible where the grid is good (smart) and can respond to immediate changes. In such an instance, it is now increasingly common for the power company to have an arrangement with a number of large subcontracted energy suppliers with the ability to reduce or totally suspend power usage when required. In effect, when a peak load situation is anticipated, the power supplier makes a call for a certain amount of megawatts of power reduction. As the grid gets smarter and remote metering and control become more sophisticated, we may reach a point where consumer choice from an electrical power perspective may be restricted. In other words, when we boil a kettle may be at the discretion of the power companies!

The global drive to roll out smart meters is more about managing and intelligently coordinating our use of the grid than measuring the electricity supply, although it does that too. The world is highly dependent on consistent electricity supply, but new and reliable sources of energy are becoming increasingly difficult to find and fund. It is desirable for people to become smart about controlling current usage and minimizing wastage. In the same way as our choice of traveling times can reduce the likelihood of encountering gridlock and thus avoid irrational demand for building new highways specifically to deal with peak demand, an effective smart grid will permit us to extend the life of existing power-generation plants and the current grid network. Many countries, as a result, have developed explicit policies for rolling out smart meters.

- In Britain, for instance, the rollout is under way and expected to be completed by 2019, with over 26 million households fitted with a smart meter
- In France, the target is 35 million units by 2020
- In the United States, over 50 million smart meters have already been installed

By contrast, in Canada, which has a similar policy, the rollout of smart meters has run into opposition from groups who are protesting the monitoring of electricity consumption on health, safety, and privacy grounds. Protestors believe that smart meters in the home can cause symptons similar to those experienced by victims of sick building syndrome (see Step 3) such as nausea, migraine, insominia, and skin rashes. It has been suggested that meters emit microwave radiation pulses at levels more than 1,000 times greater than those of a cell phone. Indeed, if you do a web search for smart meters, you will find more negative than positive entries about their installation in homes. The evidence to substantiate these conclusions and the concerns they give rise to in Canada, almost uniquely, is very limited and questionable. Nonetheless, it poses a real and serious challenge to Canadian government policy and risks imposing a large, long-term competitive and environmental burden on future generations of Canadians.

What are Smart Meters?

The traditional meter, whether it measures electricity, gas or water, is a simple mechanical device that is manually read. This is a cumbersome process, whereby a meter reader must call to the building, find the meter or meters, read them, record the figures, and carry the records back to base for entry into the billing system. Even when customers submit the readings themselves, the process is fraught with potential errors, not least because the meters are often situated in poorly accessible places.

The modern smart meter, on the other hand, includes advanced communication technology that allows the meter to send a signal directly to the utility, without the need for a callout. This is just one of its advanced functions. Other advantages include:

- Linking to an energy display monitor, giving real-time energy usage information
- Allowing two-way communication between the supplier and customer, enabling the supplier to adjust tariffs and settings remotely
- Providing the supplier (and others) with exact data on your personal energy habits
- Providing for multiple energy tariffs throughout the day and night so that off-peak times are cheaper and more attractive than more expensive peak times
- Generally no upfront costs because the price of the unit is paid for over a number of years, potentially over the full lifetime of the service supply arrangement to the building
- Ending estimated meter readings and helping utility companies make savings by eliminating manual meter readings and reducing time spent on billing disputes

Clearly, the advantages of smart meters benefit power companies and governments. One of the biggest challenges facing suppliers is to have power-generating plants available to meet peak loads, and smart meters will give them access to detailed, up-to-the-minute information on the energy usage of each household. But as noted above in the Canadian example, there is a growing opposition to the installation of smart meters, which must be taken into account.

Energy Labels

The energy-efficiency sector is becoming easier to navigate. The introduction of mandatory energy labels helps to separate genuine energy-saving products from their "greenwash" counterparts. The energy label is designed to give consumers a better understanding of the energy performance of such products as refrigerators, washing machines, tumble dryers, lights, and TVs. In time, more products such as boilers and solar panels will also sport similar labeling. The label displays ratings that run from category G (red – least efficient) to category A*** (dark green – most efficient).

In most countries, the labels follow the same format and look the same. In the United States, they are slightly different and known as Energy Guide labels. Here, total electricity usage for the year is set down and a sliding scale of operating costs is displayed, pinpointing how the rated model compares to similar models.

When it comes to household appliances, the primary measure is the amount of watts the unit uses per hour. The lower the wattage, the less energy used. However, other factors also have to be taken into account - the label must compare like with like. For instance, a 1000-watt microwave does not necessarily use more energy than a 500-watt one because the higher power also reduces the cooking time, so the microwave is likely to be running for a shorter length of time. Energy is power used for a particular length of time.

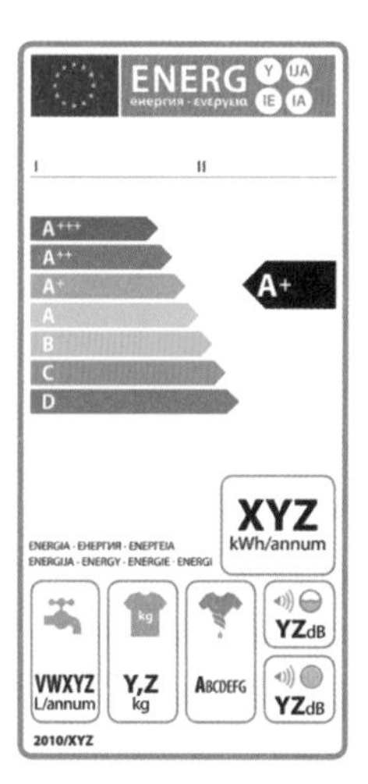

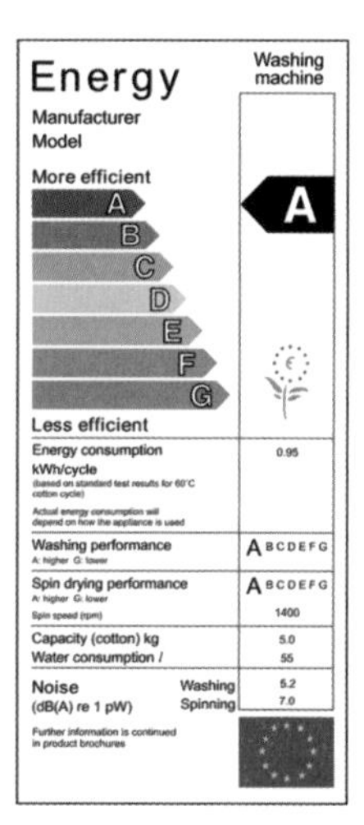

The second key piece of information on an energy label and the real reason for its existence is to display carbon dioxide (CO2) emissions. The label is less about energy use and more about government accountability for CO2 emissions from fossil fuels. It also makes consumers aware of the energy they use, and it is likely that lower energy usage will translate into CO2 reductions. The energy to run a domestic refrigerator, for example, may come from a PV panel on the roof, which is good energy with zero CO2 emissions. On the other hand, it might be powered by coal-generated electricity from the grid, which would be bad energy with high CO2 emissions. Alternatively, it might derive energy from a mixture of supply sources such as PV, wind, and gas depending on the supplier.

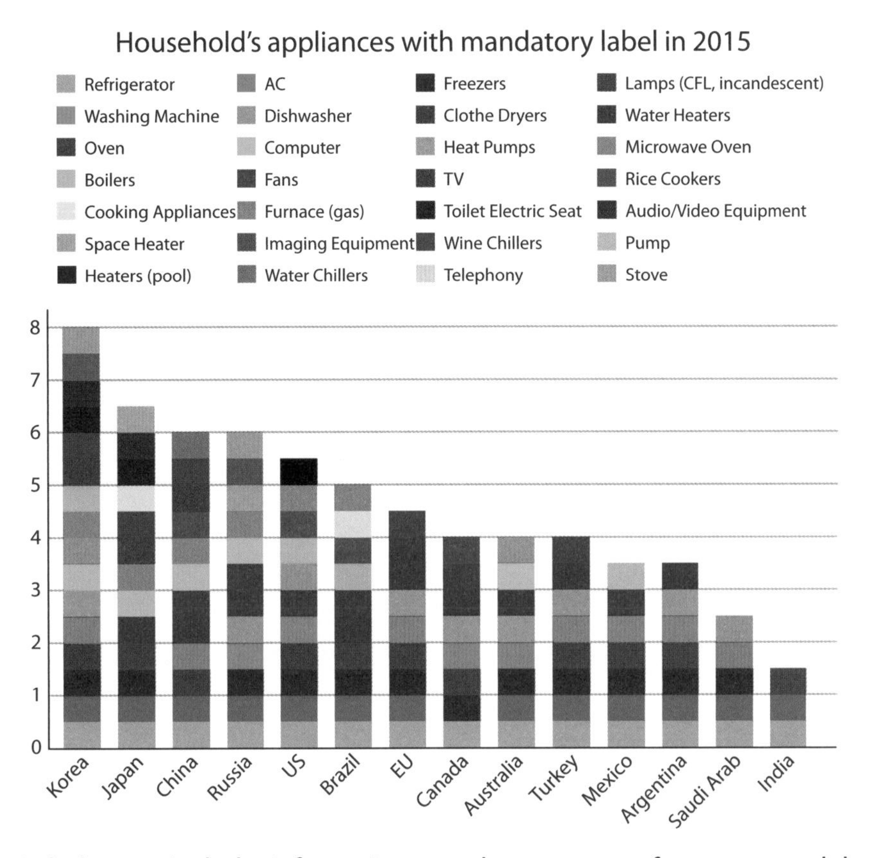

Labels can include information on the amount of energy used by a particular product per hour (kWh), and the lower the number the better. The EU label first introduced in 1995 has had many updates and a comparison between the old label and the new demonstrates that considerable progress has been made in terms of consumer awareness. For instance, the less efficient categories E, F, and G have been dropped and the single A category has been subdivided into A*, A** and A***. The U.S. energy label Energy Star estimates that washing machines today use about 70 percent less energy and 75 percent less water than their counterparts of 20 years ago.

Other very useful labels include the Energy Saving Trust Recommended label, which is only found on the most highly energy-efficient products (www.sust-it.net). In the United States, the Energy Star label is the one to look for and rates the top 25% of energy-efficient products. Better again in efficiency terms is TopTen USA, another organization helping consumers to select the most energy-efficient products on the market.

There are now many good comparison web sites similar to those for hotels and insurance to help consumers rate their potential purchases for energy-efficiecy. A worthwhile exercise before buying a new household appliance is to have a look at the energy and water costs comparative to other similar models. By doing a simple calculation similar to the one in the section below on "know your loads," you might find that an apparently cheaper model may cost as much as ten times more in energy costs to operate over the lifetime of the appliance. Reading and understanding the energy labels might be the decider when it comes to making a household appliance purchase.

Know Your Loads

An energy-efficiency drive that proposes eliminating some electrical appliances in the home such as computers and entertainment centers will not have much success, but there should be no need for such a dramatic measure if care is taken to choose the best in class energy-efficient technology available and then use it wisely. The energy use of most electrical equipment has dramatically improved over the past number of years. As discussed earlier some new appliances now use less than half the electricity of older models. There is, however, a conundrum: while electrical appliances generally use much less electricity, the number of them and the intensity and duration of their use are still rising and are expected to continue doing so into the future. This general trend in use level is facilitating an exponential growth and appetite for data transfer, in particula, one of the strongest drivers of increased consumption of electricity in our homes and buildings. Matching this known trend with the predicted increase in the cost of electricity over the medium-term future means the viability of our families and businesses is at stake here.

The number of electrical appliances are also growing and account for an ever-increasing share of the total domestic electricity bill. This figure has more than doubled in the last 35 years. With all the energy-efficient products now on the market, you would expect energy usage to fall but not so. This increase is partly the result of greater disposable income and partly because of a rise in the number of appliances in the home.

Two key factors that account for the cost of electricity are the power of the unit in kiloWatts and time it is run in hours. So a small 25W spotlight in a kitchen that never gets turned off could cost much more per year than a 1000W microwave used intermittently for 2 or 3 minutes at a time.

Spotlight 25w light used 24/7
equates to 25w x 8760 (hours per year) divided by 1000 = 219kW

Microwave—1000W (used twice a day every day)
equates to 2x3x365 x 1000/60 = 36.5kW

So the small spotlight that most people ignore actually costs up to 6 times more to run than a very powerful microwave oven.

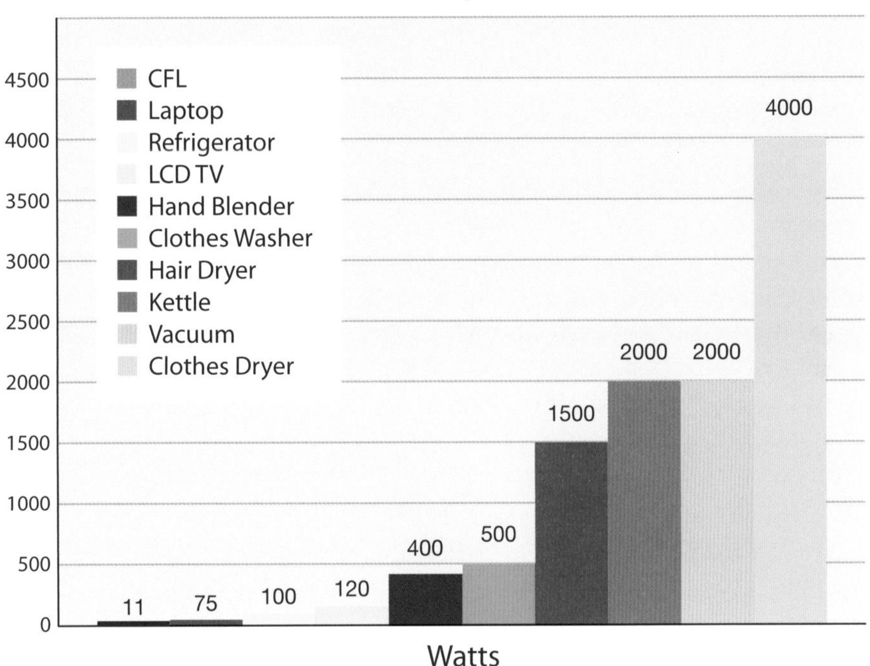

Consequently, the first rule, which will cost you absolutely nothing and is often referred to as the low-hanging fruit of the energy savings world, is to simply turn off nonessential equipment, including lights and especially all standby equipment. It was long believed that you shouldn't repeatedly switch electrical equipment on and off because the associated power surge will damage the equipment. This is almost certainly not the case with 21st-century equipment. Habits must change if we are to make any impact on reducing energy bills. If equipment is not in use, it should be turned off. Moreover, some electrical equipment will last longer if it is turned off when not in use. One example of this is new LED lights, which is discussed in detail below.

The second rule is to purchase appliances with the lowest energy ratings. This is not a limiting factor in terms of choice because, with leading brands, energy efficiency is now synonymous with quality. Look closely at the cost of running the same specification TV from different brands and you might be very surprised. For example, take two similar 42-inch TVs, one a cheaper and the other a more expensive brand. It's always hard to justify paying more up-front than perhaps your current budget allows. However, if you read the energy label mandatorily displayed on both, you might find that the cheaper brand could use over ten times more energy than the more expensive brand. That means that if you switched both on and forgot to turn them off for a year, one might cost as low as $50.00 to run while the other could cost over $500.00. That should certainly incentivize everyone to ensure the TV is turned off when not in use. While manufacturers of leading TV brands today have reduced standby power to minimal amounts, the standby power to watch out for may not always be the TV but the TV assessories such as cable boxes, modems and VCR's.

Refrigeration

Keeping food cold is one of the largest energy consumers. Our busy lifestyles lead us to depend more on preprepared foods that require refrigeration. The issue with all refrigeration units is that they use power every hour, or 8,736 hours annually. Because of improvements in efficiency, refrigeration units over 15 years old will be very inefficient by current standards. Deciding whether to change an old refrigerator for a new, energy-efficient one should be all about energy savings, which equate to cost savings. Many people get very attached to their old refrigerators, and the older the unit the greater the attachment, it seems. Most other electrical appliances reach a definitive end of life, when they fail. So appliances such as washing machines, dishwashers, and kettles regularly get replaced while the refrigerator just seems to go on and on. So great can the attachment be that when a new refrigerator is needed, the old one often doesn't get discarded but, like an heirloom, gets relocated to the shed or garage where it can provide extra storage. This is not a wise choice, the reasons for which are discussed later.

To determine how efficient your refrigerator is, it is first important to establish how much power it uses. Ways of measuring power usage and carrying out a full energy audit of all equipment is set out in detail in Step 2. To find out how much power an individual refrigerator needs, you can use one or all of the following methods:

- Most older models won't have an energy display label but may have a label on the back. Otherwise, you could check the operation manual if you still have it. There are also many web sites where you can enter the make and model of the appliance and find out the power usage on an hourly and yearly basis. The figure you are looking for is a simple value in kWs. If, for example, the figure is 125kW, multiply this by all the hours in the year (8,736), which equates to 1,092,000 million watts or 1,092 kW.
- Use an electronic, plug-in energy meter. You plug the meter into the socket for the appliance to be measured and then plug the appliance into the meter. Most meters have a number of settings, the main one in this instance being kilowatts. If you set the meter to zero, it can measure per hour, day, month, or for as long as the unit is continuously measured. Most of these units can be programmed to accept local electricity rates and display costs in the local currency amount.
- The most versatile measuring unit is the mobile display monitor, which works in a similar way to the plug-in version.

Even if you choose to have a second freezer, this simple test will quickly tell you how much it costs to do so. In any case, it is important to have the most efficient model possible. I'm not advocating for a throwaway society but for a degree of prudence in reducing wasted energy. A new energy-efficient model can typically use as little as 25% of the energy used by one from a previous generation. Therefore, it can potentially pay for itself in savings in less than 5 years. However, if the economics of replacement don't stack up, there are a number of steps you can take to maximize the efficiencies of existing units.

Temperature Awareness. Remember that a refrigerator works by taking heat out of the inside and dispersing it outside, i.e. into the room. For it to work efficiently, the room temperature must be ambient, not too hot and not too cold for heat to disperse efficiently from the condensing coils. To ensure good performance, it should not be placed in direct sunlight or beside another heat-generating appliance such as a stove, cooker, dishwasher, or tumble drier. Locating a refrigerator or freezer in a cooler outhouse or garage is generally fine for this reason.

It is also important to ensure that air can circulate freely around the cooling coils located below and behind the unit. These should be kept free of dust and dirt to allow the coils to disperse heat effectively. The recommended temperature for a refrigerator is 35o F ±1 (37° F = 2.8/3°C; much less and milk freezes in the carton) and for a freezer 2o F ±2° = -16.7°C. Temperature settings below these values will require more power for no value in return, making the unit more wastefully expensive to run.

Secure Door Seals. If the door seals are defective, it is probably the best indication that a refrigerator has passed its sell-by date and it is time to buy a new, energy-efficient model. Door mechanisms, hinges, and seals all deteriorate with age and use. If the door is not sealed properly when closed, the heat pumps are working overtime to cool both the interior and the whole room because of the air leaking through the door. Defective door seals may be obvious from a visual inspection. But a slight warping and degrading may not be so apparent. To check the seals, darken the room and place a light source such as a torch inside. Any light escaping will draw attention to defective areas. The presence of ice inside freezers, either on the door or on the produce nearest the door, is also a sure sign of defective seals. Have you ever inadvertently left a freezer door partly open for a few hours only to return and discover that the door won't close because of the build-up of ice?

Maybe the old freezer in the garage never seems to close properly because thick layers of ice continuously form around the door. Ice builds up at this point because the warmer room air carries more moisture, which condenses when it meets the cooler freezer air and forms water. This then turns to ice just inside the door. It may be that, once the ice defrosts and is removed, the door can again close securely. If the seals are defective, new ones, which are best sourced from the original manufacturer, are not cheap. Any tampering to improve seals should only be carried out by a professional, who can check the new seals and ensure that they function properly.

Minimize Frost Build-Up. Allowing ice to build up in a freezer, particularly on the coils, means that the compressor must work harder to maintain the set temperature. Regular defrosting is essential for energy efficiency. Most units today have automatic defrosting mechanisms. However, if ice build-up is a regular occurrence, it is a symptom of an underlying problem such as defective seals. The most likely source of ice build-up is moist air condensing when warmer room air meets the cooler refrigerator air. Equally, too much opening of the refrigerator or freezer allows warm, moist air in. Also, hot moist food should be allowed to cool plus it should be covered to prevent moisture escaping. It may also be that the refrigeration temperature has been set too low, causing overfreezing, and an upward adjustment may resolve the issue.

Minimize Door Opening. The majority of domestic refrigeration units are vertical, with side opening doors because this is ergonomically the most suitable arrangement. Chest freezers with a top opening are more awkward to use, given their depth, which can cause back strain to those stretching to reach in for an item. In fact, the chest freezer is much more efficient in terms of design than the upright freezer. Cold air is denser and rests at the bottom of the unit, so when the top lid is opened, the cold air doesn't escape. The same principle governs supermarket display refrigerators, which often have no cover.

The upright refrigerator and freezer has an inherent design fault. When you open the door, the cold air escapes and is immediately replaced by warm room air. Minimizing the amount of times the door is opened is paramount to energy efficiency, preventing the refrigerator from having to work overtime to maintain the set temperature. Many modern upright models also have horizontal drawers and sliding built-in container units. These allow the unit to achieve a top energy rating because, in test conditions, it scores maximum points in efficiency terms. The drawers and sliding containers provide reservoirs for cold air that is retained when the door is opened, thereby increasing efficiency. Unfortunately, these facts are not always explained to customers who often remove drawers for ease of use and because they take up valuable storage space.

Cooking

In many modern homes, busy lifestyles involve quick-fix meal preparation, and cooking habits have adapted accordingly. Often, cooking involves taking previously prepared frozen foods from the freezer and placing them straight into the oven, the cooker, or, most commonly, the microwave. The energy expended on cooking and preparation is not determined by our efficient appliances but by our choice of time-saving but energy-inefficient cooking habits and techniques.

For example, convection ovens can save up to 20% in energy usage to cook a standard meal, but this gain is immediately lost if the oven is unnecessarily preheated, extending the cooking time beyond that needed, or if only one item is cooked at a time. With a bit of planning, a full meal plus other baked items, for example, could have been cooked using the same amount of energy. The chosen energy type, electricity or gas, for instance, or the efficiency of the appliance– could offer some savings, but the real energy savings relate to technique and the length of time the cooking appliance is running. We are not used to being energy aware when cooking, so here are a few tips:

- Select the right size pot for the gas or electric ring to help reduce wasted heat. In simple terms, if a pot is half the size of the ring, it will waste half the heat.
- Always use pots with lids. This will keep in the heat and reduce the need for the extractor to work overtime, removing heat, moisture and cooking smells.
- Avoid preheating where possible unless the recipe specifically demands it (as with breads and cakes, for instance). Many modern ovens are virtually able to provide instantaneous full-temperature conditions, whereas the cookbook may have been written, or based upon, 1950's technology!
- Double up in the oven where possible. This might mean selecting appropriate pot sizes so they can fit into the oven together. If some foods need less cooking time, they should be placed in the oven for shorter periods.
- Normally we are advised not to use large flat trays or lay foil on racks because this reduces heat flow around the oven. However, these can sometimes allow dishes to be cooked at the same time at slightly different temperatures, where the top of the oven is hotter than the bottom.

- Too often, good energy in boiled water is poured down the drain. Consider reusing the liquid to cook or to preheat something else.
- If water is boiling over, keep the lid on and reduce the temperature. Remember water does not get any hotter after it is boiled!
- Never leave cooking appliances on standby. As with all other phantom loads, you might be surprised how much it is actually costing you.

It seems that very many of our TV celebrity chefs are completely ignorant of the energy- and water-use costs incurred in their endeavors. As an energy consultant, I have visited many commercial working kitchens. In every case, the same pattern was repeated: A host of heating and cooking devices is left in a state of readiness just in case diners change their mind and order something extra. All ovens are preheated and left on standby to shorten the preparation time, pots are rarely fitted with lids and boil over, the extraction system is constantly running to keep heat and moisture under control, and taps, often hot taps, are left running for chef's convenience. Even when the amateur master chef is at work, the same readiness for every eventuality is evident and every kitchen utensil is used. There may be as much energy needed in the clean up as was required for food preparation.

Clothes and Dishwashers

Washing machines use energy for a number of specific purposes: to heat water, run pumps and motors to rinse dishes, and heat coils and fans to dry dishes. More than half of the energy needed to wash dishes is expended on heating the water. It stands to reason that dishwashers using less water will use less electricity (water usage is discussed in Step 7)

Most machines provide two options for connecting to a water supply, either to cold supply only or to dual hot and cold. Which should you use? Modern dishwashers have a built-in energy-efficient heating system. This brings the water to the required wash-programme temperature. This is often the better option because there are many losses in the distribution system with a direct connection to the hot water supply. One exception is when there is a plentiful supply of renewably generated hot water, as with solar thermal, (see Step 6 and Step 7). It is also not unusual for other forms of renewable electricity generators to effectively dump extra power into the hot water system as storage This is regularly done by micro wind turbines and solar PV, when extra electricity is more cost-effectively used to heat water than exported to the grid (see also Step 5). In these situations, it is worth connecting to this often abundant hot water supply for as many uses as possible, including dishwashing and laundry.

While washing machines have numerous settings, most people have little time to read the instruction manuals and don't take time to figure out the optimum settings. There are just a few settings common to most dishwashers that can, if used correctly, save considerable costs in power and water usage. The percentages noted below are not cumulative but, combined, could amount to over 50% in energy and water savings.

- **Pre-Rinse**: Often an optional extra on many machines. It should rarely be selected, allowing you to save as much as 20% in energy and water usage.
- **Temperature Settings**: Different detergents have different recommended temperature settings. Many machines have an energy saving, economy, or eco setting where the temperature drops from 65oC to 55oC, and this can provide equally good results. Estimated saving 25%.
- **Machine versus Hand-Wash**: There seems to be as many high-level studies carried out to determine whether using a machine or hand-washing clothes or dishes is more efficient as there are bath versus shower studies. The reality is, whether it's dishwashers, washing machines, hand-washing, baths, or showers, the focus must be on efficient use, that's the winner.

Lighting

Improving the energy efficiency of light bulbs and how they are used can be the simplest way of making significant electricity cost savings. Lighting currently accounts for 17% of the domestic spend on household appliances and upward of 10% of our energy spend. The cost of lighting energy is second only to heating and cooling energy costs in most homes. Interestingly, the cost of electric lighting rose considerably over the past 40 years but reached a peak in the late 1990s and has steadily dropped since. The introduction of energy-saving bulbs and government bans on certain incandescent high-energy bulbs (old-style bulbs) can account for the savings, but there are many more savings to be made. The big problem with lighting is simple: bulbs are left on for too long. Even low-energy bulbs left on 24/7 will use a lot of electricity. Remember, time is the big multiplier in electricity costs. You save electricity every time you turn off the lights. There are many myths that suggest that turning on and off the lights uses more energy and damages the bulbs. This was true with the old style incandesent bulbs, but today's compact fluorescent light bulbs, CFLs, and light-emitting diodes, LEDs, are more robust and their energy saving credentials far outway any minor lighting on/off energy demands. Dimmable switches and motion sensors add considerable additional energy savings potential to all types of lighting systems.

In the home, there are only two choices you have to make when replacing old incandesent bulbs and that is CFL or LED. They are both tried and tested technology, produce good light, have direct replacement fixings, and save considerable energy.

Why Choose LED?

- Uses 70% – 90% less energy than old style incandesent bulbs
- Provides the same brightness (lumens) with less energy (watts)
- Lasts 10 to 25 times longer than incandesents
- Produces little heat and are durable and reasonably robust
- Many models are dimmable
- Gets fully bright instantly
- Helps reduce carbon emissions

While the purchase price for LEDs is high, the savings in terms of energy efficiency and lifetime warranty make them an easy first choice in any energy upgrade.

Why Choose CFL?

- Uses up to 70% less energy than incandesents bulbs
- Provides the same brightness with less energy, but slight delay in lighting up
- Lasts 4/5 times longer than incandesents
- Produces little heat but are also fragile
- Helps reduce carbon emissions

CFL bulbs are not quite as efficent as LED type, but because they are less expensive they represent an opportunity for significent energy and cost savings.

In the past, purchasing a replacement bulb was straightforward; you simply replaced the old one for a new one of the same wattage. Today, it's a little more complex, with many governments banning the sale of the old-style incandesent bulbs, simple replacement is not an option. As consumers, we have to balance energy costs with achieving the brightness we require with the color and appearance we prefer.

Brightness

Old Incandescent Bulbs (Watts)	Energy Star Bulb Brightness (Minimum Lumens)
40	450
60	800
75	1,100
100	1,600
150	2,600

Use the chart above to determine how many lumens you need to match the brightenss of your old incandescent bulbs. For brightness, look for lumens, not watts. Lumens indicate light output. Watts indicate energy consumed.

When buying CFLs or LEDs, first look for the lumens as an indication of brightness or light output. Watts indicate energy consumed rather than energy output, but a good rule of thumb for matching old -tyle bulb wattages with energy-efficient bulb brightness in lumens is indicated in the table below. When shopping for lights it is now neccesary to choose the color and appearance of the light emitted from the bulb. Light color or appearance matches a temperature on the Kelvin scale (K). Lower K values mean warmer yellowish light and higher K values means cooler blue light.

When it comes to outdoor lighting, it is essential that the lowest available wattages are chosedn because outdoor lights tend to be left on for lengthy periods. This is particularly important when considering security lights because floodlights, by their very nature, require more power. Motion sensors and photo-sensors considerably reduce the energy use and should be an integral part of all outdoor lighting installations. As the cost of LED bulbs and solar photovoltaic, PV, systems has fallen, the integration of solar LED is an extreemely efficient method of providing renewable energy for outdoor lighting.

Renewable Electricity

The realization that fossil fuel supplies are diminishing is the catalyst for the current drive by national governments to find new sources of renewable energy. This book is not about macro energy sources, such as major onshore and offshore wind farms and fields of PV arrays, but the smaller micro systems that can apply to every household. In Step 5, we looked at the micro sources of renewable heat generation such as biomass, heat pumps, and solar thermal. Here, we are looking at micro sources of electricity production, small-scale measures that are feasible in any home or building. The main options for producing renewable electricity are:

- Solar PV
- Micro wind turbines
- Micro hydro schemes
- Small anaerobic digester (AD) plants

As we saw in Step 5, choosing the right renewable heat source is all about ensuring a readily available supply of biomass, ground source heat or unobstructed solar aspect to harness energy from the sun. Similarily, the key first step with renewable electricity generation is to consider the availability of power resources, whether solar irradience, wind speed, or feedstock for AD plants. If your property is shaded from the sun or sheltered from the wind, solar PV and wind generation are not viable options. If there is no stream or river nearby, hydro power is out. For anaerobic digestion, because the fuel sources may change over time, dependence on such factors as the local availability of energy crops, animal slurry, or food waste, it is important to consider the longer term feedstock-fuel source availability.

For electricity generation, solar PV installations are generally the most widely applicable and simplest of energy projects to undertake. The availability of sunlight as a fuel resource is easily determined by examining maps, checking the property's orientation, and ensuring there is no shade from adjoining buildings or trees. Planning issues tend to be down to the simple matter of whether or not the installations are visually intrusive. The installation process is not complex, and the cost of the technology is reducing year on year. Unquestionably, in ten years, it will be common practice to orient all new roofs to facilitate the installation of solar panels for electricity and thermal heating.

The potential for some other forms of onsite electricity generation should always be considered. People generally know without too much analysis whether their site is suitable for erecting a wind turbine. Too many surrounding buildings or trees shading the site make it unlikely that there will be sufficient wind available to harvest. If the available open space is too small or too close to neighboring properties, or if it is designated an area of conservation, obtaining planning permission for a wind turbine might not be possible. For micro hydro power, the availability or otherwise of suitable locations on local streams or rivers is a first determinant. If they do not exist, that eliminates hydroelectric power options. But even if they do, there is a multiplicity of issues, from legal access rights to environmental matters, that makes generating power from a watercourse one of the most complicated of planning processes. Nonetheless, hydro power is always worth investigating because generating electricity from water is one of the most rewarding renewable processes and not just in a narrow financial sense.

Anaerobic digestion (AD) is a complex process in terms of both available fuel/feedstock and environmental planning processes. But like hydro power, it is well worth considering because it is potentially a 24/7, year-round operation. AD is traditionally more suitable to the larger end of micro electricity generation (500kW per hour). But as technology improves, plant sizes down to 25kW are now possible. Since 1990, Germany has had a policy of encouraging the take-up of AD and now has over 7,500 AD systems installed throughout the country. In developing countries and parts of China and India, there are millions of small working AD systems and many small homesteads and farms have one as a matter of course. With AD systems, the major gain is not just electricity generation. There are many environmental benefits, which are discussed below.

Solar Photovoltaic

Solar photovoltaic, or solar PV for short, is a cell made from silicon that generates electricity from sunlight/daylight interacting with photovoltaic panels. The word photovoltaic derives from Greek, where photo means light and voltaic means voltage. This is not the same as and should not be confused with solar thermal panels, where the power of the sun is used to directly heat water or fluids. Solar PV is a relatively new technology, advanced considerably by U.S. scientists to power satellites in space.

Photovoltaic is the direct conversion of light into electricity, using materials such as silicon that exhibit a property known as the photoelectric effect, which means that they absorb photons of light and release electrons. When the free electrons are released, an electric current results. If this is managed using a series of metal strips, for example,

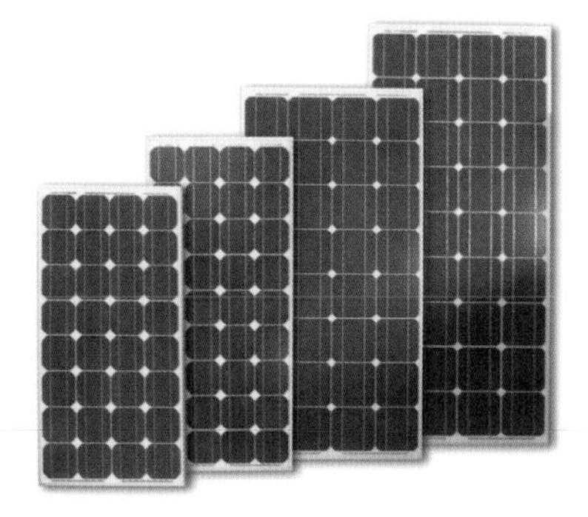

electricity can be made to flow. Each individual small solar cell will produce very little electricity, but a large number of solar cells connected to each other and mounted in a support structure called a photovoltaic panel or module will potentially combine the electrical units. These panels can then be added in sequence to produce a much larger power output, even to the extent of solar farms covering many acres of ground and producing megawatts of electricity.

The solar PV units we are probably most familiar with are very small and used to charge the batteries in watches, calculators, mobile phones, and motorway signs. The big advantage of PV cells in these situations is that no cables or other external power sources are required; the PV cell is self-sufficient in terms of electricity generation.

Measuring Solar Fuel (Sunlight)

The fuel for PV systems is simply the amount of sunlight reaching the panel. Like all renewable energy sources, harnessing the sun's energy is a local issue, dependent on the local climate, regional location, and site-specific issues such as shading and property orientation. The angle at which the PV panel is placed relative to the sun's path and the time of day/year are also key factors. Not every site is suitable, and the key to getting the best performance out of every PV system is a basic understanding of how the sun's energy can best be used. The beauty of solar photovoltaic is that sunlight is available everywhere, no other feedstock is required, and no complex machinery is needed to harness the sun's energy. A solar PV installation is the ultimate in clean technology: it needs no moving parts, is silent, and requires little maintenance. While it will provide optimum electricity on a long and clear sunny day, it will also supply electricity on dull and overcast days. The more light there is, the more power the cells can generate.

An important issue here is temperature, which affects the performance of PV cells. Too high and there is a corresponding reduction in electrical output. Hotter locations, which naturally have longer hours of sunshine, can suffer from the drawback of overheating and hence reduced energy production. In this respect, cooler countries can often outperform hotter ones because overheating is less likely to occur. In terms of local conditions, there must be no obstructions such as trees, chimneys, or building overhangs to reduce the optimum amount of light striking the panel(s). There are a number of factors that must be taken into account to optimize the power generated at any location:

- Orientation of the panels and distance from the equator
- The average tilt angle of the sun's path
- Absence of shading
- Choice of panel, system design and configuration
- Type of mounting to allow tracking/ventilation

Solar irradiance is the all-important measure of solar light radiation hitting a given surface area at a given time. Most countries have developed reliable maps illustrating the amount of solar energy available over the year at various locations. The information is cross-border, and much of it has been put together by NASA based on over 25 years of data from weather satellites. When outputs from potential solar PV units are being analyzed, solar irradience is always expressed in watts per square metre per year, or W/m2/yr.

All solar PV panels are sold with a universal international performance benchmark measure showing the peak output potential of the unit. This allows one panel to be fairly compared with another and for basic payback periods to be worked out based on electrical output versus capital purchase costs. Cheapest is rarely best, and the full lifetime of the unit should be taken into account when calculating payback time.

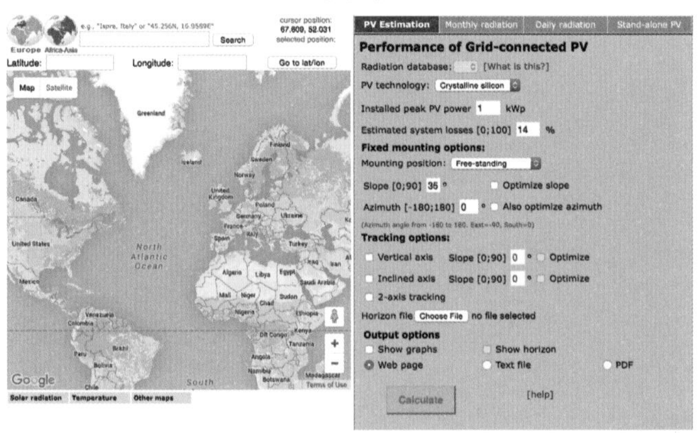

There are a number of good online simulation tools that can reasonably estimate the power output from a particular solar PV panel at a specific location. This free-to-use software is relatively simple to use: Enter the required location, the angle from the horizontal of the proposed panel, the N-S orientation, and the peak output to be installed. The software estimates the output and, depending on which simulation tool is used, may also offer a basic financial report outling indicative payback and annual income based on the local feed-in tariff and/or commercial market price for electricity. If dealing with a professional solar expert, you should request a copy of the energy analysis report for your particular site.

Types of Solar PV Panels

The solar PV market is growing fast. Governments and leading-edge technology companies around the world are involved in funding research and development into better, more efficient ways of delivering solar PV energy. This is welcome, and prices have dropped rapidly. It is estimated that the price of PV in the United Kingdom has dropped by over 50% to 2015. Given that the market is ever-changing as newer and better panels are regularly produced, comparing prices and systems is, however, difficult. Nonetheless, the popular marketing strategy for various manufacturers seems to be that they alone have the latest technology with the greatest outputs and at least X% greater efficiency than the nearest competition.

Having said that, there are still effectively only two conventional types of PV solar panels: crystalline silicon and thin film. Most common today is crystalline silicon, and this has two principal types, monocrystalline and polycrystalline. The thin film type is not yet as popular, but the technology is evolving fast, potentially allowing the technology to be manufactured on simple and cheap membranes for covering roofs, walls, bus shelters, or almost any available surface. There are also hybrids that can potentially provide even greater power using the strengths of the different technologies.

Monocrystalline

This is perhaps the most popular type of panel used today. It is certainly the most productive/m2, albeit the most expensive because it is made from a single large crystal. When the highly purified molten crystal is formed and allowed to cool, it takes the shape of a long cylinder. To make individual cells, this cylinder, or ingot as it is more correctly called, is sliced into very thin wafers of 0.3mm. These are then chamfered at the edges to allow them to be packed more tightly, which gives the monocrystalline solar panel a distinctive uniform appearance. The cells themselves are black and are usually mounted on a white background. However, increasingly, they are being placed on a black background and in a black frame and may then blend discretely into the background on a dark roof.

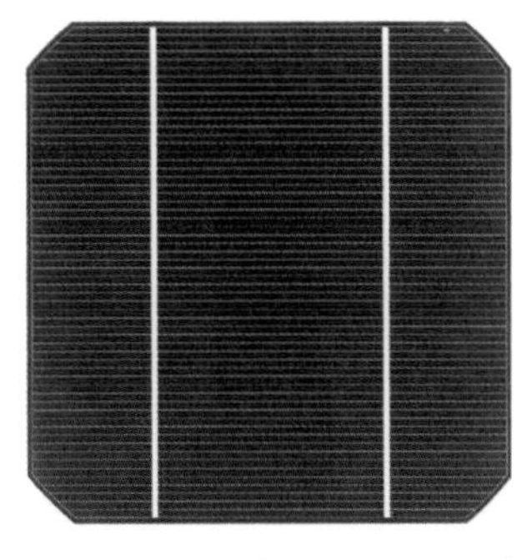

Efficiency levels of these monocrystalline panels are in the higher ranges of 18%–20%; meaning they produce electricity in the proportion of 18%–20% of the total annually available sunlight irradiation at a given location. They can extract viable energy from indirect sunlight, even on cloudy days. The basic system prices are in the $600–$700/kW peak range, installed. They are durable and should come with a 25-year warranty to match the typical feed-in tarriff time period but will reasonably last for longer. The key elements when it comes to durability are the frame, coating, and fixings, all of which should be specifically included in the warranty. The finishing coatings in particular must be specified to suit the local environment; for instance, installations in coastal regions need to be salt-resistant.

Polycrystalline

Polycrystalline solar panels are made from multiple crystals. The manufacturing process is quite different to the monocrystalline panels insofar as different ingredients are added to the molten silicon to create a mixture of smaller crystals, forming larger cube-shaped crystal. The cubic ingot crystal is then cut into very thin square or rectangular wafers, allowing for easy placement of cells on the solar panel. The efficiency of the polycrystalline cell in terms of converting light into electricity is reduced because of the random alignment of the multiple crystals present, and it is not as effective as the single monocrystalline type. It is, however, cheaper to manufacture, and the cubic shape of the cells means that they stack better on the solar panels.

Polycrystalline solar panels have a distinctive appearance. They resemble shattered glass and normally have a blue/black color. The modules typically have slightly lower efficiencies in the region of 14%–18%. The standard price averages at about $600 per kWp, depending on scale and locally available incentives. The quality of the frame is all important and warranties should cover the entire unit.

Flat Film/Thin Film

The term "flat film" or "thin film" solar PV is a general name for the use of amorphous-type materials in the manufacture of indefinite-sized solar panels. Amorphous means without structure. The formed flat film product is more akin to that of glass than crystal, and hence the flat film can be much thinner than other types of solar PV. The manufacturing process involves depositing amorphous silicon (although other materials can also be used) on a substrate, usually glass, plastic, or metal.

One of the advantages of this process is that the substrates need not be rigid, which allows for widespread possible applications, even on such flexible materials as curved PVC roofing and vinyl sheeting. A number of manufacturers are also screen printing low-cost amorphous solar films, and these have a multitude of potential uses on building façades, carport exteriors, and the surface of roofing materials such as tiles. It is a much cheaper technology, but it is currently barely half as productive per m^2 as the other technologies.

These panels are the least efficient at converting light into electricity, with typical efficiencies in the region of 5%–10%. The price range varies depending on the quality and purpose of the substrate, but the standard range is $300 per kWp installed.

Another advantage of thin film is that it is particularly good at generating electricity even on overcast days or when the panel is not in the optimium position. Even on moonlit nights, it can generate some power. This technology currently only accounts for approximately 5% of installed sites, but, given its tremendous flexibility and the rapid fall in costs, its market share is destined to increase in the future.

Wind

The principles of extracting power from wind are not new. Wind as a form of energy has been used worldwide since Roman times for such tasks as powering grain mills, pumping water, and transporting goods by sea. Countries such as Germany and Denmark now have wind power generation embedded into their electricity supply systems at a significant level, having led the world for 20 years in the development of wind technology and related management software systems. Other nations have been rapidly catching up over the past 10 years, notably the United States and China, harvesting the potential of their wind energy ron a massive scale. Britain and Ireland in particular have special advantages in terms of this resource. Over 40% of Europe's land-based wind resource exists in the British Isles, as the warm Gulf Stream is accompanied by consistently strong winds. Ireland currently draws nearly 20% of its total energy supply from wind and aims to double this figure by 2030.

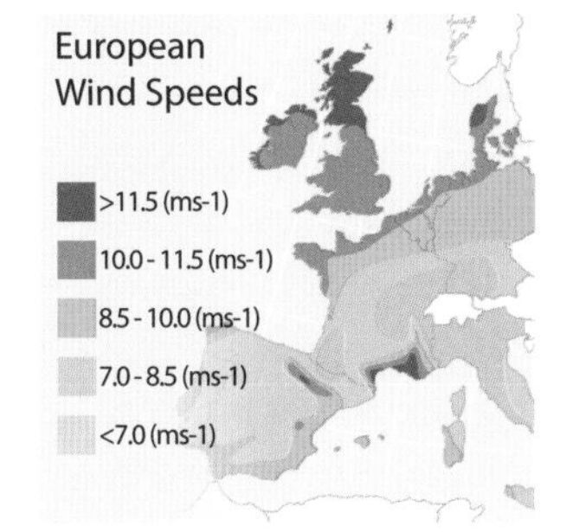

How Do Wind Turbines Work?

Modern wind turbines seek to convert the power of the wind into usable electricity. Wind is the fuel, one derived from solar energy. The turbine converts this fuel into electricity. Like solar power, good performance is dependent on choosing the right location. In other words, is it a site with good average wind-speeds? and what are the other remarkable local climatic conditions? If there is a good wind resource available – usually estimated to be a minimum average of 5m/s wind speed – uninterrupted by local topographical features, trees, or buildings, there is potential for wind power.

Wind speed increases with height, so, within reason, the higher the turbine the better. The most important guide when selecting a site is what is referred to as the "rule of cubes," which means a small increase in wind speed leads to a proportionately much larger increase in the quantity of electricity produced. For instance, if the wind speed doubles, the electricity produced by the turbine may be multiplied by a factor of 8. The opposite is equally true because, as wind speed reduces, there is the same exaggerated reduction in the quantity of electricity produced. The net effect is that wind turbines are highly viable on the better sites but are hard to justify on a "fair" site because there will be a disproportionately lower electricity output.

Unlike solar energy, which is relatively easy to predict, wind energy is more complex. Site selection is the most vital consideration, followed by appropriate turbine size. Small wind turbines on good sites can generate very little electricity, and large turbines on the same site can generate very large amounts of electricity (that is when the wind is blowing!). The bigger the wind turbine, the more energy it can produce.

What is Small Wind?

Most people today are familiar with large wind turbines, whether on a hilltop or out at sea. They are the iconic pictures presented by many power companies to reflect an image of clean, low-carbon energy that is loved by some and hated by others. Then there are small turbines that the DIY expert can buy and bolt onto the side of the house. They may not actually produce any worthwhile electricity.

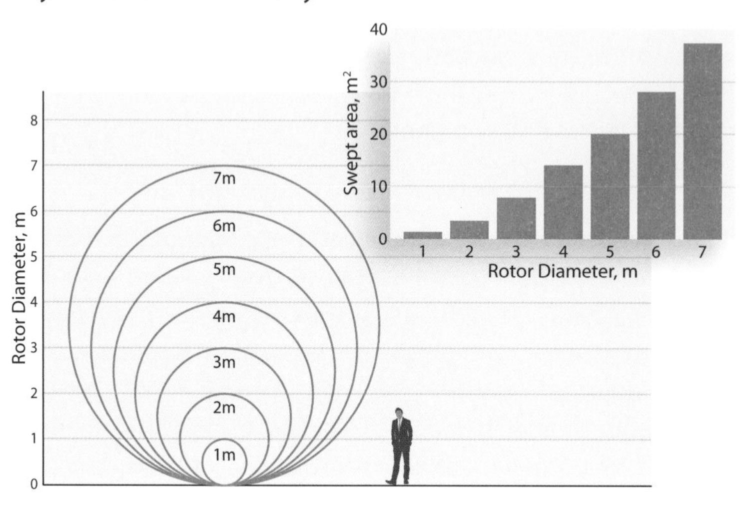

There is no real universal definition of small wind, but probably the best effort is that made by Renewable UK, which classifies micro wind as less than 1.5kW, small wind between 1.5kW and 50kW, and medium wind between 50kW and 500kW. Above 500kW is obviously large and will most likely refer to wind farms or large industry turbines. With micro- and small-wind, the electricity generated is for individual properties and the lower sizes are those covered by micro feed-in tariffs.

Power of the Wind

There is an all-important equation that defines the power of the wind, which is worth examining because it defines the golden rules upon which wind turbine design and location are based. The mathematical equation that determines the power in the wind is:

$$P = \frac{1}{2} DAV3$$

This equation gives an estimate of the power available to a wind turbine

P is the power available to be harnessed from the wind and measured in watts. However, no matter how efficient the turbine design or how sleek and aerodynamic the blade shapes, a maximum of 59% of energy can be extracted from the wind; this is known as the Betz limit. Air density D varies with temperature, humidity, and elevation and can affect the power of a wind turbine by as much as 20%. You can imagine on a warm summer's evening when the air feels light, there isn't the same mass or capacity to turn the propeller blades as there might be on a cold winter's morning. A represents the area or circle size swept by the blades of the turbine. Doubling the size of this area doubles the power output. You may remember from school that the area of a circle is defined by its radius (r). Wind turbines are often described by the length of the blades. As the blade size increases, – which is r in the area of a circle equation $A = \pi r^2$. So in basic mathematics, a 6m radius turbine can harness four times more power from the wind than a 3m radius turbine. When choosing a turbine, therefore, the bigger the radius of the blades, the higher the power output.

Wind speed, V, is the most important variable factor in the equation. Most manufacturers selling into the market measure wind speed in meters per second (m/s). There is other terminology such as knots, feet per second, and miles per hour, but the simplest and most universal is the S.I. measurement, m/s. The velocity of the wind is cubed in the equation V^3, which caters for the exponential effect mentioned earlier. Consequently, small increases in wind speed have dramatic effects on power output – remember that if you double the wind speed, the power is increased eightfold.

Types of Wind Turbines

There are two main types of wind turbines. The first, horizontal axis wind turbines, or HAWTs, are the most common. They are seen on wind farms and can be any size. The second type, vertical axis wind turbines (or VAWTs), are not as common and are arguably not as efficient, but they have advantages in terms of lower noise levels and greater potential to harness wind in even problematic urban locations.

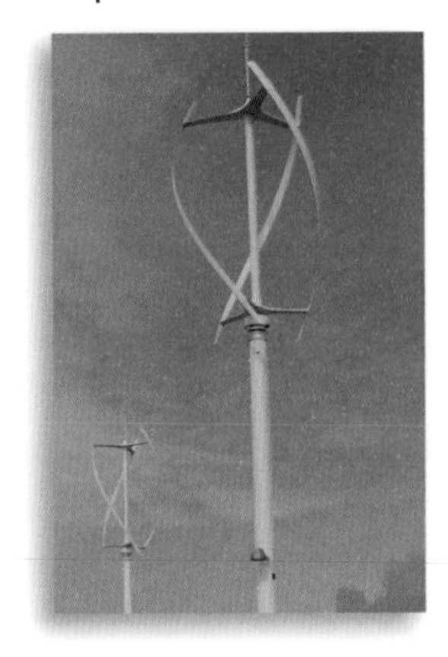

Horizontal wind turbines are considered conventional technology. Often, they have three blades, rotating around a horizontal axis at the top of the pole. The bulbous section at the top houses the mechanisms for the gears and/or magnets that convert the wind power to electricity. The natural aerodynamics of the rotor blade shape means that the turbine will always face into the wind. Some turbines have a tail piece to allow them to change direction and adjust to meet the oncoming wind. In very powerful winds (e.g. gale force 8 on the Beaufort Scale), a mechanism is triggered that forces the turbine to turn away from the wind and cease spinning for reasons of safety. Other safety measures include furling, which means the rotor blades are designed to distort or furl and lose their aerodynamic shape in high winds.

Vertical turbines are becoming more popular because of their greater adaptability to the urban environment. The actual shape can vary significantly from one turbine to the next. However, their common feature is that the main axis runs vertically, allowing the gears and mechanisms to be located at ground level. Sometimes, artistic endeavor runs a bit wild in design terms and it seems as if aesthetics can be more important than efficiency. Thus, they are often used as a design statement or as a "green" message to the public by their creators.

Rural and Urban Sites

Before deciding to choose wind as an energy source, it is essential to establish local available wind speeds. Ascertaining the wind speed at, say, a height of 40m is straightforward. The details are readily available from wind speed maps similar to the one pictured above. It is more difficult to work out the precise available wind resource at the exact height and location of the specific proposed turbine for your site or building. There are some very good web sites with free estimation tools, but before looking at those it's worth getting a basic understanding of the factors that affect site selection and of how to measure wind speed.

Wind speed in rural locations can be a little bit easier to determine than in urban areas. Common sense suggests that open sites in coastal areas, on hilltops, and in exposed areas will have better available wind speeds. This is borne out by the wind map for Europe (shown above), which shows that the wind resources for the whole of Scotland and Ireland are the best in Europe. Other factors to consider include the local topography and whether objects such as natural projections, trees, buildings, or other obstructions may intercept the otherwise smooth flow of the wind. In Britain and Ireland, the prevailing winds are from the southwest, and it is critical that proposed turbines in these locations are unobstructed and open to all winds from this direction.

A "wind rose" is a useful conceptual tool for describing the proportion of wind power (i.e. % time X average wind-speed) that impacts your chosen site from all possible directions. Most sites have impediments and obstructions, so the "wind rose" describes whether such obstructions are located in a critically important place or whether they may be of little concern. See an example of an actual "wind rose" pattern below.

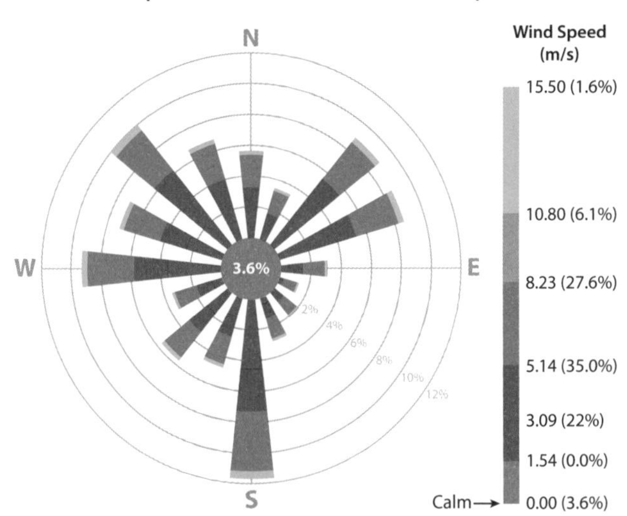

Topographical features such as water, grass, trees ,and buildings have a different effect on the wind speed as it passes over them. As you move from water, which has a minimal effect on wind speed, to agricultural grassland, which has a moderately small effect, to woodlands and urban developments, which may reduce the wind speed to zero, the height of the turbine becomes critial. The higher you go above the surface of the earth, the greater the wind speeds.

Therefore, the key factors when assessing the power you can harness from the wind at a given site are: Wind speed and pattern at the proposed location, turbine size, and turbine height. This is relatively simple to assess in a rural setting, but not so easy in urban settings where a turbine should ideally tower above the height of surrounding buildings to capture the free-flowing non-turbulent winds. This is generally not possible because of issues such as aesthetics, noise, flicker, and various other neighbor-intrusive problems.

Urban wind turbines need to be smaller and building-mounted, which places them right in the turbulence zone. Vertical-axis wind turbines are better at capturing energy from turbulent wind, are quieter, and tend to be more popular in urban environments. The biggest problem in capturing wind in a built-up area is accurately measuring the flow and wind speed. The built terrain directs the wind into all sorts of turbulent flows, and the slightest change of direction might mean that a strong wind speed goes to zero in a matter of seconds. There are very sophisticated measuring devices and analytical software available for measuring wind speeds, but because urban wind is completely site-specific, general site measurements can be extremely misleading. The measurements must be recorded at the exact location of the proposed turbine and at the precise proposed hub-height. Site-specific wind analysis in a dense, high-rise urban environment can be costly because of the volume of testing required, particularly relative to the lower potential income that can be generated from such a smaller turbine.

Small Hydro Power

It is not possible to discuss hydroelectric power without a little history. Hydroelectric power has been around for a long time, notably in the form of watermills. There were probably many more watermills in use 1,000 years ago than there are today. A survey prepared for William I in 1086 identified over 6,000 watermills in Britain. The mills were found in every location where a process needed more consistent power than man or animals could provide.

Typically, water-power power was used for grinding corn, oats, and barley. As the industrial era dawned, different examples of its use emerged, including:

- Saw mills to cut timber
- Textile mills for spinning and weaving cloth and carpet
- Paper mills for pressing and producting paper
- Cotton mills for cleaning and producing cotton
- Iron mills for creating furnaces and forges for metal tools
- Rolling mills for pressing and shaping metal
- Innovative powerful pumping stations for large urban water and sewerage schemes in the 18th and 19th centuries.

The advent of cheap and easily available fossil fuels drew people away from using water-power. The only type of water-powered construction built in any great quantity over the past century is the hydroelectric turbine for producing electricity. In many parts of the world, hydroelectric schemes account for up to 50% of total electricity generated. The construction of major hydroelectric schemes, where large waterways and river courses must first be dammed, can be highly controversial, both in terms of the negative impact on a region's biodiversity and the displacement of people from their homes.

The location of small hydroelectric schemes can also be very intrusive if not properly designed. The secret to a success is to replicate the spirit of the old watermills and reflect and respect the existing ecosystem such that there is no adverse effects on the local environment. Planning regulations, which we will discuss later, are also a key component.

How Small Hydro Power is Generated

There is a subtle difference between how a watermill works and how a hydro turbine works. Watermills are designed to operate machinery directly. There are no real losses other than friction, and there is a direct relationship between the power in the water and the power transferred to the milling device. Storage of power is not an option, so there are no storage losses. Hydro turbines, on the other hand, need a good current or head of water before they become efficient at converting water pressure into electricity. Not every site suitable for a watermill will also be suitable for a hydro turbine. If you are investigating the possibility of a new hydro site, the location of an old watermill is a good place to start.

Hydro power is the most site-specific of all the renewables. Without a suitable water source, generating hydroelectric power at your property is simply not an option. If there is a suitable water source, further questions will then need to be answered. First is water quantity. Ideally, a large volume of fast-flowing water is required. Most people will generally be aware of the presence of such a water source on their property or in their neighborhood, and features such as waterfalls are easily recognized. There can be less obvious situations that may have potential, such as where a lake feeds a canal or a reservoir discharges into a collection lake. The restricted flow may have focused hydraulic energy at these places. Similarily, at manmade weirs, a partially restricted flow could be harnessed to generate energy. Often, the fall in a river or stream may not be immediately apparent. A watercourse meandering across a farm with seemingly level fields may hide a fall in levels of 5m over 100m length, for example. This is only a 5% fall, which is not always detectable without some form of measurement, but a 5m head could provide sufficient electricity to power a reasonable generator.

When assessing the potential of a watercourse to provide sufficient electricity, an equally important consideration is the seasonal flow rate. Many rivers, streams, brooks, etc., have minimal flows in summer and can run dry in times of drought. In all situations, the biodiversity of the watercourse must be taken into account. Whether the turbine mechanism interferes directly or indirectly with the flow must be assessed before any decisions are made regarding the suitability of the site. Changing or interrupting the natural course of water must only be done with the utmost respect for all the life-supporting functions it serves. Water has meandered its way across hills, valleys, and flatlands for millennia, and it rests in lakes and reservoirs or races along in fast-flowing rivers and streams when it can. It may meander around at a more leisurely pace when the land levels out and the pressure is off. Water flowing in all its forms has its own way of dealing with flow rates. For example, the meandering shapes of river courses slow down the fast-flowing water by taking the energy out of the flow as it negotiates the bends.

Provided the flow of the water and its populations of fish and other fauna are not interfered with, harnessing the available energy can be a sustainable, secure and cost-effective way of generating electricity. The planning regulations for hydro turbines are the most rigorous of all the renewable micro-energy systems, however.

Measuring Head and Flow

The first step when designing a small hydro system is measuring the head, H, and the flow, Q. The head is the measured distance between the highest and lowest point along a section of watercourse. At a steep section, such as a waterfall, the head can simply be the height of the waterfall. In most other cases, it can be a little more difficult to establish and measure. The principle is that head height is the vertical drop of the flow of the water, measured in meters. Sites with a head of greater than 50m would normally be classed as high, from 10m to 50m as medium, and below 10m as low. Head heights below 2m would generally be considered too small to be economically viable for energy generation. If head height has to be measured over a length of river, an ordnance survey map could be a good starting point, using the most appropriate and local contours to establish the drop in levels. A simple tape measure and spirit level can give a good approximation for preliminary calculations. For the more experienced, a laser level or theodolite can provide as much accuracy as is needed.

The flow is the volume of water passing a particular point, measured in metres per second m^3/s. To get a good approximation of the flow, we need two measurements: the volume of water flowing in the water channel and the speed at which it flows. To make the measuring easier, find a straight section of stream, ideally without any brambles or stones that could disrupt the flow. I say stream specifically because trying to take measurements at a river or deep, fast-flowing watercourse without the right equipment might be dangerous for the inexperienced. To find the volume, we need to measure the width of the stream and the average depth. To estimate the flow, begin by marking two points on the riverbank, say 1m apart, then throw a light stick into the stream and record the time it takes for the stick to flow past the first point to the second. Because the bed of the stream is probably uneven and the movement of the stick in the water will be a bit random, the measurements should be repeated a few times and an average taken. For example, let's say the stream is 6m wide with an average depth of 0.3m, this would equate to an area of $1.8m^2$.

The amount of electricity generated by the turbine is dependent on the head of water, the flow of water, and the efficiency of the turbine at converting this kinetic energy into electrical energy. Most micro turbines have an efficiency of between 60% and 80% depending on the make and model and how well it is designed to match the site's water conditions. The general formula for the power in the stream is: (see p141 V2)

$$\textit{Power (kW)} = 6 \times \textit{Head (m)} \times \textit{Flow } (m^3/sec)$$

$$\textit{Head} = 6m \qquad \textit{Flow} = 1.8m^3$$

$$\textit{Power} = 7 \times 6 \times 1.8 = 75.6 \text{ kW}$$

Types of Hydro Turbines

There are two main types of hydro turbines, categorized according to how they are designed to respond to flowing water. The first type is the impulse turbine, which works when the water is brought to it via high-pressure jets. It functions best under high pressure from a large head of water, usually diverted from a river and piped direct to the turbine, via a pipe known as a penstock. The turbine consists of a wheel with a series of split cups that are driven in a continuous circular motion under the force of the water jets. The water is then discharged back to the river, a little downstream from where it was extracted.

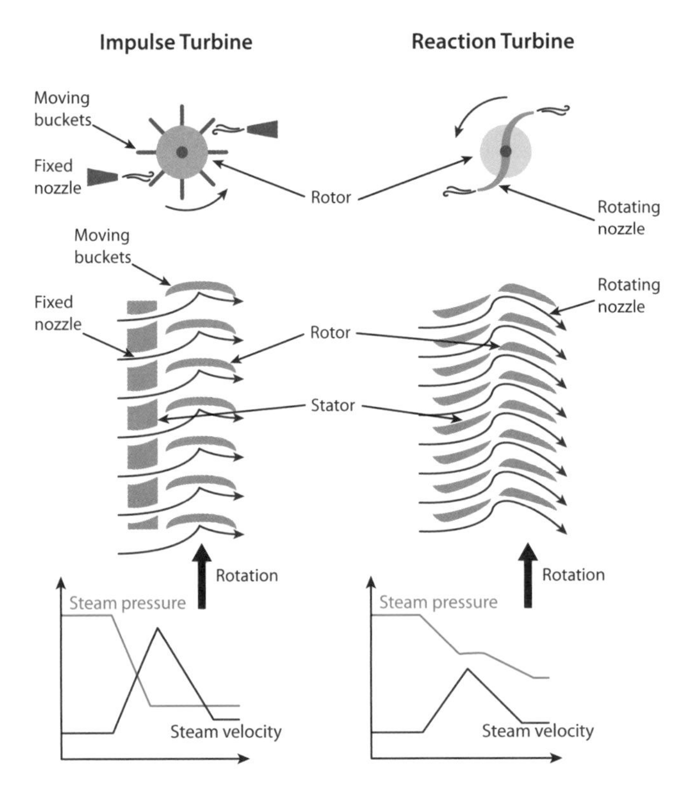

The most common types of impulse turbines are the Pelton, Turgo and Crossflow models. The Pelton and Turgo turbines are largely similar but vary depending on the angle at which the water jets hit their propellers. This angle can be important insofar as the discharged water must be dispelled quickly so that the propellers stay in continuous motion. Both types are very popular for micro-hydro systems. The Crossflow turbine is different from most other types because it does not have the standard wheel shape. Instead, it has a cylindrical shape with a large number of sharp blades. Crossflow turbines can be equally efficient at harnessing energy across both high- and low-flow rivers. They are popular for use in rivers, where water levels and flows change seasonally. Historically, the water wheel was the most common impulse-type machine. It is less popular today because it is not that efficient, but there are many places where, for conservation and amenity purposes, water wheels are being rebuilt.

The second turbine type is the reaction turbine. This is either fully submerged in the flow of the water or encased to contain the water pressure. The casing is needed to contain water flow and pressure. These turbines react to the flow of water like the propellers of a boat by extracting the water pressure to create movement in the turbine blades. The most common types are Francis and Propeller turbines.

The Francis turbine is one of the most common in use. It is a propeller-type where the water flows radially and inward. The water is received at high pressure and causes the turbine to spin before the water exits at low pressure. High levels of efficiency are achieved with the Francis turbine because of the decreasing radius of the spinning blades as the water enters the casing. The process is similar to the movement of gears on a bicycle, only in reverse.

Anaerobic Digestion (AD)

Anaerobic digestion is perhaps the least known renewable energy system. AD is very much a natural process and refers to the breakdown of organic matter in an enclosed vessel called a digester. Without access to air and the oxygen in it (i.e. in anaerobic conditions), decomposition of organic matter by certain specialized bacteria takes place in the digester. Large volumes of highly valuable biogas are produced. It is high in hydrogen and methane, and it can be used to run a conventional fossil fuel engine. In turn, the engine can produce heat, or electrical power, or both in the case of a combined heat and power, CHP, unit. The waste residue (digestate) is a high-quality, safe, and clean renewable fertilizer or soil conditioner. This process offers an almost perfect solution for dealing with streams of organic waste matter.

A similar, possibly more familiar, process is composting. The key difference is that composting is aerobic, where oxygen is part of the decomposition process. There is much less usable fuel gas produced than with AD, and much more unwanted carbon dioxide (CO_2), the prime greenhouse gas. In addition, the quality of the left-over digestate is not nearly as good.

Feedstock suitable for an AD plant can include a wide variety of organic materials such as animal manures and slurries; plant cuttings and verge trimmings; farm-grown energy crops such as maize, silage, and grass; and quite a lot of food wastes.

There are approximately 250 digesters in operation in the United States today, most of which were installed in the last three years. By comparison, Germany has almost 7,600 plants and China has over 18 million smaller units. AD is successful in these and many other countries because their governments long ago recognized the many benefits of the process. Some of the many enviro-economic benefits of AD include:

- Fossil-fuel-free gas is produced instead of valueless and damaging CO_2
- Clean, usable, and highly beneficial digestate as a by-product
- Gate fees to the operator of the plant by taking in a waste
- Cost reduction to operations which produce organic waste
- Odor control – dramatic improvement available
- 100% landfill reduction in most cases
- Carbon credits or similar entitlements available to AD plants and/or their owners

How Does AD Work?

The best analogy I can make to explain how an AD plant works is to compare it to the natural digestive system in animals. The system digests and breaks down biomass using natural microorganisms in a similar fashion to the way the digestive tracts of cows use bacteria to break down and digest their feed stock. The resultant process releases a methane rich gas (biogas).

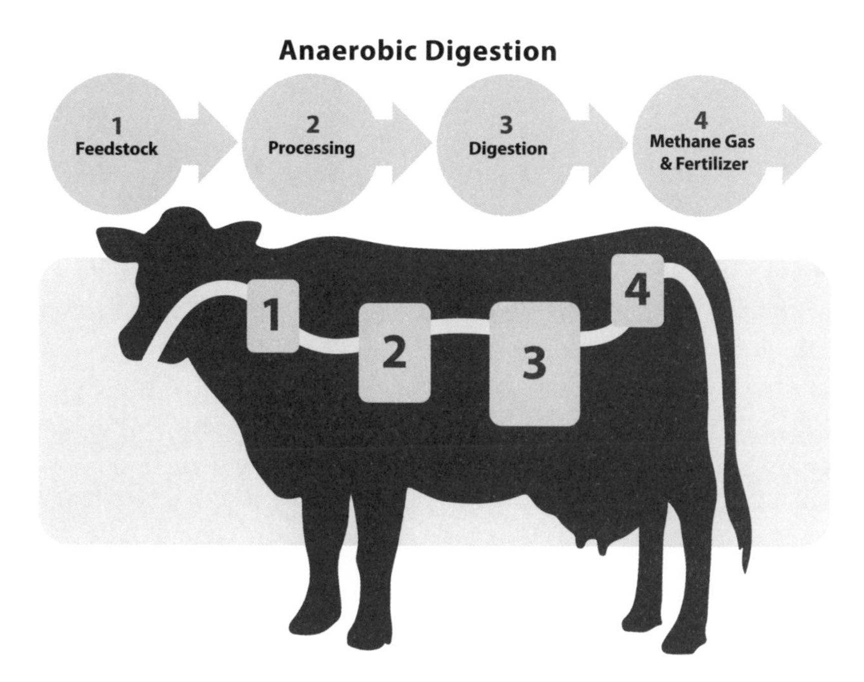

Every farmer knows that cattle must be fed a constant and regular balanced diet to maintain good health. Because summer and winter feedstock varies depending on climatic conditions, a farmer may have to add supplements to the feedstock such as cereals and protein feeds with added vitamins and minerals at different time of the year. If the farmer misfeeds or fails to feed the animals, they will not be healthy and, in extreem circumstances, may die. The anaerobic digester is no different. Failing to supply the correct quality and quantity of feedstock to the AD plant will prevent the system from operating at optium capacity. Poor management of the feedstock will result in failure of the AD plant and it may have to be de commisioned, resulting in weeks/months of lost revenue. Comparing the management of live cattle feeding with that of an AD plant is very appropriate. In both cases, you need experience gathered over time in a situation with hands-on learning and guidance where intuition is also developed.

Feedstock

Given that feedstock must travel to an AD plant, the first issue to address when considering the feasibility of such a plant is where the feedstock will come from. AD plants require a certain volume of feedstock to be economically viable. While technology is changing and different types of feedstock can produce higher quantities per ton of energy/gas, there is a rule of thumb that a minimum of 20,000 tonnes per year is required to make a modern plant economically viable.

There are perhaps five categories of suitable feedstock:

- Farm residuals, manure, slurry, animal feed waste, and bedding
- Agricultural products such as energy crops
- Municipal feedstock such as organic food waste
- Commercial organic waste such as food factory and brewing byproducts
- Municipal sewage

The AD plant works on a multiple digestion system, so by mixing materials with higher biogas potential, the overall gas output can be increased. The ideal mix will contain carbohydrates, proteins, and fats. The only organic material that digesters don't take is woody materials that the process cannot break down. Manure, while low on gas production, makes an ideal base feedstock because it contains healthy anaerobic bacteria that get the process going. From the table below, you can see that materials such as fats and greases have the highest biogas outputs. These are closely followed by bakery waste and then food scraps, energy crops, and farm manure.

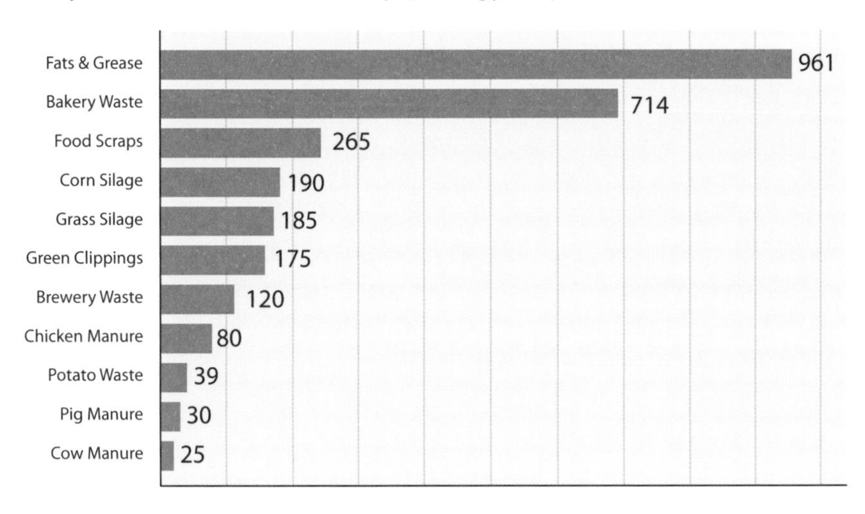

The fundamental concept behind AD is sustainability. The sources of feedstock must be available locally and not involve large fossil-fueled transport costs because this undermines the positive carbon footprint of the process. The planning authority and environmental agency will gauge this aspect of locally available feedstock, and it will be a key factor in the approval and licensing procedure. Using the biogas from an AD plant to run a fleet of vans is one option often used for extending the travel radius for sourcing potential feedstock without negatively impacting on the sustainability of the project.

Cooperatives among local farmers work very well. By pooling resources and feedstock supplies among members, larger AD plants, which are generally more economic than smaller ones, can be supported. It's not just farming communities that can benefit; any rural community within a village or town can come together in a cooperative fashion. Equally, the heat output, which is not always fully utilized on a farm, can benefit a community's houses, schools, factories, etc.

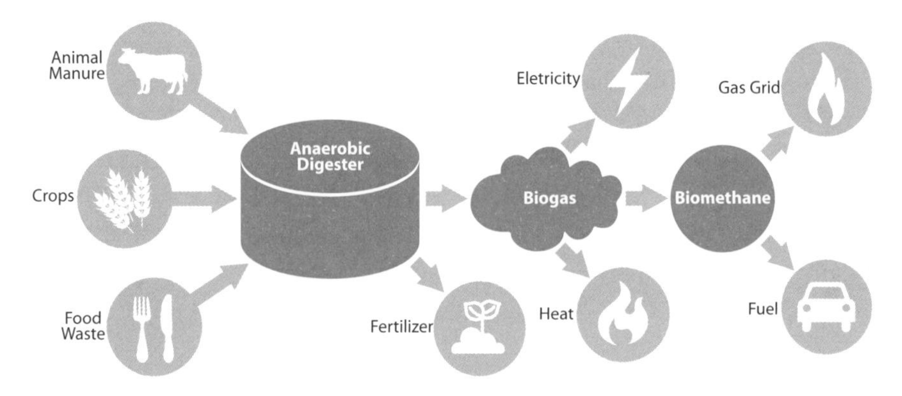

AD plants are also becoming a popular addition to many food-production plants, particularly large bakeries, producers of fresh cooked and packaged food, and suppliers of fruit and vegetables, which generate potentially large volumes of waste that are expensive to dispose of. The AD process turns this waste from a cost into an income-earning business asset. When the key feedstock ingredients have been sourced, it's also necessary to establish that there is an adequate continuous supply over time. Remember that the AD plant is a 20-year-plus business and security of feedstock supply needs to be reasonably secure for this time period.

The biogas tables are a good place to start when determining optimum feed mix based on locally available feedstock. They offer a rough idea of the quantities and types of materials necessary. To further improve the accuracy of biogas estimates, there are also some good online calculators. Enter the quantities and types of available feedstock, and the calculator estimates the gas output, the heat/electricity production, and remaining digestate quantities. No online calculator in the renewable energy industry is complete without also calculating the CO_2 savings.

Step 6 Summary

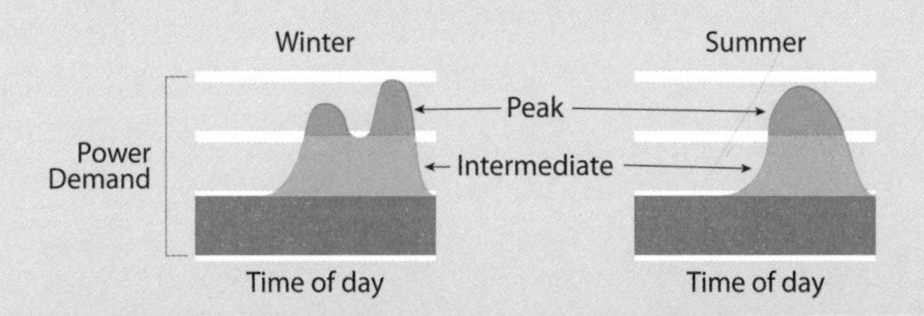

Twitter Summary
Having a basic understanding of electricity is an essential first step in reducing your energy needs and becoming self-sufficient by terms of generating your own power. Combining solar power with battery storage will have the same impact on mains grid power that mobile phone technology had on fixedline phone systems.

Smart Citizen Summary
Step 6 is about understanding the launguage of "smart". Smart grids, smart meters, smart cars, smart tv's, even smart cities all controlled by smart gadgets in the hands of smart citizens. Of course, before considering self-sufficiency in terms of electrical supply, it is essential that the recommendations set out in steps 1 to 6 have been complied with insofar as energy efficiencies have bee maximised. Additionally every smart citizen will also have to:

- Understand the basics of electricity generation and realize how its cost base can be affected by smart grids and smart meters.
- How to interpret energy labels and use them as a basis for selecting the most advantageous energy efficient products.
- Know how to calculate the energy loads of all new purchased products.
- Know how to reduce the energy usage of existing appliances such as refrigeration units, cookers, clothes and dishwashers.
- Understand the key role new lightng efficient products can play in lowering energy costs.
- Become familiar with the role batteries are now starting to play in making renewable energy technologies suitable for supply of electricity to homes, day and night.
- Appreciate that renewable energy technologies should only be considered after all other effeciencies have been implemented such that any energy generated on site will not be wasted.
- Know how to establish which, if any, renewable technologies best fit your particular building.

Step 7: Water Efficiency

"If mitigation is about CARBON, then adaption is about WATER"

John Slater

There is much talk about climate change, carbon footprint, and building a zero-carbon economy. Climate change is rightly connected by scientists to carbon dioxide emissions.. Scientists agree that greenhouse gas emissions are responsible for global warming and are causing and will continue to cause further warming for generations to come. Governments worldwide are focusing on fuel security and reducing emissions. The juggernaut of change, if it happens, will move slowly, very slowly. In the meantime, if the cause of the problem is greenhouse-gas emissions, the symptoms will be high temperatures and erratic weather conditions, leading to water-related disaster: too much water or too little water; water of the wrong quality; in the wrong place and at the wrong time; and too little water where and when it will be needed most.

The vast volumes of water required to support society are such that rivers will run dry, lakes will evaporate, and groundwaters will vanish. There are many horror stories of once great rivers running dry, watertables dropping by as much as 4 feet per year, and smaller cities facing extreme water shortages as the available water is diverted to major industrial centers. When dealing with water supply, one simple rule holds true: extraction cannot exceed recharge if we are to maintain a balanced freshwater ecosystem. A fantastic book, the first in a trilogy by Maude Barlow, Blue Gold, is about the world's dwindling water supply. It is a sobering read for anyone interested in understanding why the world is running out of fresh water.

Water, so essential for life, is turning against man as we get caught up in the earth's climate change rebalancing process. The way in which the earth balances temperatures and self-cleanses is through water – oceans, lakes, rivers, groundwater, rain, evaporation, condensation, and flooding. Erratic weather conditions are, however, causing excessive flooding, drought, tsunamis, melting ice caps, and rising sea levels. More than half of the world's wetlands, generally conceived as the kidneys of our ecosystem, have been destroyed. As intense efforts are made to slow, or even halt, global warming, long-term management of our water resources is also crucial. The term carbon footprint has been with us for some time, but the term water footprint is only now entering our vocabulary. It will feature prominently in how we experience the effects of climate change.

Some of the worst effects of climate change are on water resources, a fact that should cause no surprise because the water cycle is the climate cycle! As climate change continues unabated and temperatures rise, we easily miss the vital part water plays in the unfolding crisis. Yes, we appreciate that climate change leads to water chaos, but there is little awareness that the reverse is also true, that water change leads to climate chaos. The standard international civil engineering approach has always been to treat the hydrological cycle as one great big plumbing system. Fresh water is sourced from a watershed, well, lake, river, or stream via a series of pumps and pipes and delivered to its point of use. Once used, it is immediately discharged via a different series of pipes, referred to as sewers and drains. The discharge point is usually to the largest watercourse available, leading directly to the ocean.

The maxim "the solution to pollution is dilution" always seems to hold true when it comes to waste water disposal. The fundamental dilemma here is that water extracted from a watershed is rarely if ever returned to the same watershed. As a result, a number of issues arise that can lead directly to climate warming. The absence of the cooling effect of moisture via evaporation means that dry soil and dry surfaces heat up quicker, heating the air around them. Without a cooling influence, the local climate gets warmer, further reducing moisture levels in the soil, leading in extreme cases to desertification of what was a previously green landscape. This, in turn, reduces evaporation even more.

Rising sea levels is one of the principal threats of climate change, as is the pumping dry of vast underground stores of fresh drinking-quality (potable) water, which are ultimately discharged at sea. Worldwide, the aggressive pumping of fresh water from groundwater aquifers has more than doubled in the last 50 years, and research carried out at Utrecht University, the

Netherlands (see Appendix 2), found that 25% of the annual, global sea level rise was a direct result of depleted groundwater. Water in the local hydrological cycle is locked in a downward spiral, and the only way that process can be halted is through a full mind-set change with regard to how to treat and conserve water. Only then can we move toward protecting and preserving precious water resources.

The Water Cycle

The water cycle, also known as the hydrological cycle, is the journey water takes as it constantly moves between land, sea, air, and back again. In this cycle, water is always changing state between liquid, vapor, and ice. Within these categories, it takes multiple forms, from ancient fossil groundwaters and glacier ice, to springs, aquifers, rivers, lakes, and oceans. From clouds to moisture, mist, and fog and from snow to ice and back again, water undergoes a range of transitions, including percolation, precipitation, evaporation, and condensation. It can move by flow, seepage, infiltration, and evapo-transpiration. The water cycle is, therefore, more than just a major plumbing process; it is the fundamental element supporting life on earth.

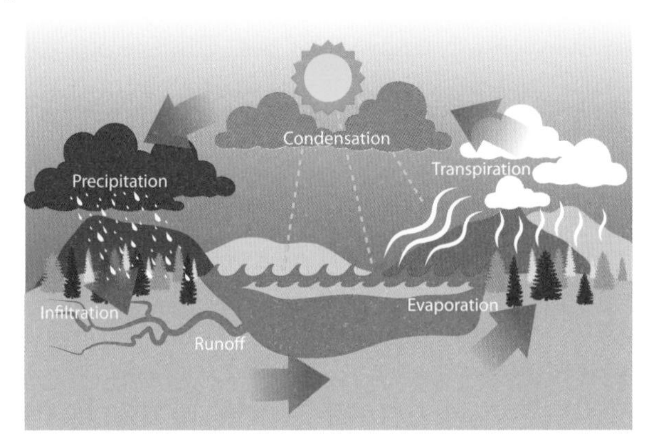

Water's form and state is ever changing. It can spend thousands and millions of years deep underground before surfacing, in which case it is referred to as fossil water.

The concept of peak oil, that oil is a finite resourse, is grasped by most people. Now, however, we are also facing the prospect of "peak water," a phrase chosen in 2010 by the New York Times as one of its new terms of the year. Some might argue that the concept of peak water cannot hold true, given that the amount of water on the earth is constant, albeit changeable within the hydrological cycle. On a global scale, water is renewable, particularly if we do not differentiate between fresh and sea water. But fresh water extraction is a local issue, and when groundwater aquifers containing fossil waters are removed, their replenishment may take eons, the same amount of millenia it took them to form in the first place. Nonetheless, the standard civil engineering approach continues to be based on extracting the largest volumes of fresh water from land and depositing them, somewhat used, in a watercourse en route to the sea. This process is interfering with the natural cycle, and the result is that there are numerous places where peak water has become a real 21st-century problem.

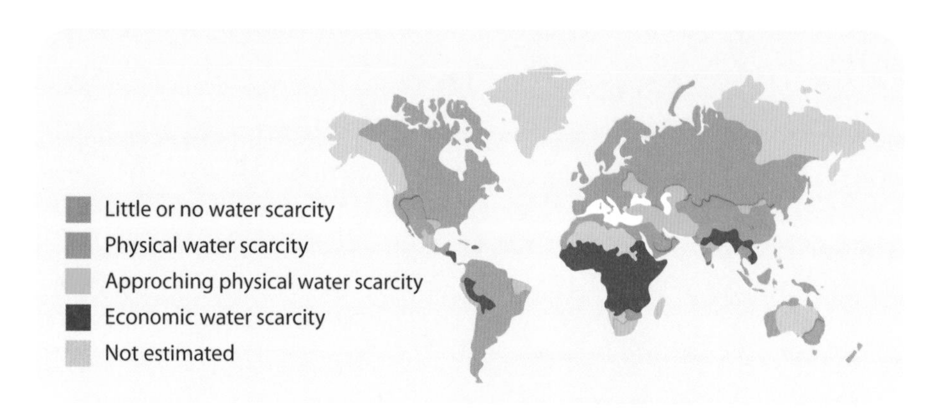

Whereas many countries are acutely aware of this dilemma, they choose to ignore it, not neccessarly out of ignorance but because the economics of correction, as currently measured, are beyond their resources. I say currently measured because global economics does not yet place an appropriate value on consequential environmental destruction. In order to tackle the peak water problem, the issue needs to gain widespread recognition, along with a willingness to take corrective action and invest in the resources neccessary to bring about change. The first place where these conditions aligned is Saudi Arabia, which is as water-poor as it is oil-rich. The Saudis' skill at managing peak oil has now been matched by their ability to manage peak water. In 2008, Saudi Arabia became the first country to establish a stragetic plan to reduce the pumping of water from diminishing aquifers for food production by 12.5% annually for eight years, ceasing the practice completely in 2016. The Saudis can now preserve most of their groundwater supplies by importing water-intense food crops. Falling watertables and depleted aquifers are affecting farming crop-viability in many countries. It is likely that a water crisis will be required before most other countries follow Saudi Arabia's lead.

Water Luxury

In the developed world, we have been spoiled by unlimited access to water. As a result, we have little concept or understanding of water's full value to us and what its scarcity could mean. Everything we are and everything we do is dependent on water. Indeed, humans are made up of between 55 – 75% water, and man's well-being and health rely on adequate water for drinking, cooking, eating, washing, cleaning, cooling, relaxing, etc. Water's dual association with luxury and survival is closely ingrained in the human psyche, a fact that the marketers have not missed. Almost all images used to demonstrate well-being and relaxation include an image association with water, whether that's a simple glass of water or a Jacuzzi, swimming pool, stream, river, lake, or waterfall. As a result, exercising a frugal approach to water use is not intuitive. Moreover, people who have lived frugally in respect of their fresh water consumption, particularly in regions of the developing world, have similar aspirations. This causes concern when these regions lack the necessary infrastructure and water supply as that found in most of the United States or Europe, for example. The end result is likely to be that, for the foreseeable future, we will continue to mistreat rivers, lakes, and groundwater as part of an ever-abundant, renewable resource in some large-scale plumbing system. When, in fact, water is not a renewable resource at all.

Our ancestors would not have made this mistake. They rightly revered water and considered it sacred. They were also intitutive about water and its properties and seem to have had a heightened awareness that water is fundamental, not just to mankind but also to the balance of nature. Most of the ancient civilizations, including those of Babylon, Greece, Rome, Egypt, and Ireland, revered water as a source of life and worshipped and treated with reverence all the places where water emerges from the ground, including springs, wells, lakes, and rivers. Most commonplace scientific and engineering approaches to the "management" of water, epitomized by the way in which is it so casually referred to as H2O, do not convey its true essential value. I'm not advocating a return to ancient beliefs, but perhaps it is time to reappraise some valuable insights to gain a better understanding of and meaningful respect for water. This might be a good starting point for recognizing our essential relationship with water.

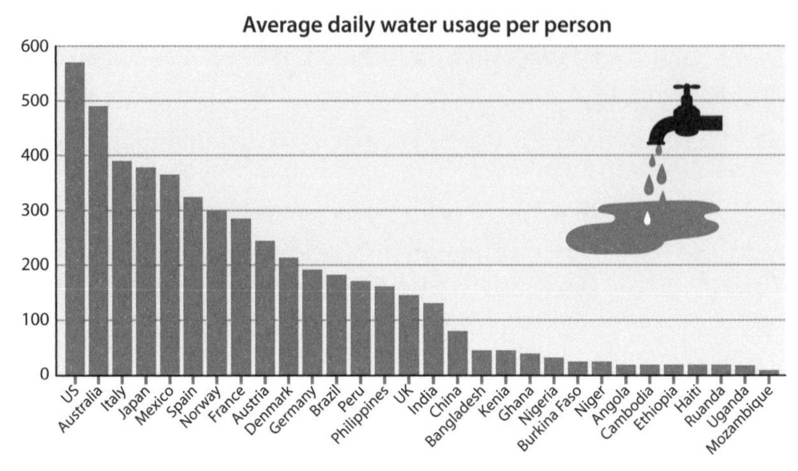

There is a tendency to treat water like a standard must-have commodity without recognition of the fact that it is a limited resource. The World Health Organisation (WHO) estimates that the basic human requirement for water is about 20 litres (over 5¼ U.S. gallons) per day. A cursory inspection of the data in the table above reveals that water-use statistics do not reflect water availability so much as wealth. For instance, Australia, one of the world's driest countries, uses nearly 500 litres per person daily. Meanwhile, the United States uses the highest amount of water per person, at almost 575 litres (152 U.S. gallons). But the amount of fresh water available is not uniform across the world, and it certainly doesn't respect or reflect population densities or their requirements. A good example of this is India, which is home to 20% of the world's population but has only 4% of its potable fresh water. In fact, India has the largest water extraction needs, but groundwater resources and water tables are falling dramatically, by as much as 6 feet per year in extreme cases. What is more, China has had the world's fastest growing economy for a generation and the largest population, but it has the lowest available quantities of fresh water. China supplies the rest of the world with consumer goods, but the production cost in terms of water used for industry is alarming.

Despite the fact that we are surrounded by water, only a small percentage of this water is suitable for human consumption. So how much water is there? It is estimated that the planet has approximately 1.4 billion cubic kilometers of water. Figures vary, but the accepted data indicates that saline or sea water acounts for over 97.5% of that. That leaves only about 2.5% or 35 million km3 for fresh water. However, of this, just 1% is available for human consumption because most is locked up in ice caps, glaciers, and permanent snow cover.

How Much Water Do We Use?

The steadily rising global population is leading to an unconstrained and insatiable demand for water. Constant overpumping and extraction have depleted water stores. Has the world's supply of fresh water already peaked? Are we running out of fresh water? The simple answer is we don't know. Unlike oil, which is measured and valued, water is rarely measured and is very much undervalued. The importance of water was, however, acknowledged in July 2010 by the UN General Assembly, which adopted a historic resolution recognizing the human right to safe and clean water. That resolution will be rendered meaningless if we fail to immediately start measuring, monitoring, and protecting water resources. The best place to begin understanding water use is to read the meter, which is now a standard fixture in most developed countries. Similar to energy bills, discussed in Step 2, the single most valuable step anyone can take to reduce water costs is to read their water bills, which are easier to understand than energy bills. In most cases, the bill amount is simply volume (gallons, litres, or cubic meters) multiplied by unit cost. So the important part, and the element the consumer has complete control over, is the actual quantity of water used, which is key to establishing a baseline from which to make savings. There are different metrics for the comparative usage of water, depending on whether you want to compare individuals or countries, including:

- Per individual, usually measured in liters or gallons per day.
- Per year, per head of population (per capita). This is an average figure of national consumption and is generally measured in cubic meters per person, per year.
- Per total volume of water used. This figure can be calculated for an individual, a process, a product's value chain, a business, or a nation. It includes the water used to grow food and produce goods and services and is referred to as a water footprint.

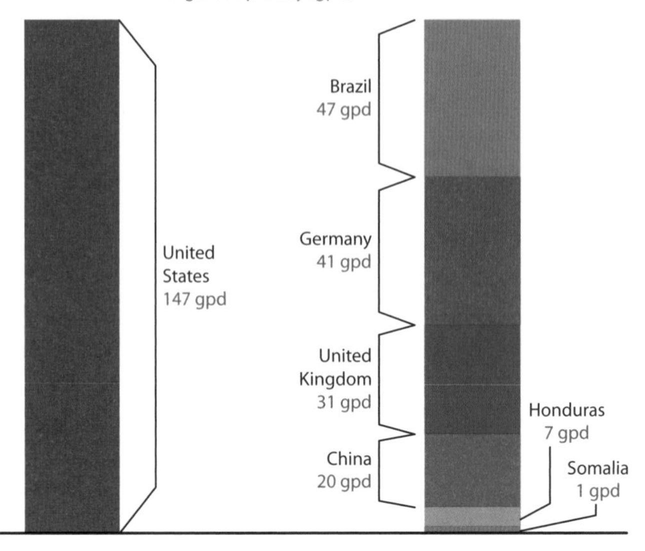

In unmetered buildings, the best way to establish a baseline of water usage is to use a web-based calculator. This estimates domestic annual water consumption based on your responses to questions about usage and the type of water-consuming appliances in the home. There are a number of free calculators on consumer-centered web sites (see Appendix 1). A typical example of an online calculator is shown below. Because these tools are generally country-specific, it is important to ensure that you use the appropriate calculator for your region.

Calculatorts can also work out whether you are paying too much or too little for water, compared to the amount you would be charged for a similar sized property with similar occupation levels in the same region. Water, like energy, follows a similar pattern in most developed countries where amounts used depend on lifestyle. The percentage lost through leaks and used for activities such as showering, bathing, flushing toilets, doing laundry, washing dishes, and drinking is similar, even if the quantities differ from country to country. They can also differ significantly within a country and within a state. For instance, residents of Rancho, Santa Fe, California, use an average of 585 gallons of water

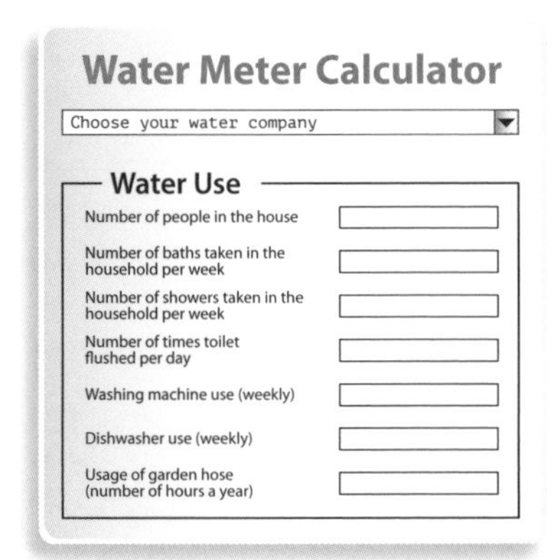

per person per day (gpd), whereas their counterparts in San Francisco use just 45 gpd.

Globally, agriculture accounts for up to 70% of total water use and industry 23%, leaving only 7% for consumer use. If we were to include the water used to grow our food, then the figures for individual water use would be a multiple of those quoted in the table above. A study from the University of Twente, the Netherlands (see Appendix 2), puts the average per-person effective water consumption at over 1,000 gallons per day. The study describes the so-called water footprint, a key measure that factors in direct water use and embedded and virtual, or hidden, use, referring to water in the products and food we buy. In a water-scarce world, we must be accountable for all the water we use, whether that's consumed as liquid or hidden in the production of rice, coffee, melons, cotton, or paper.

The carbon footprint is measured in a way that is universally accepted, and a ton of carbon in the United States has the same value and effect as a tonne of carbon in, say, Uganda. The water footprint, on the other hand, has different values that are dependent on regional climate and locally viable water supplies. It will be some time before there is a widely accepted way to measure the water footprint, so in the meantime, it will have to be accounted for locally, using such methods as labeling.

Water Efficiency Labeling (WELL)

Attaching a label to all water products is probably the most immediate way to increase consumer awareness that water is a finite resource. Water efficiency labels, though similar in many respects to energy labels, are not yet widely used. Adoption of labeling is more of a voluntary than mandatory practice in most countries, and it represents best practice rather than any legal obligation. Countries with mandatory water labeling tend to be those with major water stress issues such as Australia and Singapore, but a label will be mandatory in most developed countries by 2020. The products that generally require water labels usually include devices or machines that consume or dispense water such as plumbing fixtures and accessories. Energy efficiency labels on household appliances, discussed in Step 6, must also contain information on water efficiencies.

The plumbing industry will need to forecast future consumer purchasing trends. Not all manufacturers in the sector have signed up to voluntary labeling codes, but they undoubtedly will, as labeling becomes the norm. They will need to redesign their products to match new water efficiency trends, and, in fact, a whole new design philosophy is emerging with efficiency at its core. Out go roomy bathtubs, bucket-shaped WCs, and free and fast-flowing faucets and in comes a range of efficient designs, all of them striving for top ratings on the new labels. These labels will increasingly be the catalysts of change and shape choices. We pay for the water we use, so knowing how much water a dishwasher or washing machine uses is critical for reducing consumption.

Labeling alone will not educate us about diminishing water resources, but it represents progress toward placing a measurable value on use. The European Union and United States now have a plethora of new regulations restricting flow rates and the amount of water that products use.

Hot Water Use

Most books on the subject of energy efficiency deal with hot water supply alongside heating systems. While the two are interconnected, optimizing hot water systems without minimizing water usage is a waste of energy. In other words, significant energy will be unnecessarily wasted on heating water. Hence maximizing water efficiencies is an essential part of reducing total energy use in hot water systems. Heating water is probably the second biggest domestic energy bill, after space heating and cooling. There's a simple rule of thumb stating that it takes 65kWh of energy to heat 1m3 of water. So every time you introduce greater efficiencies to water usage, the direct cost of water heating is considerably reduced. Every 1m3 reduced represents a saving in both energy and water charges.

Hot water use in the home is completely dependent on personal circumstances: how many people share a house and their age profile, cooking patterns, house cleaning routine, and personal hygiene habits. The quantity of water used is also a function of the distribution system and type of household appliances. Traditional supply systems were designed to deliver water under reasonable pressure to each of the outlets in the building.

There was no differentiation between the designed-for pressure flow in hot and cold pipes, and standards in pipework design emerged to meet demand for water. In the United States and other countries with a record of high per-capita water consumption, plumbing systems can deliver high volumes of water comfortably around homes. Wider pipes with faster flow rates through faucets and showerheads, as well as bigger storage tanks then provide a high-pressure supply to the other water-using appliances. In effect, houses have become like the old SUVs of the building world, designed and plumbed to deliver water far in excess of what is sustainable.

Rethinking Hot Water Use

Table on page 244 above offers a good starting point for helping to quantify your hot water use. For instance, a reasonable average figure for total water consumption in many European countries is 150 liters per person, per day, which amounts to 54,600 liters, or about 14,500 U.S. gallons, annually. Assuming 50% of this is hot water, 27,300 liters is the average volume of hot water used per person, per year. There are many variables when calculating the amount of hot water used and the cost of raising the temperature from ambient to hot.

Life-Cycle Costs for 13-Years Operation of Different Types of Water Heaters					
Water Heater Type	Storage Volume (Gal.)	Efficiency	Cost	Annual Energy Cost	Cost Over 13 years
Fossil Fuel					
Gas Storage (2015 standard)	40	0.62	$1,170	$165	$3,300
High-Efficiency Gas Storage	40	0.67	$1,660	$150	$3,630
Condesing Gas Storage	50	90% TE	$2,570	$135	$4,320
Condesing Gas Hybrid	25	90%TE	$2,570	$135	$4,320
Gas Tankless	<2	0.82	$2,380	$120	$4,630
Condensing Gas Tankless	<2	0.92	$2,900	$105	$5,000
Off-Fired Storage (Current standard)	30	0.53	$1,970	$680	$12,770
Off-Fired Storage (2015 standard)	30	0.62	$2,040	$550	$11,095
Electric					
Electric Storage (2015 standard)	50	0.95	$710	$290	$4,470
Heat Pump	50	2.00	$1,580	$165	$3,740
Solar					
Solar-Assisted Electric	N/A	1.8 SEF	$4,250	$155	$6,260
Solar-Assisted Gas	N/A	1.2 SEF	$4,250	$85	$5,375

Choosing a New Hot Water System

The same guidelines apply when selecting a new water heater as apply to choosing a new space heating system (see Step 5): Never base your selection on the size and fuel type of the old system, and use an upgrade as an opportunity to rethink your total hot water requirements. If your plumber or specialist adviser uses the old system as a basis for determining the new one dismiss them immediately. Some research is necessary before you approach a specialist installer because some have existing relationships or trade deals with suppliers. This means that their advice could favor their partners and may not represent the best value for your particular situation.

The key decisions that need to be reached after you have figured out how much and at what times of the day you need hot water are: the most suitable energy type – gas, biomass, electric, or solar – whether it's storage or on-demand, and whether it will be standalone or integrated into the space heating system. Thereafter, choosing a water heater is straightforward because efficiency standards are now very much subject to government regulation. In the United States and the EU, for instance, there are minimum efficiency standards for water heaters.

Fuel Choice

The cost of energy for the lifetime of a water heater should be one of the first factors to consider before deciding on a fuel. The easy option is always electricity, not least because it is usually readily available and can represent one of the most cost-effective solutions in terms of ease of management and control. Electricity may be inefficient in terms of network delivery to an individual property, but once inside, it can represent the most effective direct conversion of energy for heating water. This is because the electric current is converted to heat in the same way that old electric light bulbs glowed with heat. The difference is that, here, water acts as a sort of heat sink, cooling the electric element as it heats up. Unlike other fossil fuels, there is no need for secondary pipes, coils, or transfer plates in the heat-conversion process, so there are fewer opportunities for heat loss.

Electricity is at its most efficient at either end of the water requirements scale. In cases where very little water is required, such as in properties with few occupants who spend most of their day away from home, an instant electric water heating system can be very cost-effective, providing water on demand, with minimal waste. Although a large heating element is needed in terms of kilowatts, its usage time is short, so the cost is low. At the other end of the scale, it might be worth considering whether and how off-peak electricity can be used to heat a large, well-insulated storage cylinder of water. This can be a cost-effective option for certain households, whose occupants are disciplined enough to use the hot water at optimum times: shortly after off-peak heating periods. Often, there are reduced tariffs available at set off-peak times, although not all energy companies offer them to domestic customers. This may be about to change because of smart-grid technologies. With electricity, it is always worth checking out reduced charge periods because heating and storing water can be one of the best and most cost-effective means of managing hot water supply.

Gas-fired water heaters can also be very economical, particularly where mains gas supply is available. Oil and gas market prices are closely linked, but mains gas supply has a number of advantages over oil. It is less expensive per unit of energy and can be delivered conveniently and cheaply through the mains pipe network. Additionally, gas has lower carbon emissions than oil and will, if Paris 2015 is effective, attract less carbon taxes than oil in the future.

Biomass is another increasingly popular fuel source. Biomass has always existed, but the technology – if you could even call it that – remained unchanged for centuries. A fireplace, with or without a back boiler, and a stove or range were the full extent of available choices. The only variable in the system was the chimney or chimneys, which adorned the rooftops of pretty much all houses built before the 21st century. Biomass is now making a big comeback, with the arrival of new products and new combinations of fuel sources. There are now numerous aesthetically pleasing stoves on the market that also deliver efficiencies in terms of economic water heating.

Part of the reason for the resurgence of biomass is because it is generally designated carbon neutral and considered renewable (see also Step 1). That is an incentive for the industry to develop and maintain prices without the threat of added carbon taxes. Another good reason to choose biomass is that, unlike fossil fuels, prices can be controlled and are commonly fixed for five years or more, providing security of supply and cost.

However, when it comes to security of energy supply for hot water systems, there can be no better energy source than the sun. Any upgrade or new works should at least consider including solar water heating in a building, essentially a cost-free supply of hot water for decades to come. Solar hot water may not always provide the most cost-efficient solution, particularly in terms of materials, controls, and the retrofitting needed for storage cylinders and pipes, but it should be viewed as a long-term investment. While the technology is improving and costs are declining annually, solar water heating still needs to be backed up by a secondary system on dull winter days and at night.

Hot Water Storage

The copper cylinder is probably the best-known hot water storage tank. Unbelievably, the original tanks had no insulation, and when lagging jackets were introduced, they were loose fitting and had to be purchased separately as something of an afterthought. By contrast, newer storage tanks and cylinders are much more sophisticated and come with an integrated insulation enclosure. The key to efficient water storage is a near-perfect, factory-made insulated vessel with fully integrated pipes, fittings, valves, thermostats, and controls. Similar to the issues covered in Steps 3 and 4, small gaps and areas without insulation cause cold bridging and lead to major heat and, in this case, hot water loss.

There are often two separate heating elements or coils in the cylinder:

1. At a lower level to heat the entire cylinder-volume when large quantities of hot water are required or when cheap/free heat sources are accessible.
2. At the top, which heats a smaller amount of water.

Given that hot water rises, this creates a phenomenon called "stratification" within the cylinder. A smaller amount of warm water stays on the top of the cylinder with cooler water remaining below, which is why hot water is always drawn from the top of the cylinder and cold water is fed into the cylinder tank from the bottom.

There are essentially two types of water heater arrangements, referred to as direct and indirect. The direct system applies an energy source directly to the water, via electric elements in the cylinder, for example. A pre-set thermostat controls the on/off timing for each element. In gas- and oil-fired direct systems, the energy is usually in the form of a flame, applied directly to a heat exchange plate or pipe that contains the water.

Indirect water heating systems are typically solar thermal and heat pumps. They generate energy in a heat-exchange fluid, which then passes that energy into the water in the storage vessel. With suitable planning and bespoke design, indirect water heating systems can represent the best value for money over the life of the system. Here, the water storage cylinder is treated like a zone in the home that requires heating. The storage cylinder often contains a closed loop pipe system, which carries hot water from the boiler and, in the process, transfers heat to the colder water in the cylinder as it passes through. With solar thermal, a closed loop pipe system takes heated fluid, usually water heated by panels on the roof, and transfers the heat indirectly to the stored water in the cylinder. Similarly, heat pumps take heat from one source, such as outside air or groundwater, and transfer it to the stored water in the cylinder. Thermostats and controls monitor when the water in the tank falls below preset temperatures and signal the delivery of more heat. With any heat pump arrangement, it's very important to fully understand the workings of the system because poor control and management can very easily result in the loss of potential operational efficiencies.

Where Savings Can be Made

No matter where in the world you live, it is necessary to take responsibility for your personal water usage. This is not just about the amount of water we directly consume but also relates to the water used in the production of the food and consumer goods. It's not unusual in hotter climates for scarce water resources to be diverted to irrigate "cash" crops for export, from melons to cotton. It is, therefore, vital to become informed about the impact of small personal choices with large consequences. It makes sense for us to treat our available water with great respect and to start reducing daily water consumption, which can be achieved very easily and with little sacrifice.

WCs

The sanitary-ware of the past 100 years is very robust and rarely needs replacing unless as part of an overall renovation or upgrade. These systems are perfect in every way apart from efficient water usage. Toilets, or WCs, are the single biggest user of water in the home, even though the size of cisterns has been reduced in capacity over the past 25 years..They still account for over 30% of domestic water use. Older toilets generally had cistern capacities in excess of 3 U.S. gallons/14 litres, compared with an average size today of 1.2 U.S. gallons/4.5 litres. Dual system flushes are now the industry standard for new cisterns, with the larger button discharging 60% more water than the smaller one. Toilet bowls have also become more streamlined to flush away waste more efficiently and hygienically.

Older style bowls are not streamlined and require a larger volume of water to flush effectively. The simplest and most cost-effective way to reduce the amount of water per flush is to place a brick or similar item in the cistern. It is also possible to buy cistern-reduction kits, usually inexpensive plastic bags that you fill with water and place in the cistern.

Urinals, in particular, deserve special mention. Hotels, restaurants, bars, and public facilities are heavy consumers of water – the continual flush systems used on most urinals are highly inefficient. This is, however, starting to change. Waterless urinals are now becoming more popular and accepted. Eco-friendly composting toilets, which use very little or no water, are also beginning to gain in popularity.

Showers and Bathtubs

A quick conventional shower is usually more water efficient than having a long bath. But not every shower is efficient. Some models have multiple jets and provide all-around water pressure and simulate a luxury spa experience, which encourages longer shower times and requires more water to maintain pressure, making a bath comparatively more efficient. Water efficiency when showering depends on the water-flow multiplied by the length of time the shower is running. A flow restrictor that can help to reduce consumption. For example, an aerator head will introduce air intermittently with the water, maintaining and even improving the water-pressure effect while saving approximately 40% of actual water usage.

Bathtubs are also being designed with efficiency in mind, with more streamlined profiles requiring less water. A common-sense addition to bathtub design is insulation. It seems obvious that a bathtub should be insulated, but this wasn't always the case. Indeed, traditional cast-iron baths with decorative feet lost heat by conduction, convection, and radiation even before they were full.

Washing Machines and Dishwashers

Modern efficient washing machines and dishwashers can use as little as 10% of the water used by 30-year-old models, and they perform equally well. Water usage is becoming at least as important as energy use, and these appliances now carry both water usage and energy labels. As we have seen, water and energy ratings are almost interchangeable.

Major household appliance and bathroom fixture manufacturers invest heavily in research and development. They have to predict likely future market trends and most valued customer features, before designing innovative products to meet them. Surprisingly, they regularly collaborate with their competitors to share the cost and findings of market research, design, and product development. This is evident from the aisles of any white goods showroom, where the similarity in product design and market offerings is remarkable.

Washing machines carry a water-usage label that details liters of water used per 1 kg of dry laundry. The typical load capacity can vary between 6kg and 12kg, with 7kg being about average. When purchasing a new model, optimizing the load-per-wash capacity is important. If capacity is too low, the machine will be inefficient in terms of multiple runs and potential overloading; if it is too large, there will be inefficiencies in terms of underloading. A full-sized Energy Star-certified washer uses 13 gallons of water per load, compared to 23 gallons for a standard machine. The average American family washes about 300 loads of laundry each year, and by simply upgrading to the Energy Star machine, savings of more than 3,000 gallons of water can be made annually.

Dishwashers similarly rate their water consumption in gallons per place setting. The average family-size dishwasher holds ten place settings, and a water-efficient machine would use 2 gallons per setting, or 20 gallons per wash. Surprisingly, hand-washing dishes uses an estimated 26 gallons per ten-place setting

Faucets

Undoubtedly, our great indifference to water stems from its apparent free and endless flow from faucets, which means that we don't have to think about where the water is coming from. If restaurant and bar staff were to leave a soda dispenser tap running while attending to another task, it would be deemed extremely wasteful, yet we routinely leave water taps running in this manner. Faucets can run water at an average rate of 6 litres per minute, and people can be careless about running water while performing routine washing and cooking activities.

Changing faucet type to reduce or control the flow is the easiest and most economical way to start reducing water wastage. In commercial buildings where there is large bathroom usage such as restaurants, hotels, airports, and shopping malls, installing water-efficient types can cover the capital costs with water-cost savings within one year. This makes tremendous economic sense when water bills are based on metered usage. There are numerous efficient faucet designs on the market, including push-down models with a pre-set timer, click technology where the pressure varies depending on how many times you click the switch, spray-heads (instead of full-flow heads), and infrared sensors that turn the water on and run it for a pre-set time and flow rate. The infra-red-controlled units have the added advantage of being more hygienic than standard models. This technology will undoubtedly become much more widely-used as awareness grows of the large potential cost savings and other benefits it brings.

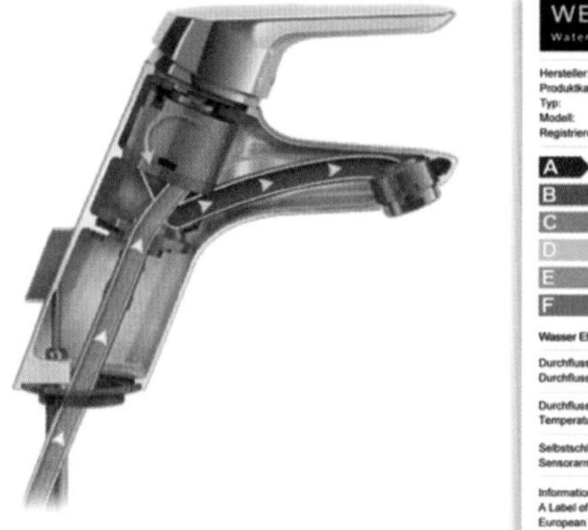

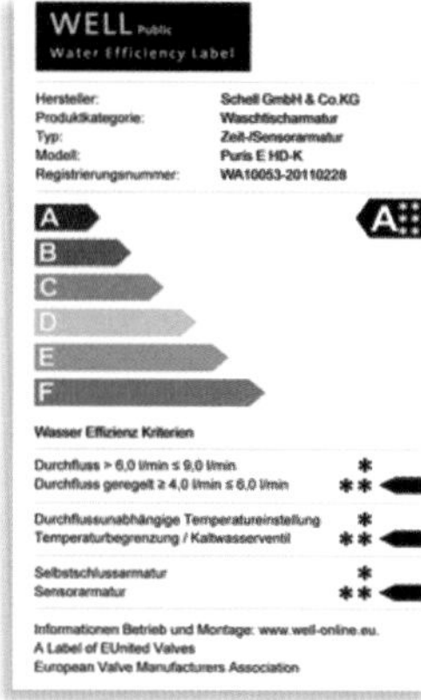

Water Sensitive Design

"There are as many varieties of water as there are animals and plants"

Viktor Schauberger

Water doesn't follow straight-line engineering theory.The oceans ebb and flow with a constant, heartbeat-like rhythm; rivers naturally meander over their length, forming flood plains and rapids as and where necessary; and rain falls, sustaining life and the biodiversity of the planet. The average person's understanding of water is limited, but this must change. Future water patterns will be key to survival. We must not leave custody of water solely to traditional civil engineering systems that treat water as a problem to be solved, resolved by a series of barriers, pumps, pipes, and engineering works. Straightening rivers, building apparently robust stone walls to restrict their courses, and trying to contain and control their direction as they flow through towns and cities represent a misunderstanding of nature.

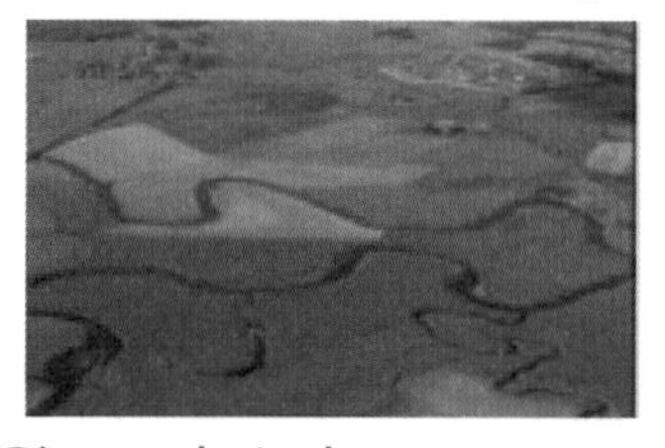

Water-sensitive urban design (WSUD), a relatively new concept that originated in Australia, has spread internationally. In the United States, the principles of water sensitive design have been embraced under the technical management concept known as low impact development (LID). Whatever its name, the principles of WSUD are the same and it is a first step toward a more holistic approach to managing water. It is a natural way of handling water on the earth's surface, with minimal recourse to a civil engineering approach; more of a "go with the flow" approach. Where possible, it tries to replicate the way in which the natural topography has shaped or is shaped by water. It is a design approach that seeks a sensible coexistence between all the phases of the water cycle and our human built environment. The phases of the water cycle include rainfall, storage, floodplains, water needs, water quality, and water disposal.

The realization that managing water more sustainably can deliver significant benefits over conventional problem-solving approaches involving underground pumps and pipe networks has not only improved the biodiversity and greening of local landscapes but has also considerably mitigated the inevitable effects and cost of localized flooding events. The challenge now is to use this thinking to develop "retrofit" solutions appropriate to existing urban landscapes. There are a number of different ways to do this. The ideal approach will vary according to the setting, but the smaller and more local the proposal, the better the chance of success.

- Pre-treatment Systems
- Green roofs
- Soakaways
- Rainwater Harvesting
- Ponds
- Wetlands
- Bioretention
- Trenches
- Swales
- Filter Strips
- Sand Filters
- Pervious Pavements
- Detenction Basins
- Geocellular Systems
- Infiltration Basins

Water sensitive design involves everything from simply collecting water in a plastic butt in the garden to retrofitting a complete urban landscape by replacing large quantities of concrete and tarmac with a sequence of swales and ponds to form a, better protected, successfully integrated urban landscape that thrives as a biodiverse ecosystem.

Rainwater Harvesting

Rainwater harvesting makes full use of rainfall within the curtilage of a property to supply the majority of its water needs. Rainwater is collected and stored for subsequent use within the property. Depending on the extent of filtration and water treatment, the water can be used for everything from cleaning and flushing toilets to washing, bathing, watering the garden, and even providing household drinking water, which would require a comprehensive treatment system.

Rainwater harvesting is not a new technology. It has been used for centuries in regions that experience short monsoon seasons of very heavy rainfall. The best examples of traditional rainwater harvesting systems are the baoris or stepwells of western India. Their design consists of a step arrangement that allowed continuous access to available water even as levels dropped to a minimum. The architecture of these stepwells is stunning, and they are adorned with ornate carvings that demonstrate an inherent respect for water.

Today's rainwater harvesting structures are usually built from either concrete or molded plastic and are practical but lack the elegance of their ancient predecessors. Rainwater harvesting is making a comeback among environmentally concerened citizens who want to support the conservation of water and exercise some control over their ever-increasing, metered water-costs.

Much of the water we use does not need to be of drinking quality, but in most developed countries with municipal water supply systems, no distinction is made between drinking and non-drinking water. All of the water is handled in the same way and treated with the same chemicals for purification. Similarly, most domestic buildings have just one pipework system and no way to separate potable water from lesser-quality water needed for cleaning, washing, and flushing toilets, etc. Given that 95% of domestic water does not have to be potable, huge savings can be made using a rainwater harvesting system. If the utility supplies only the water needed for drinking and cooking and rainwater harvesting supplies the rest, a metered water saving of up to 95% could be achieved. As building legislation catches up with climate change mitigation, many countries mandate that rainwater harvesting is essential for buildings to comply with planning and building codes.

Designing rainwater harvesting systems for new buildings is relatively straightforward. Integrating the plumbing to accommodate water from a rainwater storage tank will not significantly increase costs if done at the new-build stage. The only extra expense is the cost of the water storage tank, which should be as large as the space allows. Tanks are usually installed underground, have a minimum 50-year life span, and should be correspondingly robust and durable.

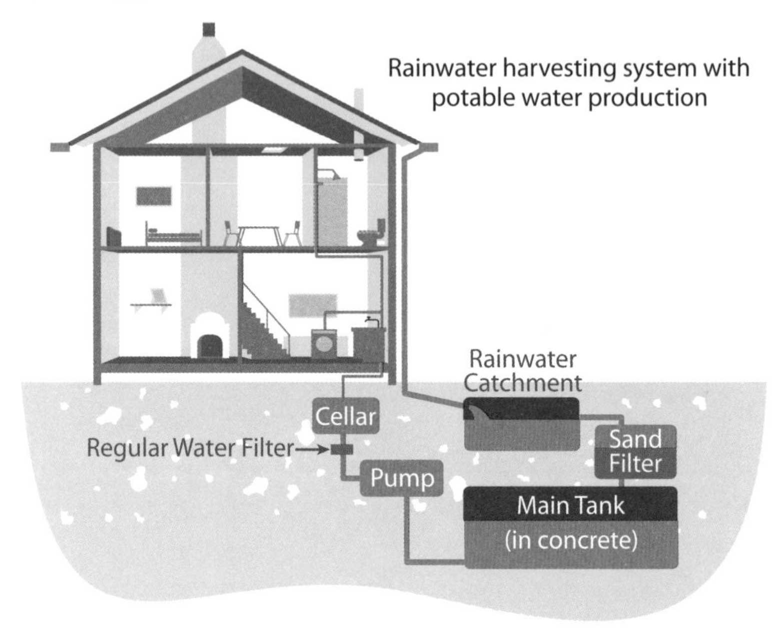

Retrofitting rainwater harvesting systems in existing buildings can be considerably more expensive because extensive internal plumbing is generally needed to separate pipework for drinking water taps from showers, baths, and toilets.

Rainwater Butts

Probably the simplest and most cost-effective first step for anyone trying to reduce their water bills is to install a water butt. These come in various shapes and sizes and are designed to collect rainwater from your house, shed, glasshouse, garage, or other garden building that has a roof with a gutter and downpipe arrangement. They are very easy to attach and connect to an existing rainwater downpipe system, and they usually have a capacity of 100 to 200 litres (about 26 to 52 U.S. gallons). The main criteria for selection are the practical details of available space and the intended use of the collected water. Simple measures for conserving water in the garden include choosing more drought-resistant plants and using an organic mulch to help plants, including lawn-grasses, to retain water during long, dry spells.

So when the newspaper headlines shout: "garden hosepipe ban could last all summer," we know that most, if not all, garden watering needs can, and should, be met from these completely sustainable measures. The temporary hosepipe ban is the epitome of poor water management by householders. There should be no temporary ban; in my opinion, there should be a permanent ban because the only time a garden needs water is the very time when aquifers and our entire water systems are most stressed due to low rainfall.

Watering your garden from a metered mains supply is an expensive exercise because most water utility companies that charge for water supply are also, in fact, charging for waste water treatment. But utilities only charge based on metered deliveries. Installing a meter to measure returning waste water and sewage effulent requires a more sophisticated and costly meter because of the possibility of solids interfering with the meter mechanism. It is standard practice for water companies to assume that water in equals water out and to then multiply the metered reading by two to account for waste water charges. Mains water used to irrigate gardens does not need utility treatment but, because of the metering method, you are effectively double-charged. Incidentally, it makes little practical sense to use mains water for garden irrigation because plants do not like a chemically treated supply; they grow far better on fresh rainwater.

Sustainable Drainage Systems (SuDS)

Sustainable drainage systems, or SuDS as its more commonly know, is the aspect of water sensitive design that specifically deals with drainage. Getting water drainage right is crucial in terms of flood mitigation. The basic principle behind SuDS is that all the rainwater that falls on an area should discharge from that area at the same pace as it did prior to development. If SuDS is handled properly, it will help us to avoid flash-flooding after heavy downpours and allow the maximum amount of surface water enough time to percolate back into the soil and, through the soil, to replenish ground-water reserves.

With SuDs, there is a pardigm shift in terms of how conventional surface water drainage is treated when buildings and their surrounds are being designed. In many cities around the world, surface water pipes and waste water, or sewer, pipes were combined. As a result, heavy rainfall would flush all sewage contents past any sewage treatment plant. Although illegal to build today, combined draining systems are still very common. Many of us are familiar with "no swimming" notices at lakes and beaches because of high algae counts from "unknown sources" following heavy rainfall. Uncontrolled pollution is caused not just by inadequate treatment systems but also by dangerously inadequate drainage systems. Sustainable drainage involves managing rainfall as it lands on your site and storing as much as possible for later use, allowing as much thereafter to percolate through the soil to the aquifers below and only then to drain away the very peak amount, which joins the nearest watercourse. There are a number of ways this can be achieved.

Slowing down the rate at which water leaves a site is key to sustainable drainage. The increasingly popular green roof is a perfect starting point because the natural vegetation, foliage, and soil absorb the rainfall and only a fraction of what lands on the roof makes it way to the gutters and downpipes. At ground level, there are now many permeable products that allow water to percolate through paved areas. Cobblestone and pavement slabs also let water percolate to the soil below, provided there is adequate spacing between them. If non-permeable paving must be used, it can be "broken up" (interspersed) or delineated by planted areas. The key here is to avoid kerbs or else provide drainage routes through the kerbs so that surface water can easily disperse to the planted areas, in a process that is often referred to as bioretention. Another popular method of slowing down the rate of surface water flow is the addition of swales. These are vegetated or permeable-surfaced areas, which are designed with a natural dish shape that attracts water runoff and then retains it until it seeps downwards and away. Swales are, in effect, mini-floodplains, allowing water to rise and fall depending on local rainfall levels.

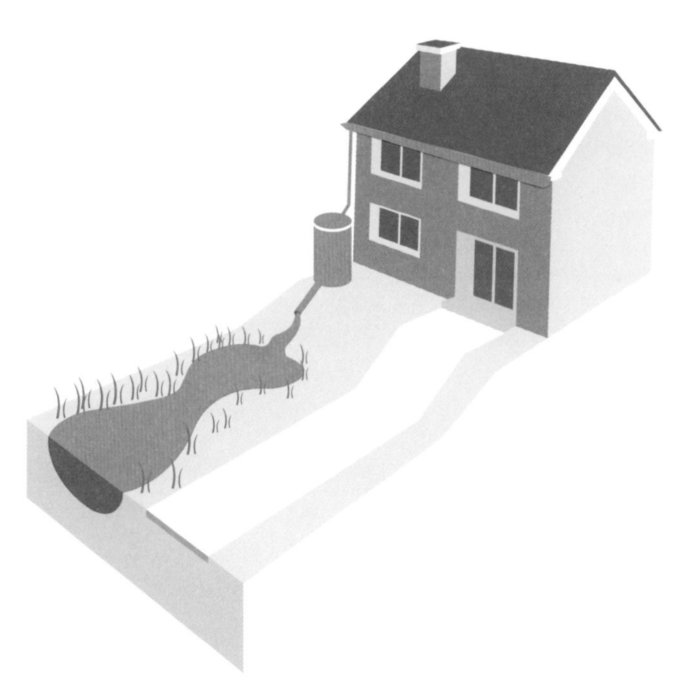

It is important for any site that needs to retain all its surface water to have a suitably designed and constructed soakaway area. Soakaways can take a number of forms, the simplest of which is a pebble-filled pit at the end of a drainage pipe. More complex designs are based on the same principle but consist of a series of specifically designed trenches with graded granular backfill surrounded by a geo-textile membrane to keep the stone free of soil infiltration. The overall size of the soakaway required is dependent on the amount of rainfall in the area and the soil's capacity to allow water to infiltrate and percolate away to the natural watercourse over time.

Flood Damage

Climate change has turned the traditional flood design philosophy on its head. In some places, flooding seems to be a more frequent occurrence, where it had once been very rare, once in a century, perhaps. During the past 25 years, floods have resulted in over 20,000 fatalities and billions of dollars worth of property damage, not to mention the distress and trauma caused by each flood event. Even after flood waters recede, many issues can remain:

- The physical damage can take months/years to fully repair
- There may be toxic contamination of the building fabric that affects physical health
- The loss of personal mementos and valuable, vulnerable assets
- Serious structural damage may simply be too costly to repair
- There may be a loss of income, particularly for small businesses
- The property may be subsequently un-insurable
- It will also have the prospect of future, repeat flood-risk
- The traumatic memory of the flood event coupled with the knowledge that it will probably reoccur at some point can cause ongoing psychological distress

It is crucial to find out whether your home or business is in a flood risk area, understand what steps you can take to reduce potential flooding, and make sure that your property and contents are more resistant to the effects of water ingress. Flooding is and will be a more frequent natural event. Although it cannot be prevented entirely, there are measures that can be put in place to limit potential damage.

Flood Risk

Most people are aware of the risk of flooding from rivers, water channels, and the sea, but flooding can also occur because of heavy rainfall, rising groundwater, runoff from surrounding higher ground, blocked underground drainage networks, or frozen and burst pipes. Before considering ways to protect your building, it is essential to assess the risk of flooding and identify likely sources. There are a number of ways to do this.

- Local knowledge is a good starting point because flooding events can be traumatic and are rarely forgotten. So consult friends and neighbors.
- Visit your local authority or environmental agency to inspect flood maps for the area.
- Determine whether potential sources of flooding are nearby.

Given the growing threat from flooding, buildings will have to demonstrate some form of flood mitigation strategy as part of a building code or regulatory regime. That's not to say every building is at risk, but with climate change altering global weather patterns, every structure should be deemed at risk until proven otherwise. Buildings require a protection strategy. While flood risk analysis and flood protection policies are relatively easy to incorporate into new building developments, it's the existing building stock that is most vunerable. Even insurance companies are examining the level of risk associated with all buildings and rewarding well-protected buildings with lower premiums, while refusing to reinsure some properties with a high risk or history of flooding.

If you conclude that your building might be at risk, it may be necessary to seek professional advice to determine how often flooding might occur, to what depth, and for how long. Water depth is a key factor when determining appropriate protection measures. The force of the flood water trying to get into a building is directly related to the depth of water, and this will dictate the reasonable measures that can be taken to reduce the risk of flood damage.

How to Protect Your Building

Most buildings have little or no natural defense against the ingress of flood water. There are numerous routes for flood waters to enter a building, including through gaps, cracks, service openings for pipes and cables, and joints around doors and windows. Because most walls in our houses and buildings are porous, flood waters can simply seep straight through the walls. Seepage can also occur from below ground and up through flooring slabs. The most destructive inflow of flood water often comes from backflow through a blocked or overloaded drain or sewer, which is toxic and causes a major health and safety issue.

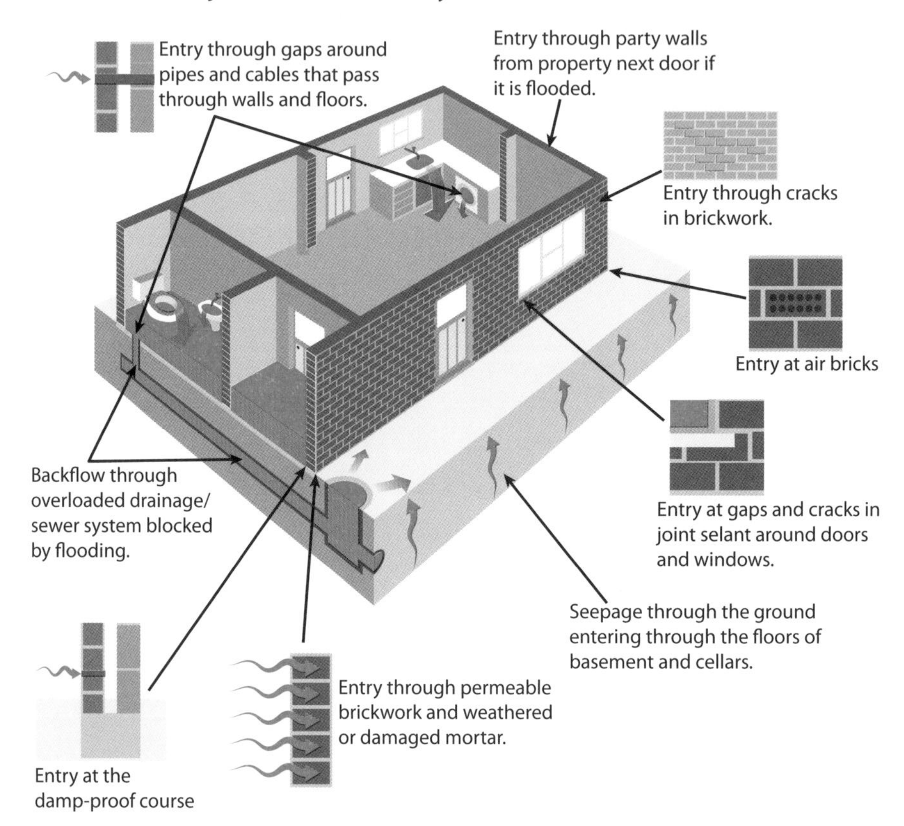

There are three different approaches to protecting your property from flood damage.

- Permanent flood protection by means of embankments, river walls and barriers. These are non-removable and normally installed as part of a community or regional flood protection program.
- Dry-proofing measures in individual buildings to keep water out, including sand bags, door barriers, and air brick seals. These

are often just temporary holding measures and will not offer long-term protection.

- Wet-proofing measures to alleviate the detrimental effects of flood water on the fixtures and finishes of the building's fabric. These might consist of solid floors in place of timber or carpet and cement-based wall renderings in place of plaster board.

There is a general rule of thumb that the maximum height of water protection measures should not exceed 1m above ground level. This is because water can exert considerable pressure on a structure's walls, windows, and doors, meaning that structural damage may be the outcome if water rises above this height. Equally, a lightly constructed building may be forced out of the ground if the water pressure is too great.

In the event of localized flooding, buildings with basemements are especially vunerable. Basements can become submerged, so specialist advice should always be sought before starting flood-proofing works. There are two principal reasons for this. First, a flood-proof basement may be hazardous if the protection devices are in any way breached or defective, potentially trapping occupants. Second, the 1m rule noted above does not apply to buildings with basements. If the groundwater rises above basement level, depending on the number of floors above, severe structural damage could result.

Water Treatment

Until there is some separation between the different qualities of water needed for drinking, washing, and flushing toilets, we will continue to waste energy unnecessarily on water treatment, infrastructure, and pumping. Earlier, we discussed the inextricable relationship between energy and water. Municiple water treatment plants are high energy users because they have continuously running motors driving multiple filtration systems with gigantic pumps and large chemical disinfecting stations. In most cases, although some might argue otherwise, water leaving the treatment plant is potable. However, less than 5% of water delivered to homes needs to be of drinking standard. Moreover, most countries have an old and leaky infrastructure and outdated pipework that commonly loses as much as 70% of treated water in some European cities. In the United States, average losses are between 15% and 20%. The net result of leaks is that less than 5% of all treated drinking water is used for its intended purpose.

Many studies have examined the most suitable location for water treatment facilities, whether it should be at the source of the water or at the point of use. Aside from inefficiency, an argument against centralized treatment is gaining ground. Water is often stored in less than ideal conditions, with crumbling infrastructure containing toxic substances such as asbestos and lead. Further compounding the problem is the fact that,water companies treat the water supply with chlorine to disinfect it and, in theory, to help prevent outbreaks of typhoid and cholera. According to Dr. Joseph M. Price, author of Coronaries Cholesterol Chlorine, there is a link between the chlorine in our water and coronary disease.

Point-of-use water treatment systems are alternatives to the current centralized model. They represent a paradigm shift in the approach to water sensitive design and take a more holistic view of human water needs and human interaction with the natural water cycle. Rainwater harvesting and sustainable drainage can work together to provide a more biodiverse urban water cycle that maximizes the use of locally sourced water. But the outstanding benefit of point-of-use water treatment is the energy savings associated with purifying only the 5% of water we use.

What water quality you require will depend on the source and intended use. Water for flushing toilets only needs a basic filter system. Water for dish washing, laundry, and personal hygiene may require further filtration, including water softeners if the water is alkaline or hard. In some countries, the water treatment industry is unregulated and only some proven systems can be sold as purifers, but this is really only a concern if you intend purifing your drinking water.

Energy and Water

Water and energy are inextricably linked. To conserve water is to conserve energy. Yet everyone from homeowners to policymakers often miss the connection. Water has a fundamental role in the generation, processing, and delivery of energy. In fact, a considerable amount of the world's power is generated directly from water via dams and water turbines. Even in nuclear power stations, water performs a central role in the power-generation and cooling processes. Its importance as a coolant was demonstrated in 2011, when the Fukushima Daiichi nuclear plant in Japan was deprived of its water coolant following a tsunami, with catastrophic consequences. Coal-burning electricity plants require enormous quantities of potable-quality water in order to function; and is a prime reason for their increasing lack of viability in water-stressed regions.

Energy is used to secure, treat, and distribute water. When you turn on your water at home, a series of pumps is programmed to kick in and keep the water flowing. Taxpayers share the burden of the energy costs associated with the cold water supply, but those associated with hot water are individual. You pay the full operational cost of the water heating system. Higher heating costs are directly related to rising demand for water.

The nexus between energy, waste, and water is never clearer than with reference to the developed world's relationship with bottled water. A disconnect is apparent in the fact that consumers are happy to pay from 500% to 2500% more for bottled water than for tap water. Perhaps bottled water is perceived to be of superior quality, but it must be noted that the bottled water industry in most cases is significantly less regulated than the tap water industry. Many leading bottled water companies source their water from tap water, in fact.

This book is primarly about saving energy. To do this effectively, we must learn to discard many of the existing philosophies and ideas we have been conditioned to believe about how the earth owes us a living. The first chapter examined the requirement for attitude change – if we don't change our thinking, we will continue to use, abuse, and waste precious, finite natural resources. This chapter opened with an examination of the strong subliminal links between water, prosperity, relaxation, and well-being. If you take nothing else from this book, please take the realization that the scarce natural resources of this earth are deserving of respect. Every householder can contribute in practical ways, making themselves and their families far more self-sufficient and helping, in some way, to improve the prospective viability of humanity in the process. Collective community action follows, as do national and international initiatives, such as the Paris 2015 conference. But the key point is that we wake up to our responsibilities and take decisions that are in our clear, personal, best interest.

Step 7 Summary

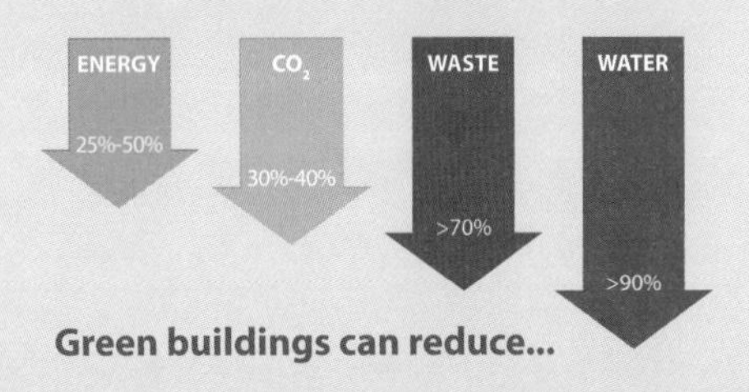

Twitter Summary

The climate cycle and the hydrological cycle are effectively one and the same thing. We must reduce non-sustainable ground water extractions and become aware that interfering with the hydrological cycle can intensify climate change.

Smart Citizen Summary

Step 7 completes the cycle in terms of steps the smart citizen must take to ensure that this Earth can be sustainably enjoyed by all, in such a way that does not cause further stress to the fine balance of its ecosystems. Water mindfulness is just as important as greenhouse awareness in terms of the detrimental consequence both play on the cause and effect of climate change. The smart citizen needs to:

- Be aware that the vast volumes of water required to support our modern lifestyles is such that rivers will run dry, lakes will fade away and ground waters will vanish.
- Know how to measure the amount of water we actually use on a day to day basis.
- Understand the concept of water labelling
- Re-think how hot water is used in our homes and understand the many ways of heating water with renewable fuel sources such as solar thermal.
- Understand the amounts of water used by common everyday apliance and systems such as showers, baths, washing machines, toilets etc and learn to reduce their water demands
- Appreciate that water senstitive design is fundamental to mitigating the adverse effects that climate change is having on this Earth.
- Consider installing rainwater harvesting and rain water butts where possible to reduce the need for mains water supply
- Know that flood damage mitigation measures will be an integral part of the design philosophy of both new buildings and refurbishments.
- Understand that energy and water are inextricably linked. To conserve water is to conserve energy.

Further Reading

A Carbon Primer for the Built Environment, 1st Ed., by Simon Foxell (2010, Earthscan).

The Complete Manual of Practical House Building, by Robert Matthews (1993, Butler & Tammer Publishers Ltd).

Consumer Guide to Home Energy Savings: Save Money, Save the Earth, 10th Ed., by Jennifer Thorne Amann, Alex Wilson & Katie Ackerly (2012, New Society Publishers).

Cut Your Energy Bills Now: 150 Smart Ways To Save Money and Make Your Home More Comfortable and Green, by Bruce Harley (2008, The Taunton Press).

Do-It-Yourself Home Energy Audits: 140 Simple Solutions to Lower Energy Costs, Increase Your Home's Efficiency, and Save the Environment, by David Findley (2010, McGraw-Hill).

Energy Audits: A Workbook for Energy Management in Buildings, by Tarik Al-Shemmeri (2007, Wiley-Blackwell).

Energy Free: Homes for a Small Planet, by Ann V. Edminster & Peter Yost (2009, Green Building Press).

The Energy-Smart House, by the editors of Fine Homebuilding (2011, The Taunton Press).

Energy Management in Buildings: The Earthscan Expert Guide, by Dave Thorpe (2014, Earthscan).

The Environmental Design Pocketbook, by Sofie Pelsmakers (2012, RIBA Publishing).

Green Building Bible: Volume 1: Essential Information to Help You Make Your Home and Buildings Less Harmful to the Environment, the Community and Your Family, by Keith Hall (2008, Cambrian Printers).

Green Building Bible: Volume 2: In Depth Technical Information and Data on the Strategies and the Systems Needed to Create Low Energy, Green Buildings (2008, Richard Nicholas).

Green Home Building: Money-Saving Strategies for an Affordable, Healthy, High-Performance Home, by Miki Cook & Doug Garrett (2014, New Society Publishers).

Heat Pumps for the Home, by John Cantor (2011, Crowood Press Ltd).

The Home Energy Handbook: A Guide to Saving and Generating Energy in Your Home and Community, by Allan Shepherd, Paul Allen & Peter Harper (2012, CAT Publications).

The Homeowner's Energy Handbook: Your Guide to Getting Off the Grid, by Paul Scheckel (2013, Storey Publishing).

The Passivhaus Handbook: A Practical Guide to Constructing and Retrofitting Buildings for Ultra-Low Energy Performance, by Janet Cotterell & Adam Dadeby (2012, Sustainable Building).

The Renewable Energy Handbook, Revised Edition: The Updated Comprehensive Guide to Renewable Energy and Independent Living, by William H. Kemp (2009, Aztext Press).

Renewable Energy Systems: The Earthscan Expert Guide to Renewable Energy Technologies for Home and Business, 1st Ed., by Dilwyn Jenkins (2013, Earthscan).

Small-Scale Wind Power Generation: A Practical Guide, by Jamie Bull & Gavin D.J. Harper (2010, Crowood Press Ltd).

Solar Technology: The Earthscan Expert Guide to Using Solar Energy for Heating, Cooling and Electricity, by David Thorpe (2012, Earthscan).

Sustainable Energy – Without the Hot Air, by David J.C, MacKay (2009, UIT Cambridge Ltd).

The Water-Wise Home: How to Conserve, Capture, and Reuse Water in Your Home and Landscape, by Laura Allen (2015, Storey Publishing).

What Colour is your Building? Measuring and Reducing the Energy and Carbon Footprint of Buildings, 1st Ed., by David Clark (2013, RIBA Publishing).

The Whole House Handbook: How to Design Healthy, Efficient and Sustainable Buildings, by Maria Block and Varis Bokalders (2010, RIBA Publishing).

Wind Energy Basics: A Guide to Small and Micro Wind Systems, by Paul Gipe (1999, Chelsea Green Publishing Company).

Wood Pellet Heating Systems: The Earthscan Expert Handbook on Planning, Design and Installation, by Dilwyn Jenkins (2010, Earthscan).

Resources

www.ashrae.org
International technical society organized to advance the arts and sciences of heating, ventilation, air-conditioning and refrigeration.

www.bre.co.uk
BRE Global is responsible for the internationally renowned BREEAM family of schemes for assessing the environmental performance of buildings.

www.cibse.org
The Chartered Institution of Building Services Engineers (CIBSE) provides best practice advice in all areas relevant to building services.

www.energysavingtrust.org.uk
The UK focused Energy Saving Trust helps people to save energy by sharing advice and information on energy efficiency issues.

www.energystar.gov
ENERGY STAR is a U.S. Environmental Protection Agency (EPA) voluntary program that helps businesses and individuals save money and protect our climate through superior energy efficiency.

www.eia.gov
The U.S. Energy Information Administration (EIA) provides information to help people understand energy policies and markets.

www.epa.gov
The U.S. government site provides energy advice across the whole spectrum of private and commercial developments.

www.iea.org
The International Energy Agency is an autonomous organization providing member countries with energy data and information to help them meet global energy challenges.

www.passivehouse-international.org
PHA is a global network of Passive House stakeholders working to promote the passive house standard around the world.

www.seai.ie
The Sustainable Energy Authority of Ireland (SEAI) provides sustainable energy structures, technologies and practices that enable citizens and businesses save energy.

www.usgbc.org
The U.S. Green Building Council is responsible for LEED, the certification program that recognizes best-in-class building strategies and practices.

www.waterfootprint.org
This site provides standard data and tools to help measure and manage our water resources and make progress towards sustainable development

www.wind-works.org
This site provides valuable information relevant to all countries on renewable energy issues and feed-in tariff regimes.

www.worldgbc.org
The World Green Building Council is a network of national green building councils in more than one hundred countries, making it the world's largest international organisation influencing the green building marketplace.

Glossary

Air Handling Unit (AHU): A set of equipment that includes a fan or blower for providing heating, ventilation, and air-conditioning (HVAC) to a building.

Air Source Heat Pump (ASHP): In cooling mode, the pump absorbs heat from the outside air and transfers it to the space to be heated. In cooling mode, the pump absorbs heat from the space to be cooled and expels it to the outside air.

Alternating Current (AC): Electricity that changes direction periodically. That period is measured in cycles per second (Hertz, Hz).

AMP: The unit that measures the flow rate of an electrical current.

American Society of Heating, Refrigerating and Air-Conditioning Engineers **(ASHRAE)**: A building services association that publishes standards and guidelines for HVAC systems. See also Appendix 2.

Anaerobic Digestion (AD): A biological process that produces biogas, which is principally composed of methane (CH4) and carbon dioxide (CO2).

Automatic Meter Read (AMR): A system that uses telephone technology to relay automatic meter readings remotely, sending data to a billing system.

Anthropogenic: Resulting from or produced by man.

Atmosphere: The gaseous envelope around the earth.

Base Load: The level below which electricity demand never drops, i.e. the electrical load.

Battery: Two or more electrical cells joined together that produce and store electricity.

Biogas: The gas generated when bacteria degrades biological material in the absence of oxygen, in a process known as anaerobic digestion. A mixture of methane and carbon dioxide, it is a renewable fuel produced from waste treatment.

Biomass: Also known as biofuel or bioenergy, it is energy obtained from organic matter, either directly from plants or indirectly from industrial, commercial, domestic, or agricultural products.

Biomass Boiler: A boiler fueled by biomass, usually wood pellets or chipped or fibrous wood.

Biofuel: See Biomass above.

Building Energy Rating (BER): See also Appendix 2.

BRE: The Building Research Establishment (BRE) is a U.K.-based nonprofit organization providing research, knowledge, tools, publications, and advice to the built environment. See also Appendix 2.

Building Energy Management Systems (BEMS): A computer-based control and monitoring system for managing energy use within a building.

Building Fabric: Generally refers to the structural enclosure of a building, including walls, roof, floors, windows, and doors

Building Information Modeling (BIM): A virtual model of a building that includes the quantities and properties of materials and components in the structure. All structural and service details need to be included for the model to be complete.

Building Research Establishment Environmental Assessment Method **(BREEAM)**: The approach used to assess the environmental performance of new and existing buildings. Credits are awarded in different categories according to performance. See also Appendix 2.

Calorific Value (CV): Amount of heat delivered by a specified quantity of gas. It calculates the energy consumed based on the volume of gas used and is measured in joules per kilogram.

Cap and Trade Scheme: When referring to CO2 or greenhouse gas emissions, cap and trade sets an overall limit and allocates an allowance that allows participants to trade emissions credits with each other.

Capacity Charge: A charge set by the local distribution network operator (DNO) for investment and maintenance of the electricity network, based on a property's agreed capacity.

Carbon Capture/Storage (CCS): A method for capturing and storing carbon dioxide as it is released into the atmosphere from fossil fuels, before or after combustion.

Carbon Storage/Carbon Sequestration: The long-term storage of carbon (CO2) in the forests, soil, ocean, or underground in depleted oil and gas reservoirs, coal seams, and saline aquifers. Also referred to as CCS (see above).

Carbon Credits: A credit or permit arising from a greenhouse gas emissions reduction scheme such as emissions trading.

Carbon Cycle: The continuous exchange of carbon between the atmosphere, land, and oceans, including its absorption by and emission from plants and animals.

Carbon Dioxide (CO2): A naturally occurring, inert, non-toxic gas derived from decaying materials, respiration of plant and animal life, and combustion of organic matter such as fossil fuels.

Carbon Dioxide Equivalent (CO2e): A universal unit of measurement used to represent the six main greenhouse gases that cause climate change and are limited by the Kyoto Protocol. Although the gases have different global warming potential, their impact potential is converted to one unit.
Carbon Footprint: A measure of the amount of carbon dioxide emitted through the combustion of fossil fuels. It can be measured on a personal or national level, and there are a variety of online calculators available to assess personal carbon footprint.
Carbon Leakage: An assessment of the carbon emissions that occur in other countries as a result of restrictive emissions policies in a country under measurement.
Carbon Neutral: An activity or process that doesn't add to the net amount of atmospheric CO2. As the organization or product responsible for the activity in question will typically have caused some greenhouse gas emissions, it is usually necessary to use carbon offsets to achieve neutrality.
Carbon Offset: Negates the overall amount of carbon released into the atmosphere by avoiding the release or removing it elsewhere, through a renewable energy or energy conservation project, for example.
Carbon Price: The amount to be paid for the emission of 1 tonne of carbon dioxide CO2 into the atmosphere.
Carbon Tax: A levy on fossil fuel usage usually based on the carbon content. Generally designed to curb use rather than just raise revenue.
Carbon Trading: The trading of personal, corporate, or national credits to maintain and gradually reduce carbon emissions. Companies, nations, or individuals who beat the targets can sell surplus credits to those that exceed their limits.
Carbon Trust: An independent nonprofit company set up by the U.K. government with support from businesses to encourage and promote the development of low-carbon technologies. A very useful source of information. See Appendix 2.
Chartered Institute of Building Services Engineers (CIBSE): The U.K.'s professional body for services engineers. It publishes guides and codes for best practice in the building services industry. See Appendix 2
Circuit: A linked series of electrical conductors, wires, and components that allow an electrical current to flow.
Circuit Breaker: A device that protects an electric circuit from power surges by stopping the power flowing.
Clean Energy: A term synonymous with fossil-free renewable energy.

Clean Technology: A term synonymous with the technology that produces renewable energy.
Climate Change: The variation in earth's climate over time. Man-made climate change is a variation directly attributable to human behavior.
Coefficient of Performance (COP): A measure of the efficiency of heat pumps obtained by comparing the ratio of heat energy output to that of electrical energy input.
Cogeneration: Also know as combined heat and power. See CHP below.
Combined Heat and Power (CHP): When electricity is generated, up to 60% of the energy can be wasted as lost heat. CHP schemes are designed to recover most of the waste heat, using it to power a turbine and generate more electricity.
Cold Bridge: Also referred to as thermal bridge. It is a pathway for heat loss through the fabric of a building and usually occurs around windows, doors, balconies, wall junctions, or anywhere that insulation details are breached.
Conference of the Parties (COP): The supreme body of the UNFCCC, made up of countries that have ratified the climate change convention and have the right to vote. Paris 2015, or COP 21, is the 21st such conference.
Conductor: A substance that allows an electric current to pass through it easily.
Copenhagen (COP 15): The 2009 UNFCCC climate change conference that was generally regarded as a failure in terms of targeted outcome. One success was the agreement to limit global warming to 2oC.

Data Logger: A device used to record meter readings and automatically transmit them to the meter reading body.
Demand Response: Generally refers to the need to temporarily reduce pressure on the national grid by switching off non-critical appliances and equipment automatically to cut peak demand.
Direct Current (DC): An electrical current that flows only in one direction in a circuit. Batteries and fuel cells produce direct current.
Display Energy Certificate (DECs): The requirement under EU legislation that certain public buildings over a certain size must prominently display on a certificate the amount of energy used by the building. The building performance rating must also be included on the certificate.
Distribution Network Operators (DNO): Companies responsible for operating the networks that connect electricity consumers to the national transmission system and provide interconnection with embedded generation.

Distribution Use Of System Charges (DUOS): Published costs made by every distribution company for delivering electricity from the grid supply point to the customer.
District Network Operator (DNO): The manager of the installation and upkeep of cabling and the distribution of electricity to the grid supply point.
District Heating: The use of heat from a central source to provide distributed/piped heat to numerous secondary sources such as houses, offices, and schools.

Electric Current: The rate at which electricity flows through an electrical conductor, usually measured in amperes (amps).
Electrical Cell: A device that produces or stores electricity.
Electricity Meter: A device for measuring the amount of electricity used.
Electricity Pool: The way in which electricity is traded between generators and suppliers as well as some very large consumers.
Electromagnet: A magnetic field produced when an electric current is passed through wire wrapped around a piece of iron.
Emissions Trading: A market mechanism that allows emitters (countries, companies, or facilities) to purchase emissions from or sell emissions to other emitters.
Emissions Trading Scheme (ETS): An EU mechanism for trading carbon dioxide and other greenhouse gas emissions.
Energy Balance: The difference between the total energy generated or bought and the total energy used. It can apply to a business or country.
Energy Crops: Plants grown as fuel to generate heat and electrical power.
Energy Efficiency: Having desired levels of lighting, heating, or cooling for minimum energy use. Cutting down on waste energy.
Energy From Waste: Energy recovery from post-recycling waste residue, an alternative to landfill.
Energy Performance Certificate (EPC): A document intended to inform potential buyers or tenants about the energy performance of a building, so they can consider energy efficiency as part of their investment or business decision. The scale is from A-G, A being the most efficient. (EPC is the building energy label name commonly used in Britain. It is called HERS in the U.S. and BER in Ireland.
Energy Performance of Building Directive (EPBD): The EU directive that promotes the improvement of the energy performance of buildings through cost-effective measures.
Energy Services Company (ESCO): A specialist in managing energy and

water conservation projects. It may perform any or all of the following services: auditing, developing packages of recommended measures, arranging finance, installing or overseeing installation of measures, educating residents and staff, commissioning equipment, carrying out maintenance, measuring, verifying, and guaranteeing savings.
Energy Star: A voluntary U.S. energy labeling program recognized worldwide. It rates domestic and commercial appliances as well as buildings and services.
Environment Protection Agency (EPA): The leading public body for protecting and improving the environment. (Known as the Environment Agency, or EA, in Britain).

Fixed Charge: A daily, monthly, or quarterly charge levied by the energy supplier in addition to the standing charge.
Fixed Term Contracts: Supply contract for a fixed price, over a fixed period of time, which gives customers a constant price. Fixed charges include standing and availability charges.
Feed-in Tariffs (FITs): The price per unit of electricity paid by government to those who generate electricity and export it to the grid. There is usually a fixed term for the payment depending on the type of generation plant. The scheme is usually designed around promoting renewable forms of electricity generation.
Fossil Fuel: An energy source formed in the earth's crust from decayed organic material. The common fossil fuels are oil, coal, peat, and natural gas.
Fracking: A process for extracting oil and gas from below ground using hydraulic methods that have controversial environmental implications.
Fuel Cells: Fuel cells produce electricity from hydrogen and air, with water as the only emission. Potential applications include stationary power generation, transport (replacing the internal combustion engine), and portable power (replacing batteries in cell phones).
Fuse: A safety device that protects electrical appliances by preventing too much electricity flowing into them.

Gaia: An alternative theory about the earth, proposed in the 1960s by independent British scientist James Lovelock. He posited that the earth is more than just a mere life-supporting environment but is part of life itself. This living earth Lovelock names Gaia, resurrecting the ancient Greek term
Gasification: Breakdown of hydrocarbons into a syngas by carefully controlling the level of oxygen present.

Generator: A machine that converts mechanical energy into electricity.
Geothermal Energy: Heat energy extracted from deep in the earth's crust.
Gigawatt (GW): 1,000 megawatts or 1,000,000 kW
Global Warming: The gradual increase in the average temperature of earth's surface and atmosphere. The majority of scientists agree that the current warming is caused by the release of greenhouse gases from the burning of fossil fuels and other industrial processes.
Green Building Councils (GBCs): Originating in the United States in 1993 and with over 70 member organizations worldwide, GBCs work with national governments and industry to develop sustainability practices.
Green Deal: A U.K. better finance initiative, which helps consumers and businesses to make energy-efficient improvements to their buildings, with the capital finance paid back through the energy bills. The green deal has a golden rule whereby the payback amounts cannot exceed the savings amount. It has not, however, been a successful initiative.
Greenhouse Gas (GHG): A gas that absorbs infra-red radiation (i.e. the sun's heat and energy) in the atmosphere. Greenhouse gases include carbon dioxide (CO2), methane (CH4), nitrous oxide (N2O), halogenated fluorocarbons (HCFCs), ozone (O3), perfluorinated carbons (PFCs), and hydrofluorocarbons (HFCs). These gases contribute to the greenhouse effect.
Ground Source Heat Pump (GSHP): A heat pump that uses the earth's natural heat storage capacity and/or the groundwater to heat and/or cool a building.
GSM: A mobile/cellular device connected to a meter that reads the meter remotely. There has to be a very good signal for GSM to work.

Half Hourly (HH) Meters: A communication device connected to the meter that allows the data collector to remotely connect to the meter, obtaining half-hourly consumption.
Heat Exchanger: A device that transfers heat from one medium to another.
Heat Rate: Energy input per unit of time, usually expressed in kWh\h or Btu\h
Heating, Ventilation and Air Conditioning (HVAC): Most professionals and tradespeople in the industry simply refer to a building's heating, ventilation, and air-conditioning systems as HVAC.
High Voltage (HV):11,000 volts or above.
Hydroelectricity: Electricity generated from harnessing the force of falling water to turn the turbine blades, usually accomplished by damming a river.

Import: Where a site consumes electricity as opposed to generating and exporting power. Import is the most common type of site.
Insulator: A material that reduces or stops the flow of electricity.
Intergovernmental Panel on Climate Change (IPCC): A scientific intergovernmental body founded in 1988 by the World Meteorological Organisation (WMO) and the United Nations Environment Programme (UNEP). It aims to provide an objective source of information about climate change to policy-makers by assessing the latest scientific, technical and socio-economic literature on the human causes of climate change.
International Energy Agency (IEA): An organization that advises governments on energy security, economic development, and energy policy.
ISO 50001: An international energy efficiency standard to help companies reduce their energy usage.

Kilovolt Amperes (KVA): Also known as Total Power. The resultant effect of the active (kW) and reactive (kVAr) power is the total power measured in kVa. Kva = kW/power factor.
Kilowatt /Hour (kW/hr): A standard unit of electrical power equal to 1,000 watts. Kilowatts are the units used to measure maximum demand. Kilowatt hour is a unit of energy consumed.
Kyoto Protocol: In 1997, representatives from over 170 nations met in Kyoto, Japan, to agree a global treaty to the United Nations Framework Convention on Climate Change (UNFCCC), laying down legally binding reductions in greenhouse gas emissions.

Landfill Gas: Municipal solid waste containing significant portions of organic materials that produce a variety of gaseous products when dumped, compacted, and covered in landfills.
Load: The amount of electric power delivered or required at any specific point or points on an electrical system. The requirement originates at the energy-consuming equipment of the customer.
Load Factor: Measures the relationship between unit consumption and maximum demand and is the percentage capacity utilization figure of a site's power consumption. To calculate load factor, take the total number of units of consumption, divide by the maximum demand, divide by the number of hours in the period, and multiply by 100.
Low Voltage (LV): Normally at 240 or 415 volts.

Mains Electricity: Electricity supplied to our homes from the national grid.
Mechanical and Electrical (M&E): The standards terminology used in industry to refer to the mechanical and electrical systems design and details.
Mechanical Ventilation with Heat Recovery (MVHR): A building ventilation system in which heat is recovered from exhaust air to heat incoming fresh air.
Mega Watt (MW): A measure of power, 1 million watts or 1,000 kWs
Micro-Generation: The small-scale generation of energy, for example solar panels or domestic wind turbines. These are often referred to as generation from renewable sources at a domestic or small community level.

National Grid: The national grid is the main electrical transmission and distribution system.
Natural Gas: A hydrocarbon primarily consisting of methane (CH4) found naturally occurring below ground at depth.
Natural Ventilation: Also known as passive ventilation, it is the supply and removal of air inside a building without mechanical assistance.
Nuclear Power: Generation of electricity using heat produced by an atomic reaction. The process produces negligible amounts of carbon, which is why nuclear is proposed as one way of reducing global carbon footprints.

Passivhaus Standard: An internationally acknowledged standard for energy efficient buildings developed in Germany in the 1990s. Passive houses are essentially highly insulated and airtight buildings, in which the form and shape has been optimized to suit the particular climate zone.
Payback Period: The number of years it takes for the return on an energy-efficient investment to pay for itself.
Pay as You Save: A generic term commonly used to describe the process whereby investments in energy-saving installations can be recovered from energy savings.
Peak Oil: The date when the maximum rate of extraction of oil occurs, after which oil production declines.
Peak Water: Similar to peak oil. A situation when the rate of extraction of water reserves exceeds the natural recharge.
Peak Demand: Point of maximum electricity demand on the national system.
Photovoltaic (PV): The direct conversion of solar radiation into electricity

by the interaction of light with the electrons in a semiconductor device or cell.
Power Factor: A measure of how efficiently electricity is used onsite. Certain types of equipment cause poor power factor, which reduces the capacity of the network to supply power. Distribution network operators can charge customers for this through power factor charges.
Power Line: Electrical wires that carry electricity from the point of generation to the point of use.
Primary Energy: The raw energy source such as fossil fuels, nuclear fuels, wind, solar, and hydro used to generate delivered usable energy in the form of electricity, heat, or motor power.
Pylon: A large metal tower that carries very high voltage power lines.
Pyrolysis: Thermal degradation of organic waste in the absence of air to produce char, oil, and syngas.

Reactive Charges: Charges applied to a client's invoice in cases where certain suppliers and distribution companies enforce a penalty for reactive power use.
Reactive Power (KVAR): The difference between the electricity supplied and the electricity converted into useful power. If the difference is large, this indicates that a large amount of power is being wasted.
Renewable Energy: The term used to describe the energy produced using naturally replenishing resources. This includes solar power, wind, wave and tide, and hydroelectricity. Wood, straw, and waste are often called solid renewable energy, while landfill gas and sewerage gas can be described as gaseous renewables.
Renewable Heat Incentive (RHI): Similar to the FITs scheme except that the payment is for heat generated rather than electricity.

Sick Building Syndrome: When occupants experience poor health that is in some way associated with time spent in certain buildings. Symptoms usually include headaches, dizziness, nausea, dry cough, asthma attacks, fatigue etc.
Smart Grid: An electricity network that includes a variety of operational and energy measures such as smart meters, smart appliances, demand response abilities, renewable energy, and energy-efficiency resources.
Smart Metering: The ability to remotely read meters. Data is more reliable and more accurate bills are produced
Standing Charge: A daily or monthly charge to contribute towards installation, maintenance, and administration costs of the local distribution network operator.

Sub Station: An important part of the national grid, they house transformers that increase or decrease the voltage of an electric current.
Sub-Metering: The term often used when a property owner installs a separate meter to monitor the consumption of a utility such as water, gas, or electricity.
Solar Gain: Heat obtained directly from solar radiation such as direct transmission of heat into a building through its windows.
Solar Panel: An assembled array of photovoltaics (PV) for converting solar radiation into electricity. Often called solar PV.
Solar Thermal: A system for collecting solar sunlight/daylight and converting into a storage medium for hot water and space heating.
Solar Cooling: A system for collecting solar sunlight/daylight and using it in a refrigeration system.
Supplier: A person authorized by a license to supply electricity or gas to the national grid network, via the network.

Tariff Structure: Suppliers quote for electricity in numerous different formats. These range from simple, one-rated structures to complex "Seasonal Time of Day" tariffs, which are multi-rated. i.e. the price changes three, six, or eight times a day.
Thermal Efficiency: Quantity of heat produced in relation to fuel input.
Thermal Envelope: The external envelope of a building, which includes windows and doors. It separates the internal temperature zone from the external zone.
Thermal Mass: The ability of material to store heat and then release it at a later time when the air temperature drops.
Therms: A unit of energy measurement. To calculate equivalent value in kWh, multiply by 29.3071.
Trigeneration: The ability to generate electricity, heat, and cooling from a single source.
Transformer: Equipment used to change the voltage of an electric current. Transformers can increase or decrease voltage.
Transmission: The transfer of electricity at high voltage from power stations via wires on pylons to points where it can be distributed to users.
Transmission Use of System (TUoS): The charges are incurred for transmitting electricity across the national grid network from the source of generation to the network of the local distribution company.

UN Framework Convention on Climate Change (UNFCCC): The international framework established in 1992 to tackle climate change and greenhouse gas emissions. The UNFCCC aims to prevent dangerous man-made climate change and commits developed countries to take the lead in tackling climate change.

Voltage: A unit used to measure the electromotive force of an electric current.
Vehicle-to-Grid (V2G): A system that enables the battery storage capabilities of electric vehicles to be used to export power to the grid. This usually involves charging the battery at off-peak rates and exporting back to the grid at peak or other beneficial times.

Waste Residue: The portion of the waste stream (domestic and commercial) that cannot currently be recovered or recycled.
Wave Power: The generation of energy from wave power.
Wind Power: The conversion of wind energy into electrical power.

Index

S